TINY STATIONS

TINY STATIONS

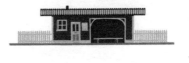

DIXE WILLS

Published by AA Publishing, a trading name of AA Media
Limited, Fanum House, Basing View, Basingstoke, Hampshire,
RG21 4EA, UK.

www.theAA.com

First published in 2014
10 9 8 7 6 5 4 3 2 1

A CIP catalogue record for this book is available from the
British Library.

ISBN: 978-0-7495-7561-8

Map illustration by Harriet Yeomans
Printed and bound in the UK

A04848

Our books carrying the FSC label are printed on FSC certified
paper. FSC is the only forest certification scheme endorsed by the
leading environmental organisations.

MIX
Paper from
responsible sources
FSC® C018072

To Rod and Vivi Boucher

It is in the petty details, not in the great results,
that the interest of existence lies.

Jerome K Jerome
Idle Thoughts of an Idle Fellow

TO LELANT

So, it's 2009 and I'm on the train from Inverness and we've almost got to the end of the line at the Kyle of Lochalsh. But I'm not going as far as the Kyle of Lochalsh, I'm getting off at Duncraig. It turns out I'm the only person getting off at Duncraig. This makes me feel special because it means the train has to stop there just for me.

When we start to slow down I can hear a buzz developing in the carriage. People look around. Is that the faintest hint of admiration I detect in their eyes when I stand? The train stops and I clamber off onto the platform. This produces another round of rubbernecking. 'Who is that special man getting off here?' I can feel them ask. The train pulls away and I am left alone in my new kingdom.

As you may have guessed by now, Duncraig is a railway request stop. If no one asks to get off there and there's no one waiting on the platform indicating that they want to get on, the train will whistle through without so much as a by your leave.

I do a lot of train travel, but Duncraig was the first railway request stop I'd ever used. So it came as something of a surprise to learn that there were over 150 of them dotted around Britain, which equates to about 6 per cent of all the nation's stations. Yet this oddest of quirks on our railway network is also one of its least known or documented.

Unless you happen to live on a line where there are request
stops, there's a very good chance you'll never have come
across one. It's not as if they go out of their way to advertise
themselves. But the next time you look at a railway
timetable, pay particular attention to the times displayed
against each station. If you see one that, instead of reading,
for example

13 04

reads

13x04

you know that that train will stop at that particular station
only on request.

Having had my interest piqued by Duncraig – a tiny halt
built by a Victorian drugs trafficker as his own private
station – I began to investigate the stories behind some of
the other request stops. The more I dug, the more treasures
I stumbled across.

Often a pen-stroke away from closure, these half-
abandoned stops afforded a glimpse into a Britain of the
not-so-distant past that has all but disappeared from view.
There were stations built to serve once thriving industries,
where the first wagons had been pulled by horses; stations
erected for the sole convenience of stately home owners,
through whose land the new railway cut an unwelcome
swathe; stations created for Victorian day-tripping attractions
– indeed, the reasons for building them were almost as
numerous as the stations themselves. The reasons for keeping
them open raised an eyebrow or two as well – political
expediency, labyrinthine bureaucracy, sheer whimsy or, in
one case, an outright rebellion in which local train drivers
simply refused to accept that the station had been closed.

It's often said that travel broadens the mind and that absolute travel broadens the mind absolutely, which is why I abandoned the Rare Books Reading Room of the British Library in favour of a grand tour on which I would visit 38 of the nation's most fascinating railway request stops (though I'll confess it now: I actually stopped off at some of the slightly less fascinating ones as well, just because I could, and hey, you only live once). It would take me on an extremely circuitous route over thousands of miles of track from the far west of Cornwall to the far north of Scotland.

Which is how I came to be standing on Paddington station one evening in the middle of May, looking up at the information screens and searching for the platform from which the Night Riviera sleeper service to Cornwall would leave.

By their very nature, railway request stops tend to be tranquil places, often found in remote areas and largely untrammelled by madding crowds, or indeed by anyone at all, for hours on end. This makes them ideal spots for two activities.

The first is quiet, reflective contemplation. To this end my rucksack was packed with a paperback copy of *The Consolation of Philosophy* by top Roman thinker and sometime consul Anicius Boethius. He was coming along because, although my adult life had been just fine and dandy, I felt that it had begun to drift a little (to I knew not where), and it was about time I made a little sense of it. There was also the fact that I had found myself at an age where I was beginning to wonder if I should have got around to getting married and having a child or two. Or at least got married. Or at least be in a relationship. I needed to focus my mind and there was no doubt that when Boethius wrote his *Consolation* he was a man whose mind was focused – the prospect of imminent execution tends to do that, so I'm told. He was clearly someone from whom I could pick up a few pointers.

The second activity to which the depopulated nature of railway request stops lends itself is the learning of a musical instrument. A bright yellow ukulele was duly strapped to my rucksack, tuned and ready for action.

I woke up at St Austell to cornflakes and tea (brought to me by the sleeping car attendant) and rain (which she did not bring). While I usually prefer the first two to the last, in this case the reverse was true. I'd forgotten to bring any soya milk with me (I don't 'do' dairy), so I popped the little box of cornflakes in my rucksack for later snackage and emptied the tiny stick of sugar into the tea in an attempt to make it palatable.

The rain, however, was good news. Despite the fact that it was mid-May, just up the road in Devon it had snowed the night before. If nothing else, rain signified a temperature above freezing, for which I was glad. Glad in the way that a man who has made a last-minute decision to unpack his bulky but toasty five-season sleeping bag and replace it with his ultra-light and super-compact but woefully thin summer sleeping bag is glad.

We arrived at St Erth, where I was due to change onto a service that would deliver me to Lelant. The train stopped at exactly 07.40 as timetabled and I opened the door. No, I didn't. It wouldn't open. It was locked. I pulled down the window and looked out along the platform to see happy, indeed smug, passengers alighting and walking off to get on with their happy, smug lives. No problem with *their* doors, oh no. I threw myself headlong down the corridor to the next carriage, my ukulele flapping up and down on the back of my rucksack like a goldfish gasping for water, only to find that that door wouldn't open either.

I had scheduled the first few days of my tour like a military campaign, allowing no leeway for hiccoughs, blunders, acts of God/*forces majeures* [delete according to taste] or my own naked stupidity. Margins for error were there none. Realising that this was perhaps a little optimistic, especially knowing how fathomless the depths of my own naked stupidity can be on occasion, I had built some more flexibility into the rest of the trip wherever the railway timetable allowed it. However, I had not troubled myself to revisit those first few days to give myself a buffer – an oversight I was already regretting.

If the train pulled off now with me still in it, and I had to disembark at the next station, I would miss my service to Lelant, my very first request stop. All my subsequent connections would then topple like dominoes, with the result that I would not end up where I wanted to be by nightfall. In turn, this would mean that tomorrow would be a mess and the next day a total disaster. Indeed, I might as well end it all by throwing myself off the train right now. I tried, but the door was still locked.

Just as I was about to charge down into the next carriage, the fifth cavalry came panting up the platform in the form of a station employee.

'Where do you want to get off?' he enquired between gasps.

'St Erth,' I called back, heroically holding back any hint of sarcasm in my voice.

It was at that moment I noticed the sign on the platform that read 'Hayle'.

'Oh,' said the guard. He didn't even have the energy to look disdainful.

When I got off at St Erth a few minutes later, the rain had stopped, flecks of blue were peeping between a thinning sheet of high cloud, and the air was drenched in the scent of English bluebells. Nowadays, whenever I see English bluebells I make a point of breathing in their scent because it's an experience that's becoming rarer. An incomer – the bolder, tougher, more wood-savvy Spanish bluebell – is slowly pushing its English cousin out of mainland Britain. The Spaniard admittedly puts on a more lavish display, since it produces flowers all around its stem rather than on just one side, as is the demure English bluebell's custom. However, like a Shakespearean sonnet delivered by a voice synthesiser, it has no fragrance.

I filled my lungs with the volatilised compound chemicals given off by the bluebells and the slowly drying tarmac, my misadventure at Hayle already forgotten.

And so began my journey into the world of the railway request stop.

LELANT

The guard had, disappointingly, shown less excitement at my request to get off at Lelant than I had expected. He merely sought to confirm that I had meant Lelant and not Lelant Saltings, the compulsory stop just half a mile before. By way of compensation, I had a surprise reception committee waiting. I knew it was for me because I was the only person alighting there. When I sprang out of the train I was greeted by a tiny ginger-haired boy and his even smaller sister, who were waving to me through the French windows of a weather-boarded house. A Scottie dog, nuzzling his way in between them, yapped at me in a friendly, welcoming way. I felt I had stepped into an Enid Blyton story.

With an admirable sense of history, the owners of the house, and the one to which it was attached, had painted the exteriors in the Great Western Railway colours of chocolate and cream, just in case their position and architecture hadn't made it clear that these were the former station buildings. The fact that they were extensive enough to have been converted into two homes speaks volumes about Lelant's relative significance once upon a time, although the village really only has a station at all due to a stroke of luck.

Three miles to the northwest sits St Ives, which, in a former life, was an important fishing harbour. The main line – then called the West Cornwall Railway – reached Penzance in 1852 but bypassed St Ives, meaning that the fish landed there had to be transported by cart to the trains. Bringing the railway to the fish would clearly speed things up, so, following several abortive proposals, work was eventually started on a branch line to St Ives in 1874. The broad gauge tracks came off the main line at Rose-an-Grouse, a place so inconsequential that it suffered the indignity of having its station named St Ives Road (it's now called St Erth).

The simplest way to avoid most of the high ground between Rose-an-Grouse and St Ives was to lay the track around the coast. This conveniently took it through Lelant, whose population of 800 or so, along with its tin works and wharfs, would provide additional sources of revenue for the railway company. The branch line was opened for 'fish traffic' on 28 May 1877 and four days later for passengers and goods, which gives a good idea of the priorities of the proprietors.

It was the last broad gauge (7ft ¼ inch) line ever built in Britain for passenger use. That the future lay in standard gauge (4ft 8½ inches) is made manifest by the fact that the section of track from St Ives Road to Lelant had a third rail so that standard gauge goods trains could service the local wharf. Anyone who thinks that people with an interest in railways are not entirely in touch with their emotions should witness the passion aroused by the debate over whether this extra rail was laid in 1877 or 1888. Whichever it was, the whole line to St Ives was converted to standard gauge in 1892.

Even though the people who planned the St Ives Railway had chosen a relatively easy route, there were difficulties in building it. The *Royal Cornwall Gazette* for 17 April 1875 published a report on the venture's early travails, including the building of bridges and embankments, the driving of wooden piles into the muddy shoreline, and the creation of a 'very high and costly' viaduct at Carbis Valley. Around Lelant, meanwhile, the news was something of a mixed bag:

> *The embankment, a little further on and towards Lelant, is in an advanced stage, and at Brewery Quay, where the Lelant Station will be erected, the navvies are actively engaged removing the earth etc from the cutting which is being made into the towans [dunes]. From this spot very little has been done until we come to the Carrack Gladden cutting – the stiffest bit of work on the line. Here all is activity, and a large number of navvies are employed in making this cutting. The ground, however, is very hard, and the rock has to be blasted.*

The digging of railway cuttings was hazardous work and the safety of the navvies who toiled away at it seldom uppermost in the minds of those who paid their wages. In October that same year, the *Cornish Telegraph* recorded the death of one John Yendall, a 53-year-old 'ganger' (work gang leader), who met his end when spoil from a cutting unsportingly fell on him.

Understandably, the navvies took to drink. This attracted the censure of the ever vigilant *Cornish Telegraph*, whose journalists knew how to sniff out a good story, especially if they could smell the demon alcohol on its breath. 'Drunkenness, to a lamentable extent, exists here,' declared its 15 September 1875 report on the goings-on in Lelant, 'the Sabbath being the favourite guzzling day. Last Sunday, from about half past two in the afternoon till late at night, drunken men were rambling about the roads much to the disgust of the decent inhabitants.'

Having failed to pin the blame for this turn of events specifically on those labouring on the railway, the newspaper made amends the following week by printing a letter from a T Andrew, who assigned full responsibility for any guzzling-related shenanigans to the navvies, describing them as 'of a class too that are proverbial for "liking their beer"'.

From the map I'd studied before I set off, I was anticipating a fine if unspectacular view from Lelant's platform. This the station duly delivered. Just the other side of the single track sprang clumps of tall reeds. Beyond these, Hayle Estuary lay motionless but for a grindingly slow current on the far side that edged its way towards the sea. The small town of Hayle poked its nose unobtrusively above the shore to the east, while a lone wind turbine and a low ridge covered by fields and woods accounted for the remainder of the panorama.

Closer to hand, about a train's length up the line, a small trawler sat up on a little triangle of beach known locally as Mackerel Boats or Brewery Quay. It earned the former moniker because fishing boats from St Ives used to beach here to avoid winter storms, and the latter on account of its having served as the quay for a brewery that closed sometime in the 19th century.

It's a nugatory little tract but may well be a landing stage of some antiquity, and has enjoyed a couple of moments in the sun, both connected with acts of heroism: barges built on the Hayle side of the estuary for the D-Day landings were moored here before their perilous journey across the Channel; and in September 1875 (a busy month for Lelant), a boy called Charles Hawes saved the life of a young man named Alfred Gall who got into difficulties while swimming off the quay.

According to the newspaper report, the young Hawes, 'seeing the peril, without waiting to divest himself of his clothes, gallantly plunged into the rescue and succeeded in bringing Gall safely to the bank'. Well done, that man. I'll admit I felt the teeniest pang of envy when I read the account of Charlie's exploits. It's quite possible I'm three times the age he was when he dived into the rushing torrent and yet I've still not got around to saving anyone's life. How have I allowed that to happen? And what great deeds did Mr Gall go on to achieve? Did it turn out like *It's A Wonderful Life* wherein an angel (second class) reveals to George Bailey that in saving his younger brother's life he indirectly saved many more because said brother went on to shoot down a kamikaze plane that would otherwise have destroyed the ship in which those people were sailing? Admittedly, there were fewer kamikaze pilots around in the late 1800s, but I like to think Alfred did something with his life that justified his being given a second go at it. I made a mental note to pull my finger out and start hanging around people who looked as if they might be in imminent danger of coming to a sticky end.

Of course, it's not only people who go the way of all flesh. Near Mackerel Boats, relics from the railway line's past were rotting slowly away – a stable large enough for a score of horses, a disused smithy and carpentry benches, all of which were used in the construction of the line, only to be dispensed with once they had served their purpose. An equally redundant slipway poked out into the estuary at the other end of the platform. This was all that was left of an old cart track across the sands of Lelant Water. It might also once have been a quay, possibly a predecessor of Brewery Quay. If so, it seems to have been abandoned well before the railway arrived and what went on here has passed into the realms of the unknown and the probably unknowable. Its snub nose now jutted out mournfully into the waters, like the floor-pressed snout of a sad dog that has been told off and can't fathom out why.

My only disappointments as I prowled the platform, keen to take in its every quirk and nuance, were a) the constant drone from traffic on the other side of the estuary; and b) the lack of a tearoom, although I'd been briefed about this beforehand so was braced for the setback. It might seem like the height of optimism to hope for a tearoom at a railway request stop, but there had been one here as recently as the previous summer. Operating out of the house next to the one in which the ginger boy and his sister had greeted me, Peter and Annabelle Jeggo served cream teas at the station for many summers, but the summer of 2012 had been their last.

'We got fed up with it,' Annabelle told me when I knocked on their door. 'It meant that all summer one of us had to be in the house and though we've been living here for 17 years we still haven't even got around to seeing all of Cornwall.'

I could see her point. However, I selfishly reserved the right to be a little sad that the only railway request stop in Britain with its own café no longer had its own café. In its Victorian heyday, the station buildings had comprised a booking office and no fewer than three waiting rooms. These latter structures were not, as one might imagine, split down gender lines (one for ladies, one for gentlemen and a racier third room in which married couples could hold hands as long as both parties were wearing gloves and neither derived any pleasure from the experience). The division was instead based on that other great Victorian obsession: class. The first-class waiting room entertained the squires and wharf owners; the second-class room sheltered the good citizens of Lelant; while the third had to make do with a class proverbial for liking their beer.

By all accounts, the buildings and platform were kept in very good order by a succession of dutiful stationmasters. A local woman called Dorothy Meade recalled in a talk she gave to the Lelant Women's Institute in 1972 that prior to World War I, 'The stationmaster was an elderly gentleman called Mr Hosking. He had a long white beard and looked, and indeed was, very benevolent. He was a keen gardener and a devout Methodist. The platform had a few palm trees and beds of gaily coloured flowers all the year round, and there was never so much as a squashed matchbox or a bit of chocolate paper to be seen.'

A later stationmaster called Mr Glasson was no less diligent or green-fingered, his speciality being the annual cultivation on the platform of a 'magnificent show' of belladonna lilies. Nowadays the station is unstaffed, as are all railway request stops. However, the platform still boasted something in the way of floral adornment: a couple of wooden tubs of mixed plants either side of the bench and a few pansies in a plastic planter attached to the fence. It might not have been a riot of shocking pink belladonna lilies, but at least it showed that someone cared.

I shouldered my rucksack and strode out of the station to take up an invitation for a cup of tea at the house of Lelant's local historian, Maxwell Adams. Walking along the quiet lane that followed the railway line I imagined myself in the boots of Willie Edmonds, part-time postman to the village around the time of the last war. Willie had a deformed foot and so, when parcels arrived at the station, he loaded them onto a little cart pulled by a pony before dutifully delivering them to their intended recipients. Even with this help his progress was apparently glacial and made him an object of pity to the villagers. I slowed my pace to a painful hobble and, since there was no one around to see, began to lead an imaginary pony onwards. Had it been a club foot that dogged Willie? Or something more severe, like elephantiasis? Whatever it was, I couldn't help feeling that it wouldn't have been easy to bear both the disability and the well-meaning sympathy of his neighbours.

Maxwell welcomed me in and told me what he had unearthed about the station and its railway line. The mystery of why a small village like Lelant should possess two stations was easily resolved. Lelant Saltings opened in 1978 as a park-and-ride facility to try to keep down the number of cars clogging up St Ives. The 'Saltings' bit turns out to be something of an affectation since the station is situated at a place actually known to locals as The Muds. It seems peculiar that a railway network quite content to countenance 'Bat and Ball' and 'Spital' as names of stations could not bring itself to admit 'Lelant Muds' into its ranks. But perhaps someone had an eye on house prices, even back then.

More excitingly, when the railway was constructed, a spur line a few yards north of Lelant station ran off to a wharf now thrillingly known as Dynamite Quay. The course of the line was still just about discernible as it peeled off around the estuary wall. The quay it led to was constructed – possibly on the remains of a much earlier example – to take advantage of the coming of the railway, the idea being that the extra trade it would bring in would benefit the village. It gained its dramatic handle as late as World War II, when it was used to store dynamite as well as black powder for fuses.

Sadly, the wharf's name was the only stirring feature it had left. The skeleton of a factory was rusting slowly into oblivion and stones that once clicked and clacked under the hooves of cart horses lay dumb. The spur line had gone too. Indeed, if it hadn't been for the intervention in 1966 of Barbara Castle, the then Labour Minister of Transport, the entire line from St Erth to St Ives would have been lost, having been earmarked for closure in Dr Richard Beeching's notorious report on unprofitable railways.

By then, the comical music act Flanders and Swann had already written the line's obituary. In their song *Slow Train*, a lament for the stations and lines to be axed by Beeching, the duo crooned, 'No one departs/and no one arrives/from Selby to Goole/from St Erth to St

Ives.' Happily, this report of its death turned out to be greatly exaggerated.*

All too soon I was back at Lelant station and set to leave behind the village ghosts: stationmasters Hosking and Glasson, limping Willie Edmonds and his pony, Alfred Gall and his boyhood saviour Charles Hawes, Dynamite Quay and Brewery Quay. If other tales told by the Victorian inhabitants of the village are true, I was also leaving behind two actual ghosts that beleaguered the lanes hereabouts – a man with a tall hat but no face and a 'phantom coach, furiously driven by a lady'.

As I was waiting for the service back to St Erth – my train-stopping arm relaxed but poised to react to the first distant rumble of wheels on rail – I thought how very lucky the Queen was. This is not a reflection that occurs to me often – after all, she may be excessively privileged but who among us could bear the endless round of official functions and ceremonies and pompous dignitaries and interminable entertainment laid on by people garbed in traditional national costumes that last saw the light of day on Her Majesty's previous visit? The smell of fresh paint she is famously said to have to endure must often, I fear, be stiffened with that of moth balls. Who wants to live like that?

Anyway, she occasionally gets lucky, as I discovered when chatting with Annabelle Jeggo on her doorstep at The Old Station House. 'The Queen is coming down the line tomorrow,' she told me excitedly. Suddenly all the union flag bunting in her garden made sense. 'They've got a new

---

* Though not in the case of the Selby to Goole line, which closed in 1964. This reduced the number of ways a person could leave Goole, which those who have been there will recognise as an act as cruel as it is heartless.

lifeboat at St Ives, so she's coming to launch it. The Royal Train is coming down as far as St Erth.'

'So, she's taking a commoners' train from there to St Ives, is she?' I asked.

'Yes,' Annabelle confided, 'but I think they're blocking off the whole first carriage for her.'

'So that's why all your bunting's out?'

'No,' she confessed with an abashed smile, 'that was for the jubilee last year but I left it up for the coronation anniversary this year. She probably won't even see it, though – she'll be looking the other way, out over the estuary.'

So, lucky old Liz. There were still going to be some dignitaries she'd have to glad hand, but launching a lifeboat is probably more fun than opening Parliament, and tomorrow she could sit back and enjoy trundling about the West of England in her very own train (or part thereof).

I was drawn from my monarchical reverie by a distant rumble of wheels on rail. I held my hand out – *et voilà!* – the train slowed to a halt. This was just as well because although there is a fairly frequent service along this line, by no means all the trains are scheduled to stop at the request stations on it, even if you take the trouble of flagging them down with your own hastily removed red petticoats. If I'd missed this train the next one that would have stopped for me was due in a little matter of eight hours. Admittedly, I could have walked the half-mile down to Lelant Saltings, where every train stops regardless of need, but that's hardly the spirit.

TO PERRANWELL

'Perranwell is nowhere,' Verena revealed to me as we stood nattering on a platform at Truro. If I recall correctly, we had just about reached the point in our conversation where I had got used to her no longer being upside down. We were not at a request stop, of course, Truro being Cornwall's county town (having lately taken over duties from Bodmin) and the Duchy's only city. My presence here was necessitated by a change of trains, my second en route from Lelant to Perranwell. It seemed harsh that I should have to change trains twice just to end up nowhere.

At this point let me give some words of reassurance. Listening to somebody's prolix narration of the changes of train they have had to make on a particular journey (in the course of which they use words like 'prolix'), and the time they have waited for each train, and how many minutes more (or occasionally even less) it was than the timetabled wait, is an unutterably tedious chore. Therefore, unless I deem it absolutely necessary to the telling of my adventures among the tiny shelters and partially abandoned platforms of Britain's lesser-used stations, I shan't be recounting each change of train and every connection achieved by the skin of my teeth. As it turned out, the vast majority of trains ran pretty much to time, and when they were late they weren't so late as to precipitate anything approaching a disaster.

So back to Verena. She was not your average chance-meeting-on-a-journey person. Indeed, I was glad that I'd been prepared for our tryst by an encounter I had with friends of hers further up the platform. Getting off the train, I was greeted by the sight of several people on a bench who were dancing with unusual vigour while remaining steadfastly seated. There was no music playing and I assumed at first that they were listening to something through their headphones, though there was no tinny tiss-tiss-tiss to suggest that that was the case.

'There's some sort of "thing" going on here,' I thought to myself, my rapier-like mind scything the air asunder. 'I bet it's a flash mob. In a few seconds, everyone else on platform 3 will start dancing in perfect choreography, the station staff will throw off their uniforms in one easy movement, revealing feline onesies underneath, the station announcer will begin to sing 'Eye of the Tiger', film crews will emerge as if from nowhere to capture my look of astonished rapture and/or rapturous astonishment and a release form will be thrust into my hand, at the bottom of which I shall notice the name of some faceless money-grubbing tax-avoiding under-scrupled corporation.'

It was then that I saw Verena. What struck me about her was not her tall, slender frame wrapped in a long black coat or even her winsomely high cheekbones. What I first noticed was that she was upside down. Better still, there was not the hint of a suggestion of a whisper of corporate faux feel-goodery about her. I said, 'Hello.' She said, 'Hello.' And so began our relationship.

She was part of a whole group here at the station, she explained – students like her from Falmouth University engaging in performance art. She was 34 (I'd mentally guessed late twenties) and had her beanie-hatted head down on the platform and her feet up in the air for quite a while. But I was the first person who'd talked to her.

'And, if it's not uncool to ask, what's with the whole upside-down thing?' I uncoolly asked.

Verena fumbled for her bag, fished around in it for her phone – a refreshingly antiquated affair from the days when mobiles were still gas-powered – pressed a few buttons and handed it to me.

'This will explain,' she said from down by my feet, the perfection of her English more suggestive of her Dutch citizenship than any trace of an accent. 'It's by Andrei Tarkovsky.'

The quotation I read was about art. Its purpose, the great Russian film-maker proposed, was not to spread ideas but to make individuals ready for their own deaths. Then there was something about the soul being ploughed and harrowed by art, thus furnishing it with the possibility of doing good.

Well, that certainly explained a lot about Russian film.

'That sums up why I'm engaged in things like this,' she told me, her powers of speech and enunciation seemingly unaffected by her posture. 'I want to explore. I want to play.'

I nodded enthusiastically. Clearly I too wanted to explore. And play, for that matter. I also wanted to talk to her about art. Most of all, I wanted to talk to her about death. After all, she'd brought it up first, so she clearly had some light to shed on the matter. And, hey, it could still be a fun chat – death doesn't have to be morbid, does it? I pictured us at a pavement café – me in a beret, Verena smoking a pipe, laughing occasionally at a witticism or throwaway equivoque of mine, the owner letting us stay for hours over a single coffee on account of the cachet we bestowed upon his establishment with our high-minded intercourse.

Perhaps aware that I was going to prove more than a passing hi-smile-bye punter, Verena flipped over onto her feet and took off her beanie, unveiling a fetching mop of extremely short dark hair. It was almost as if she knew I had a weakness for women with extremely short dark hair. But what could I say to impress her? Sartre, *naturellement* [note to self: must *not* say *naturellement* out loud], would be the name to drop – I could recall his notion that we should all kill ourselves at the moment of our greatest happiness. Or maybe not – a little *de trop* on a first date [second note to self: must *not* give inkling that I am considering this conversation a date]. Something from friend Boethius, then – after all, a copy of his book was burning a hole in my rucksack and more or less every line touched on the certainty and, in his case, imminence of death. At least, I assumed it did, because I hadn't quite got around to starting it yet, which was an impediment when quoting from a work. Maybe I could fall back on that John Stuart Mill quotation I made myself learn as a teenager – I usually manage to slip that into almost any philosophical debate.

'Hmm, interesting,' I heard myself say, supremely confident that the only reason I ever interacted with art was to have my soul ploughed and harrowed. 'Do you have harrows in Holland?'

They did. The Dutch word was apparently *eggen*. I was explaining the derivation of the name 'restharrow' – trust me, it's fascinating: the woody stems of this member of the pea family are so strong that they can literally stop harrows – when Verena was saved by the arrival of Rosie.

Rosie was wearing walking gear and a rucksack with a host of labels fastened to it by pieces of string. She had taken her inspiration from a woman who, once a year, embarked on a 25-mile solo walk along the coast from Penzance to Falmouth to clear her head.

'So I'm asking people to write down on a label something that's worrying them and attach it to me,' she explained.

She was then devoting this day to marching up and down the platform until she'd covered 25 miles, thus fulfilling her promise to the worriers to take their worries for a walk in the manner of her role model.

'And what sort of worries have people got?' I asked her.

Rosie turned her back to me and let me read a few of the labels. None of them were signed, so I didn't feel as if I were violating the sanctity of the confessional.

'The oddest one so far,' she said over her shoulder, 'is *I'm worried I don't have time.*'

It was certainly enigmatic. Was it from someone handed a gloomy prognosis and worried that they didn't have sufficient time to carry out some lifetime's work? Or was the writer simply anxious about never having enough hours in the day to fulfil all the duties their lifestyle demanded of them? If this were the case, it must have been some consolation that Rosie was doing their worry-walking for them, leaving them with more time to rush about fretting. Or perhaps they were prone to fits of ontological angst and had begun to worry that their existence was taking place wholly outside of Time (and presumably, therefore, Space)?

We agreed that the sense of a lack of time was a prevalent malaise in modern Britain. Although I didn't say so at the time, I rather admired the fact that, in the eyes of the scurrying masses, Rosie was wasting the greater part of the day on what they would consider an absurd quest. And I had to admit that I, for all that I have lived the life of a full-time writer for years now, am one of that teeming throng of the perennially busy myself, even if my busyness often only manifests itself in the aimless occupying of my waking hours with the billion distractions of cyberspace.

I asked Rosie if she was enjoying her trek up and down the platform.

'There's not quite so much to look at as on the coastal walk,' she confessed. Then she invited me to add my own worry. I inked it onto a blank label and she dutifully headed back up the platform, the worries flapping about her in the breeze with an unseemly gaiety.

Verena and I were alone again. Despite my misadventures in the worlds of harrowing and restharrowing, we were both very comfortable chatting and we picked up the threads of our conversation with ease. I already knew that I wanted to kiss her on the cheek when I had to say goodbye and catch my train to Perranwell, even though I had rarely before exchanged so intimate an act with a stranger on so short an acquaintance. Also, I was turning into Jane Austen, which was another novelty. Some redeeming of the situation was required.

'Consider whether you are happy and you will cease to be so,' I remarked with studied insouciance. 'That's what John Stuart Mill thought. It's a pity you can't apply that to being worried as well.'

Seamless.

My train would soon be leaving from a far platform. I leaned forward, we kissed each other on the cheek and hugged briefly. I hadn't bargained on a hug as well, so that was a bonus. I left her standing in a bin that bore the legend 'General Waste'. I was quietly proud of this, for when Verena had asked me for ideas as to what she could do next, I had proposed that she stand in the bin. I didn't know what it would mean, exactly. To be honest, I hadn't given any thought to whether, as art, the act of standing in a bin might prepare a person for death – ploughing and harrowing her soul, rendering it capable of turning to good. I just saw the bin and reckoned it might make people think if they saw someone in it. Or at least make them smile.

Looking back on it now, my suggestion seems unfortunate, to put it lightly. I had met someone I really liked and, on leaving her, I had asked her to stand in a bin. Come on down, Dr Freud.

PERRANWELL

Verena's contention that Perranwell was 'nowhere' was a source of rather more excitement to me than she had doubtless intended. I enjoy going to places that are nowhere. What people usually mean when they say that somewhere is nowhere – or posit the even more abstract notion that somewhere is in the *middle* of nowhere – is that humans haven't got around to building anything significant nearby. Given the propensity our species has for leaving things less beautiful than when they started – I may not agree with Ruskin on much but I'm with him on his man's-enterprise-invariably-ruins-Nature's-handiwork shtick – arriving somewhere that is nowhere can be quite a treat. In my mind's eye, I already had a vision of Perranwell as a cluster of houses on a windswept plain, a few craggy tors dotted around it like grim-faced sentinels and perhaps a youthful river cutting a scar across the moors. There was no room in my head for any fears that her pronouncement might be more in line with Dorothy Parker's summation of Hollywood, to wit, 'There's no *there* there.'

As it turned out, the truth was somewhere between the two.

I discovered that my mind's eye was in serious need of glasses. The village of Perranwell is, in reality, arranged around the sides of a little valley, its main roads forming the silhouette of a sprinter racing eastwards, breasting the tape (represented by a track running to St Piran's church) and raising her arms in triumph. However, Perranwell station itself is perched on the side of a hill half a mile to the northeast. The railway line, fresh from passing over large and graceful viaducts in both directions, has had to pick its way carefully around the side of a steep slope, following its contours and thus bypassing the village below. It meant that when I stepped down onto Perranwell's single platform, there did indeed appear to be not much *there* there at all. There might have been a goodly smattering of houses nearby, but they belonged to a quite separate entity that had grown up around the station. In order to forestall any doubts visitors might have about this fact, this community has been called Perranwell Station, though that's not even the oddest place name in the district – that honour belongs to Greensplat.

Perranwell station (with a small 's') came into being on 24 August 1863 when the Cornwall Railway opened a broad gauge line from Truro to Falmouth Docks, principally to serve the packet ships that berthed there. This extended the Cornwall Railway's standard gauge (then known as narrow gauge – as opposed to broad gauge) line whose far eastern terminus was at Plymouth in Devon. The line had crossed into Cornwall over the seemingly insuperable barrier of the Tamar by the construction of the famous Royal Albert Bridge. The company, in its wisdom, had commissioned Isambard Kingdom Brunel to design the bridge (it opened just before he died) and the main line still runs over it a sesquicentenary later, which is testament to quite a lot of things. As was the way of the tiny 19th-century railway companies, the Cornwall Railway later became part of a much larger concern, being hoovered up into the Great Western Railway in 1889.

Perranwell's signal box was a curious affair slung up high over a track, allowing trains to pass beneath it. The structure disappeared back in the 1960s along with the station's sidings and one of the line's doubled tracks. The old goods shed was still hanging grimly on though, which was quite a feat since there had been no goods traffic through here for nearly 50 years. The platform was graced by two other relics from a slightly more glorious past: the remains of a large metallic lollipop that was apparently once a drinking fountain, and a marvellous green and white signboard bearing the station's name in embossed letters. The sign was of indeterminate age but we can be sure that it wasn't the original because the station here was first called Perran. This was clearly the source of untold hilarious mix-ups owing to the fact that the next station down the line is its near namesake, Penryn. Perran became Perranwell six months after opening and the hilarity ceased forthwith.

I made up for this humour deficit by marking my visit to the village of Perranwell with an unintentional act of idiocy.

It all started off encouragingly enough. I had a leisurely poke around Perranwell, which, while not striking me as really *somewhere*, could not honestly be dismissed as nowhere either. It had a pub, a post office-cum-village store with a window display of fake bread, fake fruit and fake eggs; and a poster bearing the legend 'Dog Portraits – acrylic on canvas 12" by 12" £75 – call Suzy' below the portraits of three dogs, one of whom bore an uncanny resemblance to the pocket-sized former England maestro Kevin Keegan circa 1978–82, the bubble perm years.

I also made it to the village's Siamese twin, Perranarworthal. Perranarworthal is home to the aforementioned St Piran's church and, at the foot of a little copse festooned with campion, snowdrops and forget-me-nots, St Piran's well, after which Perranwell is named.

It was just after my visit to the site of Perran Wharf that disaster struck. I had taken it into my head that the train back to Truro left at 12.50 and not, absolutely not, definitely not at 12.40. I shan't go into the wearisome intricacies of the deliberations that led me to this conclusion but they were largely based on the time a Truro-bound train had mistakenly stopped for me at Perranwell while I was still having a shufti around the station. (I'd tried to indicate to the driver that I didn't want to get on, but my confidence in my ability to express the thought 'Don't stop the train, I'm just shooting the breeze with this large metallic lollipop' entirely in hand-signal form turned out to have been a trifle misplaced.)

It was at 12.37 that I decided to haul my itinerary from my rucksack to reassure myself that the train did leave at 12.50. I think you can probably guess the rest.

'This,' I thought, as I powered sweatily along, my rucksack growing heavier with each desperate stride, 'is how I plough and harrow my soul.' Unfortunately, I wasn't convinced that the stress caused by my habitual cutting fine of things rendered my soul capable of turning to good. Usually, it just left me saying to myself, 'Why am I such an idiot? Why do I always do this? Is there a support group for this sort of thing?'

I missed the train, of course. Running a mile down dale and over hill with a large rucksack and a ukulele in three minutes flat was always unlikely, if I'm honest. I had barely started to climb the incline when I saw my train tootling along the track above me in a carefree manner that I suspected was for my benefit.

I carried on up to the station anyway, even though I knew that there wouldn't be another train for an hour – and that would arrive at Truro a quarter of an hour too late. On my very first full day, at the second railway request stop of dozens, I had tipped over a domino. If I didn't get to Truro within the next 45 minutes my entire trip would resemble a pile of toppled dominoes – rail tickets for the wrong days, accommodation for the wrong nights, train-filled Saturday timetables transformed into tumbleweed Sundays, with the Four Horsemen of the Apocalypse laying waste to any tract of the nation in which I placed my cursèd foot.

My immediate thought was that I should hitchhike the five or six miles to Truro. This would have been a sound idea had there been any traffic passing by, but traffic there was none. And then miraculously, out of nowhere as it were, appeared a bus. A bus going to Truro station. And here was I, accidentally at a bus stop. A bus stop on the right side of the road for Truro-bound buses. Take that, Dawkins – proof beyond all dispute that God exists.

'That's £2.90 and £2.90 for your friend,' deadpanned the bus driver when I told him my destination. The quip was a reference to my rucksack, apparently. It's dry, the Cornish sense of humour.

I arrived at Truro station with ten minutes to spare. I felt as if I had used a life up. Verena had moved platform and was eating lunch. She invited me to sit with her.

'One of the station staff eventually asked me to get out of the bin,' she began. 'They said it might break. It was fun while it lasted, though.'

She revealed that she was a vegan but occasionally caved in and ate cheese. I told her I was also a vegan but had still somehow resisted the siren call of halloumi. Then I felt a bit self-righteous and wished I hadn't mentioned it.

'I live in a caravan,' she told me. It was cheap but still meant that she had to find ways of earning money to make ends meet. She found this depressing. Or possibly merely 'pressing' – I didn't quite hear and I was conscious of the fact that my train was sitting at another platform and would leave in three minutes. As I left she gave me an organic apple to take with me. I reached down into my rucksack and hurriedly pulled out the first item of food that came to hand: a half-eaten tub of hummus. I proffered it in return and she graciously accepted. We kissed goodbye and I hurtled up the platform to my train with the please-earth-swallow-me-now demeanour of someone who has just given another human being a half-eaten tub of hummus as a gift. I'd got her email address, though. That's good going for me.

TO LUXULYAN

A single-coach diesel multiple unit (if you don't know what one of these is it's a sure sign that you're a functioning member of society) was sitting in Par station waiting to take me the single stop up the Newquay line to Luxulyan. A 12-year-old boy in metal-framed glasses and an ill-fitting uniform stood on the platform, anxiously checking his watch every 20 seconds until, precisely 18 seconds early, he could take it no more. He lifted his whistle to his lips and blew. He raised his black-and-white paddle thing (there's probably a proper word for this among railway folk) and bid the train be gone. The doors closed and half a minute later the train pulled away.

The boy smiled. He was doing his dream job. Who couldn't be happy for him?

LUXULYAN

Despite having lived with friends for a year in a south London house that went by the name of Luxulyan (we never found out why), the first thing I learned on my arrival was that I'd been pronouncing it wrong.

'I'd like to get off at Luxulyan, please,' I asked the guard just as the train was burrowing, worm-like, through a short tunnel and a magnificently claustrophobic cutting.

'Luck-*sil*-iun?' he replied, emphasising the errant second syllable and replacing my 'u' sound with a short 'i'.

'Ah, I didn't know. Do you know why it's pronounced like that?'

He shook his head.

'Cornish is quite similar to Welsh,' I ventured, 'and Welsh is very fond of tripping up English tongues with its u's that sound like y's – perhaps it's like that,' but by this time the doors were opening and he had other conductorial duties to perform, so all I got was a sort of half-shrug performed out of politeness. I doubt the terms of his contract expressly demanded that he engage passengers in philological discussions, so it would be wrong to grumble.

The sun peeped meekly from behind a cloud as I stepped onto the platform at Luxulyan. This is one of the longest-serving stations in Britain, but although it was still very tidy, freshly painted and well cared for, it's safe to say that it had fallen on quieter times. A gorse bush marked the point, just under halfway along the platform, where order ceased and the wilds took over. Grasses now grew where once was gravel and small trees brought the countryside to the railway.

Just as I was about to leave the station to explore the village, I heard a roar behind me; a few seconds later a red and yellow diesel engine blundered through, hauling what seemed like a never-ending trail of china clay hopper wagons behind it. When fully loaded these trains can apparently weigh up to 1,400 tons, which is heavier than I can properly comprehend. This train was presumably running empty on its way to pick up china clay so was relatively light, though you'd never have suspected it from the clatter it made as it careered through.

The loco was a maroon and gold Class 66. I'm not a train buff but I'm certain of my facts here because it had a giveaway '66086' emblazoned on its side in large numerals. Next to them were the letters EWS. Conveniently, I used to work around the corner from the offices of EWS, so I know it stands for English, Welsh and Scottish Railways. You could barely ask for a more British-sounding name, so it comes as no surprise to discover that the company has been wholly owned by Deutsche Bahn since 2007. Let us not cavil, however, for the train's passing was a timely reminder of how Luxulyan station came to be here at all.

The name Joseph Thomas Treffry may not mean much nowadays but he was a very big wheel in his time, having been heir to the Treffry family fortune which included Place House in Fowey (if you've ever been to Fowey you'll have seen it — it's the one that looks like a Gothic castle).

Treffry used his new-found wealth to buy up local mining concerns and build a new harbour at Par on the south coast. Once he had possessed himself of the all but abandoned harbour at Newquay on the north coast, he hatched a plan to connect his two ports and his mines and quarries by means of a tramway. His first attempt, begun in 1835, came up against too many logistical obstacles and eventually had to be abandoned. Undeterred, he tried again along a slightly different route starting from a canal basin at Ponts Mill and crossing the River Par, a feat that was accomplished by throwing up a daring 650ft-long viaduct that flew 100ft above the waters. Beneath the viaduct's tramway track, the ingenious Treffry also had a channel built to carry water from the River Par to his five Fowey Consols copper mines and to power the machinery that hauled wagons up the inclined plane, a slope too steep for horses to attempt. The viaduct-aqueduct was completed in 1842 and the first horse-drawn wagons began operating on the tramway two years later.

Treffry's Tramway eventually grew into an extensive network of tracks linking the harbour at Par with both copper ore mines and granite quarries, and the enterprise prospered. The tramway's crowning glory, the graceful Treffry Viaduct, still spans the River Par, although some of its sturdy grey columns, built of stone from the nearby Carbeans and Colcerrow quarries, are now well nigh obscured by tall trees. But it was not until well after Treffry's death in 1850 that his dream of linking the ports of Par and Newquay was realised.

The honour of achieving that dream fell, rather disappointingly perhaps, to a London-based speculator and multiple bankrupt called William Richardson Roebuck. Arriving in Cornwall in 1870, Roebuck had corralled sufficient funds to buy up the entire Treffry estate and two years later set about forming the Cornwall Minerals Railway in order to turn a profit from ironstone deposits near Newquay. He established his headquarters at St Blazey – a village between Par and Luxulyan – and, once he had secured permission to do so via an Act of Parliament, started converting the tramways into railways on which he could run locomotives. However, to avoid the steep incline from the Ponts Mill canal basin, he decided to forge a new line to Luxulyan. This veered off soon after St Blazey, followed the floor of the Luxulyan Valley and came out on the left bank of the Par to pass underneath the Treffry Viaduct. This route – which is the one still used nowadays – necessitated the digging of the short tunnel and deep cutting through which, 139 years later, my own train had come.

The Cornwall Minerals Railway line from Fowey to Newquay was opened on 1 June 1874, but it was only because of the almost instantaneous demise of the ironstone enterprise that the good people of Luxulyan got to use the railway themselves. Casting around desperately for a new source of revenue, Roebuck launched a passenger service in 1876. The station at Luxulyan he called Bridges, a name it held until 1905 when it became Luxulyan. There's still a community called Bridges clustered around the station, though to the casual observer it is indistinguishable from Luxulyan itself.

Unfortunately, back in the 1870s Newquay was by no means a tourist magnet – that transformation would happen only after World War I, when the Great Western Railway gave the village a great big station and started to promote it as a holiday resort. Predictably, Roebuck's passenger service proved as financially disastrous as the ironstone venture. Another visit to the bankruptcy courts was only averted thanks to china clay, of which Cornwall has the largest deposits in the world. The passenger service was hurriedly hived off to the Great Western Railway and Roebuck concentrated on moving the clay to ships docked at Fowey.* Even this came to an end in 1896, though, when the entire Cornwall Minerals Railway operation was gobbled up by the Great Western Railway.

It's a pity that most passengers race eagerly through to Newquay without troubling the conductor with a request to stop at Luxulyan, for it has much to recommend it. The joys of a wander along the Luxulyan Valley were being trumpeted as long ago as 1928, with renowned travel writer S P B Mais declaring it to be 'one of the most glorious walks in all Cornwall ... where the rarest and most graceful ferns grow in wild woodland glades carpeted with hyacinths, bluebells, and daffodils'. Evidence of the Treffry Tramways – not least in the form of Treffry Viaduct – and the valley's industrial past can still be picked out among the woods and undergrowth.

The village had a convenience store that promoted an assiduously minimalist lifestyle to its clientele. I picked up a packet of pink wafers and realised as I was paying for it that it represented about 2 per cent of the shop's stock. Not, that is, 2 per cent of its pink wafer stock but 2 per cent of its entire stock of everything.

---

* Fowey has no station nowadays, but trains filled with china clay still ply the wonderfully picturesque line from Lostwithiel down to the town's port at Carne Point.

Feeling slightly guilty about this, I hiked across the road to the church. I love a poke about in an old church. I love to read the inscriptions on the walls commemorating a long-serving rector or a beloved organist. I love the kneeler covers stitched by members of the Women's Wednesday Prayer Group. I love the smell of the battle against those twin maledictions Damp and Cold. I love to inspect the obsolete weapons used by the parishioners in this eternal conflict – a cast-iron radiator here, an antediluvian one-bar electric fire there, a storage heater that has long since lost the will to heat or even store, and that last desperate throw of the dice: the draught excluder. But where to place it when *everything* is draught?

Most of all, I love to find a place to hide. I imagine to myself that I'm on the run (for an offence of which I'm wholly innocent, of course, or at least largely innocent; or sometimes from an oppressive regime that I have upset in some unspecified way – it all depends what mood I'm in) and that I must flee across the country on foot. At night, while my pursuers prowl the hedgerows and back alleys in futile search, I sleep in churches, my head resting on a kneeler stitched by a member of the Women's Wednesday Prayer Group. In order to effect this, I must first evade any casual inspection carried out by whoever has been charged with locking the church doors come the dusk. Hence the place to hide. I have searched for sites of potential ecclesiastical concealment for many years in hundreds of churches throughout the land and I think I can claim (without being accused of undue self-regard) that I have made myself one of the nation's foremost experts in this field. I shan't be giving away all the secrets of my research here, but I can reveal that often the only feasible location is behind the altar. Even this can be an unsatisfactory choice at some of the humbler churches where worshippers make do with a table covered by a cloth that doesn't quite reach the floor.

Having chosen my spot – and noted with approval the Ribena, bottled water and plastic cups left out for visitors and fugitives alike – I perused the guest book of the parish church of St Cyriacus and St Julitta (say what you like about the Cornish but they have the best saints' names by some margin). Many of the recent entries were taken up by Australians parading lineages that led all the way back to individuals who knew these very stones. This was not to be wondered at given the exodus of Cornish tin miners to the Antipodes in the latter half of the 19th century. 'Descendant of Samuel Prior, baptised here 1822,' read one. 'Ninth-generation great-granddaughter of Rev. Peter Wellington BA – 1623,' another claimed.

I wondered at the motives that drove this scrambling around for roots in unfamiliar soil. When I worked in an office in the same cul-de-sac as the Society of Genealogists' National Family History Centre I would sometimes look out of the window and play 'guess the person tracing their family tree'. I learned it was generally not the very old who cared to find out where they came from. Maybe they were already too concerned with where they might soon be going. It was those approaching late middle age who nursed a desire to research their ancestors. Were they looking for clues among the marriage certificates and baptismal registers that might reveal what had made them who they were? Were they perhaps vying against the chaos of the universe by placing themselves in a structure that they hoped would bring meaning or comfort or some sense of belonging? Did the Australians who had signed the visitors' book in this 15th-century church draw strength from inhabiting the very same space their all-too-distant relatives had passed through? Or had they come to curse their forebears for turning them into Australians?

I signed the book – I always do, on the grounds that some day it might come in useful if I need to prove an alibi. Next to it lay a wedding card and an invitation to write something in it, so I signed that too, wishing the happy couple all the best. I hope they didn't spend too much time agonising over who the person was whose name they didn't recognise. ('Are you sure that squiggle really says "Dixe" anyway, darling? What sort of a name is that?')

Sunshine had begun to penetrate the nave at last, if not the knave in it, when I found a booklet that answered the mystery of the curious pronunciation of Luxulyan. Apparently, back in 1162, the village was spelt Luxylyan, a name derived from St Sulian, who is purported to have founded a monastery here in the sixth century. Critically, Sulian was Welsh, and so his name would have been pronounced 'Silian'. It appears that although that early Luxylyan lost its crucial first 'y' to become Luxulian, Luxulion and even Lossulyan before settling on Luxulyan, the true pronunciation of the name has been handed down unchanged for hundreds of years.

Luxulyan may have lost its tramway, its quarries and its mines, but its grip on its spoken name remains as steadfast as ever. Living in a nation that has largely lost its habit of handing down stories by word of mouth from generation to generation, I can't help but think that Luxulyan's unbroken oral tradition is rather admirable.

BUGLE

The eastern end of the station at Bugle – the very next stop on the line and named after the venerable Bugle Inn – is now in so advanced a state of re-naturalisation that it pretty much counts as countryside. It's curious then that the remainder of the station has so much of an urban feel to it. A blackened and boxy bridge carries a main road over the railway at the western end of the platform; every single pane of glass is missing from the ugly Cubist shelter; on the other side of the track, beyond a *cordon sanitaire* of unruly bushes, a row of uninspiring white-painted houses looms over the length of the station and goads us to enjoy the view. It's not edgy, exactly – I've lived in the east end of London for long enough to recognise edgy when it leaps out of a darkened alleyway – but it's a long way from the cosy country station of the collective imagination.

It's unlikely the village it serves would be here at all had it not been for the industrialisation of this little parcel of Cornwall in the 19th century. Back in 1840, when The Bugle Inn opened, it all looked very different – there were just a few houses grouped around a turnpike road. The pub is still very much in existence, still called The Bugle Inn and still offering accommodation, though it no longer acts as a coach house and stables. I dutifully paid a visit and splashed out on half a pint of one of the local beers, though the fact that this same ale has become so successful that I've sampled it in many a pub not far from my home did somewhat dilute the exoticism of the experience. I consoled myself with the thought that at least I was in a pub with a bit of history to it.

In 1864, a shoemaker named William Cock had his ear bitten off in a brawl at The Bugle Inn. His assailant, the 20-year-old Edgar Retallick, claimed that Cock had started the fight: '[Cock] potched me with his stick,' he averred when an Inspector Sherstone took the offending ear from a folded piece of paper and confronted him with it. The mono-auriculate cobbler presumably went through the rest of his life enduring hilarious jokes about him being '... a gentleman not so much cock-eyed as cock-*eared*. D'you geddit, sir? D'you geddit?' On the other hand, it's difficult not to feel sympathy for the young Retallick, for no one likes to be potched with a stick.

Eleven years later, The Bugle was again the scene of a meaty altercation, though fortunately of a less violent nature. The contretemps betwixt a prospective sojourner at The Bugle and that hostelry's less than welcoming landlord was the subject of a brilliantly splenetic letter to the *Royal Cornwall Gazette*. The author claimed to have witnessed the barney and wrote to rebut assertions made in a letter published previously by another witness, who had signed himself 'Visitor'. The newsprint so dripped with sarcasm and outraged honour (especially in the matter of the subject's girth), and so all-consuming was the cold flame of his fury, that it is difficult to believe it was not penned by the offended party himself. It's true that the address he gave, Gwinear, is a tiny place comprising three streets, so it would almost certainly have been possible to verify the identity of the writer, but the village is far enough removed from Bugle to deter anyone from putting themselves to the bother of doing so.

But, anyway, I shall let you make up your own mind (while also enjoying the excellent use of the word 'abraded' and the superbly catty PS).

Sir, A 'Visitor,' in your number of the 13th inst., has stepped forward as the defender of 'Mine Host' of The Bugle; but his defence is of the most singular conceivable. He says, "the proprietor, having a gentleman occupying apartments in his house at the time, did not think it would be judicious to admit the 'stout party,' and the broken kneed hackney which accompanied him!". 1. Query. Was there a gentleman occupying apartments there? I doubt it; for no such reason was adduced for the refusal to entertain the traveller in question. 2. Is a traveller to be refused entertainment because he happens to be stout; or a horse 'accompanying' him, because he had the misfortune to injure his knees? Does the "proprietor" think that the licensing justices would admit that [sic] such allegations in justification for refusing to supply food and lodging to a traveller? I think not. I cannot understand why "Visitor" insinuated that it would be well for me to "adhere to the truth." As I did not violate the truth in my statement, the caution seems superfluous.

"Visitor" says, "I would advise the worthy 'Traveller' to stay at home until his equipage can be such as a licensed vicualler

[sic] would not consider a disgrace" to the Bugle Inn! The Bugle is too respectable for common-place vehicles! Perhaps the paint was slightly abraded, or there was no silver-mounted harness to correspond to the grandeur of the Bugle. Let all travellers see to it, that before expecting any accommodation at this grand hotel, they be careful to have smart vehicles, horses silver-mounted, and they themselves free from obesity (for there is no room for "stout" men).

I am not the traveller in question, as "Visitor" supposed, but I know the facts as stated by me, and am prepared to affirm that the traveller who was denied accommodation is [a] highly respectable gentleman – and that his equipage was by no means shabby. He was ready to pay for what he required. I advised [sic] "Mine Host" to reform his habits that he may become as respectable as the rejected traveller.

Gwinear, 12th March 1875

TRAVELLER.

P.S. – I may add that the want of accommodation at the Bugle is a subject of common conversation in the neighborhood.

The tramway arrived four years after The Bugle Inn opened. Up until that point, the industry that surrounded the hamlet – in the form of tin mines and the streaming works that separated the ore from the base rock – had left it untouched. When the local china clay deposits began to be exploited and brought down to the waiting wagons at the tram head, the settlement became a fully paid-up member of the toiling classes. Houses for the workers were joined by a chapel and schools, though the village was prevented from mushrooming into a town by the presence of other villages nearby that were also attracting labourers, shopkeepers, clerics and all the various folk who go to make a community.

I had a saunter but failed to be enraptured. Perhaps my expectations had been unfairly inflated by the fact that the village has such a great handle. It was the first place I'd been to that's named after a brass musical instrument since the afternoon three summers ago when, venturing west of Ledbury, I came upon Trumpet.

As far as I could gather from my recce, Bugle consisted of the pub, a couple of busy main roads, a Citroën garage, a used-car showroom, a 'pine and bed centre', an apostrophe-free working men's club, a light industrial estate full of companies with instantly forgettable compound names, a Spar and an awful lot of pebbledash. I can only surmise that pebbledash is a by-product of the china clay industry and that it comes highly discounted. Or perhaps the village had once run the risk of being entombed beneath a mountain of waste pebbledash and had been saved only when a panicked parish council rushed through a by-law forcing all householders to use some of it on their exterior walls. I bet that was it.

It was more eye-easing to look to the hills. Bugle is dominated by the table mountain that is the former Goonbarrow china clay works. There are plans for this to become part of the St Austell and Clay Country Eco-town, which would entail the building of 5,000 or so houses on five worked-out china clay quarries. I didn't notice any obvious opposition to these plans – perhaps the locals were actively encouraged by the prospect of a new venture. After all, theirs was a village that seemed to thrive only when in the grip of some fresh activity.

There was even a chance that tin mining could be making a comeback locally. I spent the night at a campsite near St Columb Road, another request stop two stations further along the line. As I chatted to my amiable host Royston beneath the intense gaze of his three alpacas, he pointed out a drilling rig a few fields away.

'They're prospecting for tin,' he told me. 'There's meant to be a billion dollars' worth of it beneath these fields. It's all because of the mobiles and laptops and tablets people have nowadays – they all use tin, so demand has rocketed. When they first started looking at this area in 1982, tin was worth $2,000 a tonne. Today it's over $20,000 a tonne.'

'And how would you feel if they opened a tin mine over there?' I asked.

'It wouldn't be great,' he confided. 'You see, they could just get a compulsory purchase order and take my land off me. I've lived here over 20 years but I could lose it all overnight.'

That night, lying in my sleeping bag, I attempted to make a start on *The Consolation of Philosophy* by the light of my trusty solar torch. Bugle had not been a terrible place by any stretch of the imagination, and perhaps my new friend Royston wouldn't lose the few acres he and his wife had made their home, but I felt that a cold shadow had passed over the landscape in the last few hours and it seemed a good time to go in search of warmth and light.

TO LYMPSTONE COMMANDO

'Why am I ... like this?' I gasped as I hurtled along, dripping with sweat and bowed beneath a rucksack that gained in weight with every stride.

The calm I had accrued the previous night – borne off into the realm of sleep at last on a carpet of consoling thoughts and watched over by heedful alpacas – had evaporated before the sun had reached its zenith. Even though the train I had to catch was at an extremely civilised 10.26 and I was camping a mere 40-minute walk away from the station, I still somehow found myself leaving the campsite at just after ten.

I say 'somehow' but I can't get away from the fact that that somehow is, basically, me. Though in general terms a glass-half-empty person, I'm always hopelessly optimistic about how long a given activity will take and inevitably end up rushing pell-mell at the end of it. This not only applies to catching trains, getting to appointments and meeting up with people* but spills over into almost every area of my life.

The fact that I started off from the campsite by going in completely the wrong direction didn't help either. Happily, my limbs gained strength from the knowledge that if I missed this train the next one was a full three hours later.

---

* Allow me to use this opportunity to apologise to everyone who's ever had to wait around for me – your patience shall, I'm sure, be rewarded.*
*Terms and conditions apply

Thus they valiantly powered me along the rutted track to the station sufficiently speedily to land me on the platform of St Columb Road a good 45 seconds before the train turned up, which in my world didn't even qualify as a close-run thing.

From this point onward I shan't bore you with tales of trains I nearly missed due to my misplaced spatio-temporal optimism, but you can take it as read that such near calamities occurred with depressing frequency for the remainder of the trip. Still, on the plus side, it does help maintain a basic level of fitness. With gym membership being as pricey as it is, I see this as a prudent means of limiting my outgoings in an age of recession.

LYMPSTONE COMMANDO

Is this the only station in the land which is not simply a request stop but one for which passengers must seek official permission to alight in advance of their journey? Well, yes, it is. So I was thankful that I'd stumbled across this fact before setting out. I tracked down the telephone number of a woman who, in turn, kindly rang some high-ranking officer at the commando base with my request to spend a little time taking a few photographs on the platform of his training camp's dedicated railway station.

'They'll let the sentry on duty and the CCTV people know you'll be getting off the 13.40,' the woman had told me when she got back to me a week or so later.

I had secretly hoped that somehow or other this message would not get through and that as soon as my foot hit the platform, commandos would storm out, arrest me at gunpoint, take me to the camp's underground interrogation cells and pump me for information about my one-man terrorist plot to blow up the station. Only then would they discover that my rucksack, far from being packed with explosives, contained mainly couscous. At that moment a phone call would come through to say that the piece of paper confirming my permission to alight from the 13.40 had been found behind a fridge or a gun or whatever they have there, and we'd all have a good laugh about it. They'd stop tasering me and they'd show me around the camp as a gesture of goodwill; they'd probably even let me fire a bazooka at a passing fishing smack or something. It would be ace.

I was luxuriating in this dream scenario, letting each glorious element lap about my imagination, when the train guard came through asking to be shown tickets. I held mine up. As I did so, I said, 'Lympstone Commando, please,' just in case her glance did not take in the station name.

'I knew there'd be one of you on here somewhere,' she replied cheerily.

It was only after she had passed on down the train that I fully digested her comment. 'One of *you*,' she said, 'one of *you*.' She thought *I* was a commando. If I were a lover of exclamation marks I might be tempted to splash out on a couple there. For the sake of clarity I should point out that I am *not* a commando, nor was I dressed in anything that might have been mistaken for military garb. My hair is short but not army-short and my rucksack, though green, is conspicuously backpacker-y and not the sort one might wear while, say, scaling a cliff on the way to knocking out a radar station. I can only conclude that it was my exceptional physique – honed almost exclusively by my late-for-everything training regime – that caused her to miscalculate my status as a commando by around 100 per cent. I wish that I had got her to guess my rank, then I could have basked in her admiration as she cooed, 'Oh, but you look far too young to be a lieutenant-colonel ...'

Nonetheless, the realisation that I could so effortlessly pass myself off as a commando was very gratifying and I like to think that at some point in the future I might find a use for this gift. It certainly went some way to consoling me when I hopped down onto the platform and not a single sentry rushed out to ask what I thought I was up to.

There is just the one platform at Lympstone Commando. It serves the one track that runs through here from Exeter to Exmouth alongside the wide expanses of the Exe estuary – a combination of the mighty Exe and the plucky but rather less mighty Clyst. Sadly, what might have been a glorious panorama of the estuary is denied to passengers on Lympstone Commando station by the presence of an impenetrable screen of trees and shrubs. At its northern end, however, where the trees come to an abrupt halt, I could at least glimpse a sandbank stretching far out into the water. But even had the estuary been in full view, my eye was always more likely to have been caught by the urgent red and white signs attached to every single lamp-post along the platform.

'Persons who alight here must only have business with the Camp,' was their bald declaration.

I know what you're thinking: that 'only' has found itself in a very curious location. I'm with you on this. It rather suggests that if you have business with the camp but also some other business you'd care to attend to at the same time – a kite you feel constrained to fly, perhaps, or research you've promised yourself that you'll carry out into the possibilities of time travel – permission to alight is dependent on your forswearing these perfectly legitimate pursuits, which seems a bit harsh. I spent a few agreeable minutes remodelling the command into happier English.* Some people will call this pedantry. I prefer to think of it as showing that I care.

---

* As a treat for those who bother to read footnotes, here's my final version: 'Only persons who have business with the camp may alight here.' For good measure, I've dispensed with the capital C in Camp as well.

Having taken some quick photographs in case a sentry did rush out at some point and forbid such activity, I acquainted myself with the one feature of note in the station – a long and not particularly attractive shelter with a bench running its whole length. Few request stops, I was to discover, offer much in the way of protection from the elements for the masses, simply because there are rarely any masses to protect. At Lympstone Commando, however, there was room for a good 30 to 40 people in the shelter if they all bunched up a bit. It had a large black dustbin in it too, which, given the general paranoia on the railways about bombs being placed in rubbish bins, seemed an incongruous thing to find at the gates of a place I'm sure must feature on some 'sensitive targets' list at GCHQ. The only other structure on the platform was what appeared to be some sort of sentry box that had fallen out of use.

The station as a whole is a recent venture in British railway terms, having been opened on 3 May 1976 to serve the camp. Up until then, the commandos had to trek all the way from Exton station (another request stop), a full 800 yards away. Since they're famously trained to run 300 miles over any terrain in a single day wearing a 180lb pack while carrying a missile launcher over one shoulder and a wounded comrade over the other, you would have thought that a stroll half a mile along a flat road wouldn't have taxed them unduly – but then I'm no expert in these things, whatever the guard may have believed.

Unsurprisingly, it's the camp itself that dominates the station. Just a patch of grass and the width of a cycle-cum-footpath away from the platform, it's surrounded by two wire mesh fences. The first is topped with three strands of barbed wire; the second, a few strides behind it, is crowned with yet more barbed wire in the form of a mighty spiral of lacerating steel. Combined with some small buildings of no apparent specific purpose and some bland blocks that might be barracks half-hidden by some trees, they give the place the unsettling look of a concentration camp. CCTV cameras perch like vultures upon their own miniature towers, each one pointing its single unblinking eye down on its own portion of fence. There was a time, I suppose, when these cyclopic spies might have appeared sinister but in the brave new Britain of today we'd probably notice if they weren't there. A sentry box, which looked to my untutored eye more like a sentry office, takes up position just inside the gate that gives on to the station, so even if you got off the train here with entirely nefarious motives pulsating around your fevered head you'd be no nearer entering the camp than if you'd pedalled your way along the cycle path.

The concentration camp image is a little dissipated by the appearance of an assault course just inside the wire. This looks as impossibly impossible as you might expect for an assault course at a commando training camp. Disappointingly, no one was tackling it that day. This was probably unusual, since there are typically 1,300 recruits, 2,000 putative recruits and 400 potential officers attending training courses here each year who at some point or other are presumably sent over it.

Today's trainees follow in the footsteps and handholds of thousands of others who have passed through here since work began on the camp in 1939, just before the outbreak of hostilities with Germany. Back then it had the rather humble title of Royal Marines Reserve Depot, since only reservists trained there. By September 1941 it had been promoted to the slightly awkward-sounding Depot Royal Marines Lympstone and 800 Royal Marines a month spent time there en route to the various theatres of war in which their newly acquired amphibious talents could be put to use. But these Royal Marines actually received very little training before being thrust into the maw of conflict. Early recruits had a meagre six weeks before they were considered battle-ready. By 1943 they were given an eight-week course, and in 1944 this was extended to 18 weeks.

After the war, the Commando School at Achnacarry was closed down – all that's left is the famous statue at Spean Bridge of three commandos looking nonchalantly brave – and during the 1960s pretty much all commando training was relocated to Lympstone. Finally, in 1970, the camp got its first proper name – The Commando Training Centre Royal Marines – and it's stuck with it ever since, courageously turning a blind eye to the fastidiously odd word order.

The training centre's section of the Royal Navy's official website trumpets the fact that '... Officers and Recruits deploy direct from the parade ground to Afghanistan, North Africa and the Indian Ocean'. Afghanistan and the Indian Ocean I could understand, given Britain's involvement in a war in one and anti-pirate operations in the other. North Africa was more of a puzzle. Did I miss a memo? I wasn't aware that we'd landed anyone on Libyan soil and I don't recall us declaring war on Egypt recently, which is probably just as well considering how it turned out last time. I suppose it's possible that we conquered

Tunisia while I was on holiday somewhere but I like to think the news would have filtered through to me by now. If not, and we do indeed now own Tunisia, allow me to extend my apologies to my Tunisian readership. Console yourselves with the thought that you'll soon have a cricket team that can give your imperial masters a tonking, particularly in the one-day format.

According to the same website, facilities at the 77-acre base include a gymnasium, 'a modern urban combat training complex' and 'a swimming pool for combat swimming tests'. This last detail alone is enough to put me off becoming a commando. I enjoy a good swim as much as the next man, but having a fight with the next man while swimming, no doubt carrying a wounded comrade over my shoulder at the same time, is a life experience I'll let pass me by, thank you.

Apparently, the camp is built on land that used to be part of Sir Francis Drake's estate and one can't help thinking that the old seadog would have approved. However, as a sometime pirate himself* he might have raised an eyebrow over the anti-pirating efforts. Meanwhile, one of the wooden huts used during World War II has been kept 'as a mark of respect to the pioneers'.

Staring into the camp, the only emotion I felt was relief that I wasn't inside it. Aside from the fact that it reminded me too much of my old school (albeit that the grim defences there were to keep us in rather than intruders out), it just made me sad that as a species human beings hadn't yet advanced to a stage where some of us did not have to devote our all too brief lives to doing violence to

* Greetings, footnote readers. Here I shall be principally addressing the Sir Francis Drake fan base: I know the English preferred the euphemism 'privateer' but the fact that it was a knowing euphemism suggests that he was indeed a plain and simple pirate, albeit one who enjoyed the blessing of the monarch.

others. I'm sure commandos do lots of other things apart from butchering the staff of enemy radar stations and I'm sure that many of these other things are of genuine worth, but when it comes down to it, they're being trained to do in the other guy or woman before he or she does them in. Part of me feels that I should be a bit more enthusiastic about all that, if only for genetic reasons: my brother and I are the first of four generations of men on my father's side of the family who have not been in the armed forces. Perhaps once every four generations, the gene for war mutates into one for bunny-hugging.

At any rate, aside from a couple of blurry heads I had spotted through the windows of the sentry office, the camp seemed to be entirely unoccupied. I only realised that it wasn't when I was suddenly joined on the platform by a real live commando. He was dressed in civvies – jeans and a green T-shirt – but I knew he was a commando because:

a) he had a proper commando haircut, as modelled by the Action Man Commando doll himself

b) he had the physique of a man who could sleepwalk the impossible assault course with a wounded comrade over his shoulder

c) he had appeared on the platform before I was even aware he was anywhere near the station

d) he had the word 'Commando' tattooed in big letters on his right arm.

Given that I had attracted a complete and utter lack of interest from the camp authorities thus far, I played with the idea that they were adopting a softly-softly approach and had sent this chap down to spy on me. This was much more exciting. He exchanged perfunctory greetings with me before sitting down at the very far end of the bench, about 15 yards away. Almost immediately a train heaved into view. I warned Green T-shirt that I wasn't catching the train so if he was intending to get on it he'd have to stop it himself. He thanked me, stood up and went onto the platform. The train drew in but rather than call it to a halt he let it rattle through. 'Ah,' he said, turning to me and smiling, 'it's not stopping.'

A commando who didn't realise that he had to put his arm out to stop trains passing through his own station? Unlikely. If ever there were evidence that he was spying on me, here it was. He sat back down on the bench, apparently entirely sanguine about the fact that his 'mistake' meant he'd have to wait an hour for the next train to Exeter.

He was joined at length by another commando in civvies, and then another. None of them spoke to each other. I didn't even notice a cursory grunt or a nod pass between them. They were evidently following orders. Each man, I noticed, had his own cover.

Puffer Jacket sat and consumed banana milkshake and liquorice – the all-day breakfast of champions. He devoured both noisily, as if to ram home the message that he was JUST A MAN SITTING DRINKING MILKSHAKE AND EATING LIQUORICE AND NOT SOMEONE SENT TO SPY ON YOU, YOU OBVIOUS DOMESTIC EXTREMIST WITH YOUR NOT-SHORT-ENOUGH HAIR AND YOUR NON-LEATHER WALKING BOOTS.

Trendy Glasses, meanwhile, had his MP3 player turned up so loudly we could hear his ears bleed. 'Look at me,' he appeared to be saying, 'I'm just a man whose ears are bleeding. I'm clearly not the kind of person you would expect to be carrying out a covert surveillance operation against you, you obvious domestic extremist.' He showed no signs of the agony he must have been going through, but then that was what he'd been trained for.

Then an elderly couple arrived. He wore a turquoise jacket, dicky bow and brown brogues you could eat your dinner off, if that's your thing – the kind of outfit you might rig up for a retired colonel if you were putting on a revival of some between-the-wars melodrama in rep at Sheringham. She was equally resplendent in brown cardigan and rhinestone-studded glasses. He was clearly the spymaster general and she was his cover.

But on second thoughts, no – that's exactly what they wanted me to think. *She* was the spymaster and he was *her* cover. I was becoming amused at the lengths to which this elite body of marines was going simply to catch me off my guard.

Dicky Bow took me in with a single glance: my zip-off trousers (so handy for those moments when you suddenly wish your trousers were shorts or vice versa), my bottle-green fleece, my lightweight canvas walking boots (all right, non-leather walking boots like mine probably aren't made of canvas nowadays, but the materials they are made of probably sound like the formulae for chemical weapons, so we'll stick with canvas until otherwise instructed), my less than military posture. Where was the class, the style, the élan? I venture that he may even have been considering pulling me up on my second-rate appearance. But then I guess it's kind of tough to tell a scruff the big mistake he's making. Also, he was doubtless under orders not to make direct contact with the suspect.

Before long the shelter was packed with Friday afternoon soldiers, ostensibly bearing weekend leave passes. They all certainly showed something to the sentry on the gate as they passed through and I imagine it wasn't a photo of their mother. But again that was probably for my benefit. What *was* their game here? Whatever it was I felt we were reaching a crisis point and that at any moment the dam must break.

And indeed it did. In an instant, as if in response to some secret signal, they all got up. Thirty seconds later I was alone on the platform. Every single one of my adversaries had got on a train to Paignton.

Coincidence? I hardly think so, do you?

THE RAIL ALE TRAIL – TARKA LINE
YEOFORD, UMBERLEIGH, LAPFORD, COPPLESTONE & NEWTON ST CYRES

All right, so it's a clever marketing gimmick. Get people to visit pubs close to railway stations on a single line (in this case the one from Exeter up to Barnstaple); have each pub confirm the visit by stamping a sheet of paper; and offer a free commemorative T-shirt to anyone who gets ten different stamps. I'll confess it now: such manufactured quests are not usually my bag. It's not as if this one is even unique. Down here in the West Country there's a whole web of rail ale trails, some of them on lines you didn't realise existed going to places that probably don't. For instance, have you, or has anyone you've ever known, visited 'Gunnislake'? I rest my case. It's clearly a made-up name and not a very good one either. Yet the Tamar Valley rail ale trail professes to end at that very stop, with the trail's creators boldly suggesting no fewer than five pubs there at which to slake your thirst, ending with the unimaginatively named Cornish Inn.

One thing decidedly in the Tarka Line rail ale trail's favour is that the route from Exeter to Barnstaple (North Devon's one remaining coastal station) is so chock-full of railway request stops that it seemed churlish to visit a load of them without scoring myself a free T-shirt at the same time. And anyway, who doesn't like country pubs?

Several hours after making this decision I was still attempting to work out a system by which I could get my ten stamps in one day. Although there's an hourly service, by no means all the trains stop at all the request stops, even if requested. On two occasions I thought I'd cracked it only to discover that I'd landed myself at a station at a time when its watering hole was shut up for the afternoon. I had clearly stumbled across southwest England's version of Fermat's Last Theorem. I nearly threw the whole thing over in favour of doing the jaunt over two days – which I later discovered is the advice the rail ale trail people give anyway – until I found out that if you eat in one of the pubs, they'll give you an extra stamp, though you can do this at only one pub. At the sixth or seventh attempt I came up with a schedule that involved a good deal of shuffling up and down the line but which would give me at least an hour at each station to hit a pub, down something liquid and lush, get the all-important stamp, cruise back to the station, and get my sheet of paper filled in a single day. If nothing went wrong, that is. At any point.

So it was with a sense of anticipation mixed with the knowledge that something almost certainly would go awry, but that any disaster would surely serve to augment my pitiful reserves of moral fortitude, that I headed off from my campsite in Topsham, a pleasant little village wedged between the Exe and the Clyst. It was a bright sunny Saturday, the end of a week in which the weather had been blithely unaware of what season it was meant to be and so had given us a bit of all four.

On my way to Exeter I was pleased to note that Digby and Sowton station had acquired its own beautiful tortoiseshell cat, or, better put, the cat had acquired it. This morning she was sitting in the shade patiently waiting for the train to pull out so she could have the place back to herself again.

It seemed fitting that the first stamp on my sheet should be given to me at the bar of Exeter's Great Western Hotel. Or at least that's what I'd thought until I discovered that the Great Western Railway never actually got its paws on the line. In fact, the company didn't even exist in 1845 when Parliament granted the right to the Exeter and Crediton Railway (E&CR) to build a modest five-and-three-quarter-mile broad gauge line from Cowley Bridge as far as Crediton. The main line, from which this was to be a spur, was operated by the Bristol and Exeter Railway. A year later, while the navvies working for the E&CR were busily laying the tracks, Parliament passed an Act that permitted the Taw Vale Extension Railway to construct a much longer (31-mile) line from Crediton all the way to Barnstaple.

At this point it gets a bit messy. A third company, the London and South Western Railway, poked its nose in by purchasing a majority shareholding in E&CR and promptly changing the gauge from broad to narrow to match its own existing lines. This was all part of a generalised ballyhoo in the southwest about which gauge should prevail (think of it as the Victorian version of the VHS vs Betamax struggle). The Board of Trade duly stepped in and made London and South Western change it back, which they did. Sort of, anyway – they hedged their bets by converting just one of the two tracks back to broad gauge (the Betamax of the drama) and opened for business as a single-track goods line in 1851, having left the actual running of trains on the line to the Bristol and Exeter Railway (remember them?).

As if things weren't confusing enough, the Taw Vale Extension Railway changed its name to the North Devon Railway. The company duly opened a broad gauge line from Crediton to Barnstaple and Fremington in 1854.

So, back at the ill-named Great Western Hotel, I ordered half a pint of ale. Now, being aware that there are few things with greater potential to bring on a sense of mind-crushing *ennui* than having to listen to someone drone on about their pub crawl, I'm going to make this snappy. And I also promise not to end the day by lurching towards you and telling you that a) 'You're my very best friend in all the world,' b) 'I've never said this before but I really really love you,' or c) 'I've just been sick in your wimple.' Though I confess it baffles me why you brought your wimple along in the first place – it was simply asking for trouble.

I determined to drink only a half at each of the nine pubs, on the grounds that nine pints would be about four pints more than I've ever drunk in one day (I know – get me, the Super-lightweight Challenger of the World). In order that you can gauge what effect this had on my tender person, I've given my degree of inebriation on leaving each pub a score out of ten. So, without further ado, this is what ensued:

Pub 1: Great Western Hotel, Exeter – 11.02am
The barman is balding and surly. Perhaps surly because balding. Two young lads sit in the corner eating huge breakfast. They talk in Welsh but swear in English. Is that normal? **Intoxication: 0.5/10**.

Pub 2: The Jolly Porter, Exeter – 11.32am

Truly an odd pub. Bar area small. To the right, two separate flights of stairs lead to two rooms out of sight, in one of which a stag do has already got out of hand. To the left another flight of stairs leads to a room that is decked out like a Chinese restaurant. On closer inspection, room *is* a Chinese restaurant, access to which is through the pub. Two elderly Chinese men sit in restaurant wishing the beaded curtains could deaden the noise from the stags. The stags like Michael Jackson, throwing darts, shouting and Jägerbombs. Things that don't sound like darts begin to be thrown in the stag do room. Barman buries head in local paper. He is well beyond retirement age and even more years past caring. **Pixilation: 1/10**.

Pub 3: The Mare and Foal, Yeoford – 12.47pm

A dog named Sweep – some sort of poodle-based mongrel – opens the door for me. Inside, I form 50 per cent of the puntership: 'The county show has a lot to answer for,' the barman murmurs darkly. Tells me Yeoford was a request stop, then a statutory stop, then became a request stop again about 18 months ago. He doesn't know why. Introduces me to John Mountjoy, local man of flowers and current champion of the Tarka Line Station Gardens Competition. He wears Crocs with socks, a look not many men would be able to carry off. I shake his hand. I don't ask him why the planters on the platform are all empty. Landlady chimes in: 'You're doing the rail ale trail *on your own*?' Does not attempt to hide tone of pity in her voice. I tell her that I do have friends but that they're just not here right now. Landlord goes upstairs to get WiFi code for me. Comes down several minutes later with piece of paper decorated with long handwritten chain of numbers and letters. Then he sees I've only ordered a half. 'Should've only given you half the code,' he quips drily. The Mare and Foal is rendered The Mare and Fowl on my stamp sheet, conjuring up a somewhat different and altogether surprising post-natal experience for the mother horse. **Tipsiness: 1/10**.

Pub 4: The Rising Sun, Umberleigh – 2.30pm

My fancy cloudy cider tastes like slightly fizzy urine. Too frightened to point this out in case asked if the reason I am able to make comparison is that I've drunk actual urine. Meanwhile, young man in Hawaiian floral shirt and friend discuss shortcomings of British judicial system. Attempt to put together watertight complaint re cider/urine problem to take to bar. Have never drunk actual urine having never been in life/death situation that required same (product of sheltered upbringing). Have definitely *smelt* urine though, so have good idea what it might taste like. It tastes like this cider. Leave pub without making complaint, telling self I don't have time before next train. On way back to station browse in antiques shop for 20 minutes. **Sloshedness: 1/10** (urine apparently more fizzy than alcoholic).*

> **Train to Barnstaple:** *An elderly man out for a Saturday jaunt is in a suit. Love how, for so many elderly men, dressing casually means donning a slightly less formal suit and a tie that's not quite up to the standard of their best one (which has a crest on it). The meagre two pints I've drunk so far have been soaked up*

---

* Just days after I visited The Rising Sun it was announced that it was no longer a rail ale trail pub. Of course, you can still drink there in an unofficial capacity, though if you have ever been compelled to drink urine in order to survive, you can avoid distressing flashbacks by steering clear of the cloudy cider.

*by bread rolls I've filled with beetroot from a jar. Spilled
a few drops of beetroot juice on the platform at
Umberleigh. It looked like blood. Hope no one thinks it's
blood. You don't want blood on the platform.*

Pub 5: Marshalls, Barnstaple – 3.50pm
Real ale. Really loud radio. Fifth out of five pubs to charge
me £1.60 for my half-pint. Cartel? Otherwise forgettable.
Sozzledness: 1.5/10.

Pub 6: The Corner House, Barnstaple – 4.12pm
Friendly. A lot of Tom Jones songs on the jukebox (well,
two – 'It's Not Unusual' and 'Green Green Grass' – but it
feels like more). Major breakthrough: charged £1.55 for
half-pint. Cartel theory dented. **Plasteredness: 2/10**.

Pub 7: The Old Malt Scoop, Lapford – 6.04pm
Lapford perched on hill, thus furthest of all the pubs
from its station. Hence stickiest one to do in hour
between trains. Train late, leaving me with substantially
less time. Saved by discovery of shortcut footpath up
field. Run up hill. Thank perpetually-late-based fitness
for ability to do this. Resolve to remain perpetually late
forever. 16th-century pub. 16th-century atmosphere
somewhat diminished by huge television right next to bar
broadcasting 'madcap' home videos programme. Pretty
woman sweetly playing hangman with friend makes me
feel slightly lonely. Wonder what Verena's doing right now?
Half-pint = £1.65. My 5p gain from The Corner House
wiped out in one go. **Wreckedness: 0/10** (due to sobering
run up hill).

Pub 8: The Cross, Copplestone – 7.07pm

So undrunk. Fair to say I've rarely felt less like I'm on a pub crawl. Never intended to become incapable but feel am letting side down by complete and utter sobriety. Have upped quota to full pint at last two pubs in desperate bid to seek wisdom from reduced inhibition that alcohol brings. Regret not availing self of the '5 Jaggerbombs [sic] for £10' advertised in non-rail ale trail pub passed in Barnstaple. **Tankedness: 1/10**.

**Pub 9: The Beer Engine,
Newton St Cyres – 8.12pm**

The only intermediate stop on the old Exeter to Crediton line revels in thrilling three-foot drop from train to platform. Middle-aged woman on station, who claims she has 'left crampons in other handbag', appeals to guard: 'You'll have to give me a bunk up.' Make myself scarce on grounds that public bunking up is best done with fewest possible eyes to see it. Beer Engine has own micro-brewery but resultant micro-beer sadly not vegan. More crucially, nothing on menu vegan but have to eat meal to earn bonus tenth mission-completing stamp. No time for chef to knock up a special before last train. Disaster loometh. Enter talks about talks with barmaid. Disaster averted by compromise deal: barmaid will give stamp for order of chips, olives, bread. **Carbohydratedness: 8/10. Sousedness: 2/10** (≈ 0.6 sheets to the wind).

And so, five and a half pints and some chips, olives and bread later, the trail had ended. I tucked my sheet of paper stamped with the requisite ten stamps safely into a back pocket and hailed the last train back to Exeter. I hauled myself up onto it, changed onto a Topsham-bound train at St Davids and sauntered back to my tent. By the time I arrived I was so sober it hurt. I'm not one for getting horribly drunk, but I had hoped to render myself at least a little merry. Yet by the time I realised that a half-pint every hour was not going to do it, especially when interspersed with aerobic activity, it was all a bit too late. My full pints at the final two pubs had so much work to do simply rehydrating me that they might as well have been lemonade. As a result, I never achieved that degree of alcohol-inspired lack of inhibition that causes imbibers to be more honestly themselves for a short while, before another drink tips them over into rank sentimentality or rank stupidity or moroseness or rage or whatever other state they enter when enough alcohol is introduced into their metabolism.

I had planned to read some Boethius once I had achieved this slightly heightened yet pleasantly mellow condition, imagining that it might render me more receptive to consolatory philosophy. However, on my way from Lapford to Copplestone I realised it was not going to happen that day and started reading the translator's lengthy introduction instead.

So, what of the five request stops themselves?

The River Yeo runs right beneath the platform at Yeoford, which, during the age of steam, was a busy place with ample sidings that resounded to the mooing and anticipatory keening of cattle being loaded. Today there's just the single line passing through and not a siding in sight, though the shed that serves as a shelter harbours a little library, which is a heart-stirring touch.

Umberleigh still bore the signs of its more glorious days. One was immediately obvious: a wonderful old name board of green metal with raised white lettering emblazoned across it. The other was subtler: the road bridge at its northern end sports two arches wide enough to allow the broad gauge tracks that first ran beneath it.

Lapford's goods yard enjoyed the distinction of serving the Ambrosia cream factory from 1928 until it regressed a couple of steps in the food chain by becoming a fertiliser distribution depot in 1970. A coal merchant once carried out its trade from the yard, but the current occupiers are a removals and storage company whose bright yellow vehicles stand outside the bright yellow doors of the scintillatingly unlovely windowless extension. What is progress? Discuss.

Copplestone's claim to fame is that the creation of the cutting at the station's southern end was the very first action carried out in the building of the line from Crediton to the north coast. Copplestone's signal box was closed in 1971, the year the line here was singled. The goods yard had gone six years earlier, while an abattoir that sprang up in its wake has since been demolished, leaving nothing but the station itself for visitors to gawp at, and there's not much of that either, as its station house has long since been converted into a comfortable residence.

Newton St Cyres was the pick of the bunch and it was serendipitous that my complex system for completing the trail had saved it until last. Along with its audaciously low platform and ivy-covered bridge, it was blessed with a venerable name board like Umberleigh's, though with green lettering on a white background, which looked cheerier. The pièce de résistance, however, was a proper little garden planted with bulbs and forget-me-nots and much else that had yet to flower. 'If John Mountjoy wants to hang onto the Tarka Line Station Gardens crown he'd better get a wriggle on,' I thought as I strode up the sloping path from the station to the doors of The Beer Engine. I confess that I had never before spent any time speculating as to who might or might not win a station-based floral competition. It's right what they say: travel broadens the mind.

The station's Edwardian days are recounted by one A G Abraham in a memoir published in 1972. Born on 16 June 1893 in what was then The Agricultural Inn, his Devon burr is almost audible as he shares his recollections from around the turn of the century:

> *Connection with the outside world was, in my young days, very limited. There was no bus service and Newton Station was about three-quarters of a mile away. This was L.S.W.R. [London and South Western Railway] and there were about two stopping trains daily each way. We children often walked to the station just to see the trains go through. What a thrill it was to stand on the narrow platform when express trains thundered by, especially if that magic word "London" was showed as their destination. Here I saw the foot warmers that were for use in the railway carriages if you paid for them. Corridor coaches had not yet arrived. Here I would mention that, near the station, there were only a few cottages, one hotel and a Methodist Chapel.*

> *Later the post office was taken over by Mr Cork. His grandmother was the village midwife who brought me into the world. With no chemist's shop in the village, the nearest doctor three and a half miles away at Crediton and transport by cycle or horse, hers was a big responsibility. The post office had no telephone or telegraph. For the latter we could walk to Newton Station (L.S.W.R.) where a message could be sent in Morse code by the signalman from the Railway Signal Box.*

Of course, the heyday of these stations lies far behind them – shunted off into a siding, until the siding itself was removed and the memories of whistles and steam and smoke and smuts were crushed to make way for the A377 that runs alongside the railway all the way to Barnstaple. The line's reduction from two tracks to one in 1971 was a hammer blow to any aspirations it might have had to making a comeback. The best its many request stops* can hope for is a life like Yeoford's, enjoying brief periods as a statutory stop like the fitful blinking of a faulty neon light.

My sludge-brown rail ale trail T-shirt arrived in the post a few weeks later. All the pubs are on the back, including, I'm pleased to see, The Rising Sun at Umberleigh, instantly making it a collectors' item. This is a stroke of good luck because I'd always thought I'd never be able to afford to retire. Now I know that if I keep my T-shirt in mint condition, I can pretty much name my price when I hand it over to Sotheby's on my 65th birthday. It just shows that if you live right and maintain a certain standard of hygiene the gods will smile on you from time to time.

* There are nine in all – the ones I only passed through were Morchard Road, Kings Nympton, Portsmouth Arms and Chapelton.

TO ST ANDREWS ROAD

Before I set off on my trip and was still sitting in the British Library researching the journey, I'd spent quite some while staring at a black-and-white photograph of St Andrews Road station taken in 1964. It shows an unremittingly dull industrial station bristling not far from Bristol. Concrete lamp-posts lower over a shelter so militantly minimalistic it appears to begrudge whatever pitifully insufficient shelter it might afford. It's not a station you'd get off at unless you absolutely had to, and even then you might think better of it. Undaunted, I'd added it to my list of places to visit for two reasons. Firstly, the vast majority of request stops are in rural locations, so St Andrews Road was very much bucking the trend; and secondly, there was no possible chance of being disappointed by it because it simply couldn't have become grimmer than it was nearly 40 years ago.

The previous night I'd stayed at the house of my friend Mo in Bristol, which is how I came to be at Temple Meads station at 8am on a Monday morning, swimming like a salmon against the on-rushing morass of whey-faced, desolate folk on their way to the first of yet another five days of work. I was wearing a bottle-green fleece and carrying an olive-green rucksack with a bright yellow ukulele strapped to it. I was clearly not going to work. Although, of course, what the conscientious masses almost certainly wouldn't have guessed was that I was actually hard at work right there and then: pluckily taking on the hard-labour-bound hordes to get to my train while making the requisite mental notes for this paragraph. I realise that that might not be everyone's idea of what constitutes work but, in my defence, it's as much a job as being a personal shopper, say, or a search engine optimisation consultant, or deputy prime minister.

When I eventually reached my train I found that the half-hour journey along the Severn Beach line was a lot more picturesque than I had imagined it. Severn Beach is where Bristol people with memories of school trips had many of those memories formed. It's the end of the line and the first station properly out of both the city and the docks. Though it's never all that satisfying to walk down someone else's Memory Lane, I felt slightly sad that I would have to get off one stop beforehand. However, once we had got beyond the suburbs of Bristol the scenery cheered me no end. Everything outside my near window was some shade of green or blue and an impressive river had started stalking our left flank. The tide was out, so the great V-shape of its sandy banks was exposed not only to my gaze but also to various species of gull hopping about in search of a gullet or two's worth of worm.

ST ANDREWS ROAD

Everything has turned its back on St Andrews Road station. It is a desolate place with no friends. It is nowhere, as St Verena of the Rubbish Bin might have put it. It serves no houses and, as far as I could tell at first glance, nothing else either. There may have been changes since that 1964 photograph but they are merely cosmetic: as deep calls unto deep, so it has morphed from one sort of ugliness to another. It's certainly no worse 40 years on, but if it disappeared in a sink hole tomorrow I fear it would go unmourned. Lying like jetsam by the side of half-a-dozen tracks and a utilitarian footbridge whose sole remarkable feature is that it straddles the lines in a single unsupported span, the platform has to endure the sight of freight trains shuffling up and down on tracks it does not serve while the passenger trains that ply its own line come by infrequently and rarely stop. To add insult to injury, its track is the only one on which grasses grow.

The footbridge is its sole lifeline to the world – without it the platform would be truly adrift on a no-man's-sea of gantries, antennae, oil containers, half-hidden warehouses, structures whose proper names and functions are known only to those who read obscure trade magazines. This is no scene of post-industrial devastation, merely current industrial devastation. So great is the sense of dislocation here that it was only weeks afterwards, when I happened to look at the station on a map, that I noticed it's just 650 yards away from the Bristol Channel.

My old friends from Luxulyan, the Class 66 locomotives, were shunting about here in abundance. I snapped some general scenes and viewing the photos later realised I'd captured EWS 66093 and EWS 66006 to add to the EWS 66086 I'd seen in Cornwall. It dawned on me that I had become an accidental trainspotter. I already owned a flask and a pencil, so it was bound to happen someday. I shall embrace it.

The smelting works and the other industrial concerns that gave St Andrews Road its raison d'être have long since melted away, while the new ones that sprawl around it have no need for the station. This explains its demotion to the status of request stop, the only one on the Severn Beach line. By 2007–08 an average of just eight people a day used the station, though this has since risen to the dizzy heights of 16.

On this overcast Monday morning the empty station seemed the loneliest place in the world, or at least the loneliest in the Bristol area. It was difficult to imagine it throbbing with the life lent it by the one or two people who used the platform every couple of hours. I was in for a shock, however, as I passed the blue windowless shelter and glanced in, for in the darkness was a slim, lightly bearded young man. This put paid to my decision to break out my ukulele, which had been based on the expectation that there would be nobody about to hear my inexpert twanging.

I wouldn't normally talk to strangers at railway stations – I was, after all, born in the southeast of England and I have a reputation to protect – but I felt compelled to ask him what on Earth he was doing there, though I couched the question in politer terms. He looked up at me with a puzzled expression. He had been sedulously scribbling away in a book and I thought that perhaps he had been too absorbed to hear what I said. It soon became apparent, however, that the difficulty here was one of language. I asked him, slowly and clearly, where he was from.

'I am from Spain,' he replied.

Now, I'm afraid I'm a terrible show-off when it comes to Spanish. During the 1990s I spent six years in a Spanish-speaking country and, although it's apparently one of the easier languages to learn, it took me an awful lot of hard work before I was any good at it. As a result, whenever I get a chance to flaunt it – albeit in the somewhat rusty form to which it has degenerated over the intervening years – I do so. It's not so much that I'll speak Spanish at the drop of a hat but that I'll speak it at the mere prospect of a hat falling or even at the rumour that someone somewhere has a hat and is known to be a bit clumsy on occasion.

We duly continued the rest of our conversation in Spanish. It carried on for rather longer than I'd anticipated because we ended up getting on the same train back to Bristol. I warmed to him because he graciously let me do the putting-the-hand-out-to-stop-the-train business, which was still quite exciting for me, this being only my eleventh request stop.

Pablo was from Madrid. He had a cleaning job at a recycling firm near the station – one of those half-hidden warehouses I'd seen when I got out. He worked for three hours a day from Monday to Thursday. 'It's not enough for me to survive on. I've been desperately looking for any sort of job at all and this is the only one I've managed to get so far,' he observed ruefully. Every day he had a one-hour English lesson but he struggled with the language's irritating habit of throwing up words that are not sounded as they are written. The Spanish language is impeccable in this regard, so I could do nothing but apologise and commiserate.

The book in which he had been writing when we met was an English grammar – he'd been grappling with conditional situations such as: 'Had I been there, I would have prevented it.' The sentences had words missing that he was obliged to fill in. I told him that a lot of people who spoke English as their first language would struggle with that exercise, but he didn't seem to take as much heart from this comment as I'd hoped.

We bonded over our shared support for the re-nationalisation of the railways and our affection for unfashionable football teams with mildly exotic names from capital cities: him – Rayo Vallecano ('Vallecano Lightning'); me – Leyton Orient. However, we kept returning to his work situation, about which he was getting pretty desperate. With the rate of unemployment so catastrophic in Spain, particularly for those like him who were under 25, he'd come to Britain hoping to improve his lot. Instead, he had found work extremely hard to come by, especially with his limited language skills, and rents extortionately high, even when sharing with several others in the grungiest part of Bristol.

Unsurprisingly, he'd swiftly become disenchanted with The British Dream, such as it is, and was already drawing up plans to make another fresh start, this time somewhere in South America. I couldn't say I blamed him. There aren't many of us who, as children, dream of working as a part-time office cleaner while gradually wasting away. Pablo didn't even have the consolation that in his time off he was writing a novel or painting the masterpiece that would lead to his genius being recognised at last. As a consequence, his time in England had little meaning for him outside his English studies and, by his own account – and the evident relief he displayed when I spoke to him in his own tongue – he was not likely to land a job helping compile *The Oxford English Dictionary* anytime soon.

Existence is very odd, of course, and yet we sentient and self-aware human beings still manage to define ourselves by what we do rather than who we are, as if our work were in any way important in the grand scheme of things. Generally speaking, people's jobs are not even all that important in the small-scale scheme of things. I suppose all this concentrating on the things we do to keep body and soul together at least distracts us from the uncomfortable realisation that who we are isn't desperately important when viewed in the context of the unimaginable vastness of the universe either.

It's instructive that when Rosie asked me for a worry with which she could walk up and down Truro station, what I wrote on the label was a concern I had about my work. And that's me coming out with that, a preternaturally lazy person who almost certainly wouldn't work at all if some other method could be devised for paying the bills. I'm a disgrace to idle thinkers everywhere.

TO SUGAR LOAF

And so into Wales by the back door: one nothingy English station (with apologies to the good burghers of Filton Abbey Wood whom I'm sure would live nowhere else, even if you paid them), then over the border to Newport, a place once cuttingly described by a friend from Aberdare as being '*almost* in Wales'. Newport's two glories are a slice of ruined castle on the edge of the Severn and a clock tower that it believes is more distinctive than it actually is. As a meeter and greeter to those who have come to taste of the delights of South Wales it utters the unequivocal message, 'Manage your expectations.'

A change of trains later and I'd burrowed further west to Swansea, the guard announcing our arrival over the PA with a deadpan, 'We're arriving a couple of minutes early but we'll have to live with that.'

It might be me, but every time I come back to Swansea the place seems to identify a little bit more with Abertawe, its equally mellifluous Welsh name which also helpfully locates the city at its position at the mouth of the River Tawe. Here I could pick up a train that would take me to Llanelli, then along the length of the Heart of Wales Line – home to a positive amphora of request stops. There's Bynea, Llangennech and Pontarddulais; Ffairfach and Cynghordy; Llangammarch, Garth (Powys), Cilmeri and

Builth Road; then five in a row – Pen-y-bont, Dolau, Llanbister Road, Llangynllo and Knucklas – before the line lurches over the border, runs through the far less poetical Hopton Heath and Broome, and finally comes to a halt at Shrewsbury.* Of the 32 stations on the line, 17 are request stops. And of those the one I was most keen to stop at was the least requested of all: Sugar Loaf.

Stranded somewhere between Cynghordy and Llanwrtyd, Sugar Loaf is not only the line's least likely station – it was built to serve a mere four railway workers' cottages – but also its most remote. A reminder of this came 45 minutes into the journey when our smiley and breezy guard had to jump out at Llandybie, her blonde ponytail bobbing behind her, to unlock a box and push a button inside it. This was to warn all concerned that our train was about to enter this section of single track and that it would make everyone's day if nothing came down the other way to hit us.

I stared out of the window, doing what I always do when I have the luxury of gazing out of a train window with nothing particular on my mind: I imagine myself running alongside myself. I rush across fields, hurdle hedges, swim rivers, slalom through woods. Obstacles too large to vault I carefully circumnavigate, compensating for the detour by tearing across whatever terrain comes afterwards to catch myself up again. Today I leapt streams, raced through the gardens of lonely houses, crossed abandoned tennis courts. I scattered a family of rabbits, their white bobs flicking on and off to raise the alarm as they hopped away. I surprised a buzzard from its lair in a spinney. The only thing my

---

* Some authorities consider that the Heart of Wales Line starts at Swansea and ends in Shrewsbury, while others count only the section from Llanelli to Craven Arms, which is not shared with any other lines. I'll leave you to decide for yourself which side you're going to cheer for.

frenetic progress across the landscape lacked was a rousing musical score. The calm rhythmic rattling of the wheels over the joins in the rails hardly did justice to the athletic prowess of my outside self.

My reverie was broken only by the stations we happened upon on our way. You might imagine that rural stations are pretty much like peas in a pod, but there's an amazing variation on the Heart of Wales Line. Each one has had to be adapted to slot into its often precipitous surroundings. Some attempts at this have been more successful than others. The best stations give the impression that they arrived here just as the hills and valleys around them were being formed.

SUGAR LOAF

An hour and 40 minutes after leaving Swansea we crossed a viaduct over a vivid green valley, ploughed through Cynghordy and pulled up at Sugar Loaf. When I'd proffered my rover ticket to the still breezy guard she'd asked me twice if Sugar Loaf was really where I wanted to get off. I assured her that it was and she duly wrote the station on her hand to remind herself to notify the driver. Walking away, she turned and said, 'I'll need to have a word with you before we get there.'

This sounded thrilling and pregnant with possibilities. Did Sugar Loaf harbour some secret element of extreme danger about which she must warn me? Or had she seen this moment in a thousand dreams and knew that her part was to propose an immediate elopement as soon as the train came to a shuddering halt? So thrilling and pregnant were these imaginings that they brought me up short and I realised that I always get a bit too excited about human interaction after I've been on my own for a few days. When it came to it, Breezy's 'word' was merely to inform me that I'd have to go right to the front of the train to get off: the platform was shorter than our train, even though the latter was just a single carriage long.

'Not many people get off here,' she confirmed in an accent so South Welsh it could cut its own coal, or would do if they still did that sort of thing.

When I stepped down onto the platform the driver poked his bald head out of the cab to find out what kind of being it was that got off here. Seeing my rucksack he allowed himself a smile so enigmatic I didn't know whether to be affronted or flattered. (I accidentally captured the smile in a photo. Looking at it now it's still impossible to tell what he intended by it, so I've taken the decision to be flattered.) In a flash the polished pate disappeared, the engine was awoken from its brief slumber and the train bumbled away down the slight declivity-clavity-clivity.

Watching the train rumble out of sight and then out of earshot, I felt rather like Robinson Crusoe as the sails of the ship from which he had been unceremoniously dumped dipped beneath the horizon. The island I had marooned myself on was in a deep cutting. Beyond the line of trees that skirted the railway rose a bluff bare hill that blocked off the world to the southeast. Behind the diminutive platform a 20ft bank of grass and shrubbery shut off the world to the northwest. Looking back down the line I saw a bridge not far from the station, beyond which a slight bend hid from view the tunnel we had just come through. In the other direction, the track curved right then left and disappeared before 200 yards had passed. These were the four walls of my new world – it was as if I had been dropped into a huge slender crater carved out by a blow from a giant's axe.

I knew from having looked at a map beforehand that there was no Sugar Loaf village – the station had been named after a nearby hill, presumably because there was nothing else after which to name it. It was a situation that hadn't changed in the intervening 114 years. I looked at my watch. We'd arrived on time – it was now three in the afternoon. The next (and final) train up to Shrewsbury would haul itself from the Aber of the Tawe, along the banks of the Afon Llwchwr, along the banks of the Afon Tywi, along the banks of the Afon Brân, along the banks of the Afon Gwyddon and up to Sugar Loaf station in approximately five hours' time.

A five-hour wait at a station is the sort of thing that drives people to write aggrieved letters to newspapers. However, Sugar Loaf was one of the stations that I had been most looking forward to, principally *because* I knew I would have to spend at least five hours here without anything to entertain me once I'd climbed its eponymous hill.

My sense of eager anticipation was based on an experience I'd had some years before while travelling around the whole of the coast of Britain using only local buses (don't try it at home – it took me 196 buses and six and a half weeks). A few weeks into the journey I'd found myself at Ullapool in the far northwest of Scotland. The interesting nature of the timetables meant that, after the solitary southbound morning bus had dropped me off at a road junction in the middle of nowhere before beetling inland, I had to wait nine hours for a bus that would take me further around the coast. Instead of becoming upset and viewing the holdup as something to be endured, I decided to see what would happen if I approached it with a Zen mindset. The result was a thoroughly enjoyable interlude in which my stillness and quietness were rewarded with a very welcome sense of calm and a prolonged encounter with a stoat. By coincidence, almost exactly the same thing had happened the following day, though without the stoat. Sugar Loaf, while offering up a mere five hours of under-stimulation, presented a good opportunity to repeat the experiment.

In the five years since that bus trip, the term Zen has been largely replaced with the less snappy Mindfulness, presumably because it sounds marginally less like something someone who'd done a gap year in India would come back preaching. It's basically the same thing, though: concentrating on every single moment as you live it, rather than letting time slide by in a rush while your mind wanders off on other things or you wish yourself into the past, the future or some other place.

The classic way into this is to practise with a raisin. First you look at the raisin, noticing its colour, sheen, shape, texture, etc. Then you pop it in your mouth but hold it there without chewing it, concentrating on its texture (again – Zen folk love texture), flavour, how it makes your mouth feel, etc, etc (and there are always a lot of et ceteras to consider). At last, ten to fifteen minutes after you began the exercise, you are allowed to chew the raisin. Cue explosion of mouth-watering partially-dried-grape flavour. So heightened are the senses in the build-up to this event that when the moment of mastication arrives it does actually render the raisin tastier than any raisin you've ever eaten before in your life. But be still thy beating heart and let the mind concentrate on the qualities of the flavour, on the disintegrating shell of the raisin, on the trickle of juice over the tongue and down the throat. I know that Zen is not meant to be about delayed gratification, but it is amazing how tasty that humble raisin becomes when savoured in such an intense way. It certainly makes you think about how little pleasure we normally bother to extract from eating food.

As one who all too often starts a month overflowing with tremendous intentions only to realise at the end of it that all I've done is read the entire *Guardian* website and send a few tweets, some practice at not letting the days drain away into the sands is timely, if you'll excuse the pun. After all, it's not as if we're on this planet indefinitely, so killing time while we are here seems a bit of a luxury. And, yes, I am aware that it does all sound a bit bonkers but, trust me, it's rather satisfying once you get into it.

So I began my time of Zen with a thorough and measured examination of the platform. The first thing I noticed was something that was not there, namely any sort of name board to tell passengers where they were. There was a metal pole which might have been expected to support a station sign, but it merely held a rusty frame where presumably a timetable or notice had once been. A station with no name – how Zen is that?*This, unfortunately, drew me away from my Zennish intentions, starting me off on a chain of thought regarding the changes of name the station had suffered when I should have been concentrating on the feel of the platform beneath my feet (like walking over the top of a shed, since you ask, because the platform, which was wooden, was covered with what looked like, and may well indeed have been, roofing felt).

Sugar Loaf station began its life with the misleading name Sugar Loaf Summit. As can be imagined, this gave the romantic impression that the station was right at the very peak of the hill after which it is named, which would

---

* Answer: Quite Zen. If you were to mark it out of ten, which is not, to be truthful, strictly the Zen way, not having a name would probably be an eight or a nine.

have required a mighty fine stroke of engineering. However, the name actually refers to the fact that the station marks the highest point of the 950ft-odd climb that engines have to make on their way up from the coast. I stood next to the precise point of the summit, which I had read was adjacent to the southern end of the platform, and studied it in a Zen-like fashion, appreciating the texture of the rails, the texture of the ballast, the texture of the sleepers, and so on. Although I enjoyed just staring at the track and appreciating its innate summitness, I had to admit that with the eye alone it was impossible to tell exactly where the line stopped climbing.

Anyway, at some point in the last century, someone somewhere decided that it wouldn't do to mislead the public in this way, even though the use of the station was restricted to railway workers. As a result it became Sugar Loaf Halt. This was a minor event in the station's history, however, when compared with what happened in 1965, for it was in this year that the halt was deemed surplus to requirements and shut down. The station was not dismantled, though; it continued dormant until 1984, when it was partially reopened as a Sunday-only request stop for ramblers and cyclists. Five years later, the 'Halt' bit fell away, thus creating the third name in the station's existence.* Eventually, its stationhood was fully restored and now passengers may board or alight from any of the four trains that motor up and down the line every day except for Sunday, when even that meagre service is halved.

Unusually, the railway line here is rather older than the station it runs through – it had already seen 31 years of

---

* The railway term 'halt' had disappeared by 1974 but made a comeback in 1978 with the opening of IBM Halt, which served a computer-manufacturing plant near Scotland's Wemyss Bay. In 2008 the word was restored to Cornwall's Coombe Junction and St Keyne Wishing Well.

service by the time the station came into existence in 1899. The first stirrings of the modern Heart of Wales Line occurred back in 1839 when the Llanelly (sic) Railway and Dock Company, which was mainly in the business of shifting coal from pits to ships, built a line from Llanelli to Pontarddulais, a distance of about eight miles. The construction of the railway progressed roughly north-northeast but was so snail-like that by 1858 it had only reached Llandovery, a little under 30 miles from Llanelli. A year later, work started on a branch line off the popular Shrewsbury–Hereford line, heading southwest from Craven Arms in Shropshire and pushing onwards a handful of miles to reach roughly one new town or village every 12 months.

In 1863 came the grand plan to join these two lines up, bridging the 27½-mile gap between Llandrindod and Llandovery, which included the stretch to which Sugar Loaf station now clings. This involved the creation of the extraordinary curved Cynghordy Viaduct – perhaps the highlight of the entire line – and the 1,001-yard Sugar Loaf tunnel. The Central Wales Line* was finally officially opened on 8 October 1868, and Shropshire and the South Welsh coast were connected at last, to the accompaniment of cries of jubilation and gasps of joy all round. To put this achievement into context, when the Llanelly Railway and Dock Company began building its line to Pontarddulais there was not a single railway track laid in the whole of India. By the time the 90-mile line from Llanelli to Craven Arms was completed it was possible to travel by train from Bombay to Calcutta, a distance of over 1,200 miles.

* Renamed the Heart of Wales Line for marketing purposes.

Despite not passing through any major towns, the Central Wales Line was initially prosperous. However, it suffered in the recessions of the 1920s and '30s and has never really recovered. The Beeching Report of 1963 recommended its closure, but it was saved from the chop, largely because it ran through half-a-dozen marginal constituencies. Such is politics – sometimes the faults in the system inadvertently work for good.

Though the line was more or less secure, things were looking dicey for Sugar Loaf itself at the end of the last century, when it was declared the least used station in Britain. The 1998–99 stats showed that just two passengers per week were coming here, bringing in less than £2 a week in revenues. The Railway Forum, an umbrella group of privatised railway companies, called on the government to allow the station to close. Happily – indeed, surprisingly – their lobbying efforts failed. The most recent figures show what a sage decision that was, with Sugar Loaf now at the nose-bleed-inducing heights of Britain's tenth least used station (albeit still the least frequented station in Wales). Some 60 people board trains in this little cutting every year and another 60 (or, who knows, perhaps the very same 60, or even one industrious person 60 times) get off, which in Sugar Loaf terms constitutes a veritable throng. It was a heady thought that my own visit would add one to each of those columns for the 2012–13 figures and might possibly push them towards eleventh place, a position currently held by the Lincolnshire metropolis of Havenhouse (66 passengers in, 66 out). See how easy it is to become distracted when you're trying to be Zen-like?

So, to give you a taste of the Mindfulness experience that, after some early mishaps, I did eventually get into, I'm going to spread my journey out into the realms of being-in-the-moment. Rather than rushing to get to whatever thrills are in store at Penhelig, the next station up, try to take as much time over each of the following pages as you would on a normal one. Have a gentle wallow in the mystery that is language. Read the words aloud and luxuriate in their euphoniousness. Delight in the malleable qualities of English grammar. But don't stop there – spend some time appreciating the paper each page is made of. The paper that makes up books comes in different colours (there are probably more shades of white paper than God originally intended), different sheens (think it's just gloss or matt? think again), different textures and different degrees of translucence. If translated into usable energy, the effort put into the choice of paper for this book could power the lights of a small town for several weeks, even if it was Christmas and they had their illuminations up. And let's not even get started on the choice of font ...

A row of pansies forms purple, pink, white and green splodges against the dry friable earth at the foot of the embankment. The pansies have no scent but the warm soil smells of sunny Saturday afternoons lying on grass in municipal parks.

A line of beige tiles runs the length of the platform. Each tile has a regular pattern of 36 raised dots to give notice to the visually impaired that they are nearing the edge. The dots press gently into the soles of the feet of the blind and the sighted alike. The effect on walking boots is subtle indeed.

A black caterpillar the length of an index finger makes its way

purposefully across the platform, heedless of predators. The purposeful black caterpillar takes several minutes to cross the platform, finding its progress impeded. The beige mountain range is in the heedless black caterpillar's way. Despite the large and generous passes between the mountains, the black caterpillar the length of an index finger makes its way not through the passes but purposefully across the mountains. Because they're there. The black caterpillar's many segments give it the look of a tiny armadillo, a tiny armadillo the length of an index finger but about as tall as a mountain. Eschewing the passes, the black tiny armadillo caterpillar the length of an index finger and about the height of a mountain climbs purposefully across the mountains, each mountain in its turn, because they're there. Each faded orange dot at each end of each segment of the black armapillo, the tiny caterdillar, is a warning shot. It is a warning shot above the heads of predators, of whom the black caterpillar is heedless, that this particular tiny caterpillar, this particular black armadillo, is poisonous. Or it could just be bluffing. If I were a caterpillar that's definitely how I'd try to evolve.

On top of a pole an electronic screen – its modernity out of place here – gives me a phone number to ring for information. The screen clears. Then it gives me a phone number to ring for information. The screen clears. Then it gives me a phone number to ring for information. Every half-hour or so the screen clears, then is possessed by a crazed spirit. The crazed spirit tells me that

XXX86930   hfsalf
   kkkkkTrqTJGWOEG3
   33 3 3   €€
        €€€XX
        XXXXXXXX.

Since I have no phone on me, this is useful.

There are

one,
two,
three,
four,
five,
six,
seven,
eight,
nine,
ten,
eleven,
twelve,
thirteen,
fourteen,
fifteen,
sixteen,
seventeen,
eighteen,
nineteen,
twenty,
twenty-one,
twenty-two,
twenty-three,
twenty-four

steps from the platform up to the exit contained in a single flight.

Beyond the top of the steps, on the other side of the forlorn squeaky picket gate, are squared-off outlines in the ground. They trace the foundations of the cottages where the railway maintenance workers once

lived with their families. (I didn't do this bit very Zenfully – the thought of railway maintenance workers coming home for their tea made me realise that it was gone four o'clock and I hadn't had my lunch yet.)

Some

people

say

this

whole

Zen

business

is

a

load

of

bobbins,

but

I

disagree.

Having investigated my domain – the platform, the single steep flight of 24 steps, the short track to the edge of the main road – I returned from the edge of the main road along the short track, down the single steep flight of 24 steps to the platform to cook a slow and very late lunch. I set out my stove and pan, took out my trusty Swiss Army knife and began to prepare the meal as Zennishly as I could. I was interrupted by the 16.18 to Swansea.

Being on a platform of a railway request stop and not having a passing train stop for you is harder than you might think. At earlier stops I had suffered the minor embarrassment of having trains skid to a halt and guards leap out excitedly at the prospect of a customer, only to have me shake my head and call a 'Sorry!' to them. At first I had thought that merely not sticking my arm out would be enough. When I discovered that it wasn't, I deployed the tactic of turning my back on the train. Neither did this work. At one station I fled into the shelter but the train driver had seen me and, no doubt being a thoughtful person, imagined I had rushed off to pick up my luggage and so thrust the brake on with a sense of purpose that the black caterpillar with the orange spots would have admired.

At Sugar Loaf I tried out a new stratagem. The train slowed down as I feared it would. When I could make out the driver's shining cranium – for it was the same driver whose enigmatic smile I had failed to interpret earlier – I made the wagging index finger motion that continental footballers are wont to make when they see the referee reaching for his red card. The driver responded by mirroring my gesture. At the same time he raised his shoulders – the body language equivalent of going up at the end of your sentence – and I confirmed his question with a nod. He waved and the train began to pick up speed again. I had won. I had stood at a railway request stop and successfully requested the train not to stop. I felt as if I had won the lottery of life, and the fact that the winning prize was merely a platform ticket mattered not one jot.

As the single-carriage train zipped past me, I saw Breezy smiling and waving vigorously at me, so I smiled and waved vigorously back at her. It was nice to know that even though I was thoroughly alone here, I had two friends, albeit only once every few hours for a couple of seconds. It made me begin to wish the train had stopped so we could have exchanged a few words.

I returned to my meal:

Shallots, 2 (finely chopped)
Garlic, 3 small cloves (left whole)
Mushrooms, 2 (sliced)
Courgette, 2 inches thereof (diced)
Sun-dried tomatoes, 3 (roughly chopped)
Olive oil, 1 dab
Veg stock cube, 1 (crumbled)
Cajun spice, generous pinch
Chives, half-a-dozen scapes (cut up)
Couscous, enough for one
Water, enough for the couscous

Instructions: I suspect you can work these out for yourself – you seem the sort who would be more than competent in the kitchen.

Best served with four red kites circling in the sky above you. If you have no red kites, a pair of buzzards or hen harriers will do nearly as well.

Repast savoured, though admittedly not quite as thoroughly savoured as the Zen student's raisin, I packed up my things and made my way up the single flight of 24 steps. I left my rucksack on the platform, safe in the knowledge that it would be there unmolested on my return and would not have been removed and/or destroyed by the security services, as is the sure and certain fate of all unattended luggage on every major urban station in the land. Though part of me had fancied the idea of spending all five hours of my wait on Sugar Loaf station, a slightly larger part of me felt I really ought to visit the hill from which it takes its name. I placated the minority part of me by telling it that I would remain in a Zen-like state of mind for the entire trip.

I thus found myself walking slowly along the A483 – a disappointingly major road for such a remote spot, but with thankfully less than major traffic passing along it – and attempted to take in and appreciate everything I could see, hear, smell, touch, taste. I confess that there was little in the way of tasting going on, though I did my best by opening my mouth wide to gulp in some of the atmosphere.

As hills that have bestowed their names upon railway stations go, Sugar Loaf is not overly dramatic, certainly when viewed from the little car park and picnic area at its foot. However, about 90 seconds' worth of steepish climb later, the view of low mountains and hill forts and wooded valleys that can be seen from the flat-topped summit goes some way to compensate for its lack of grandeur. Technically a mountain (its peak is 1,080ft above sea level), it used to mark a dividing line between the lands of the Welsh princes and the nouveau-riche Norman nobles whose forces harried them from the Wye Valley.

I lay on my back in a grassy hollow and let the breeze play over me. After a few minutes, the quiet was broken by the sound of an articulated lorry painfully hauling itself up the valley. A lacuna, like the pause when a child draws breath between sobs, indicated a change of gear before the engine strained again until at last the brute roar died away, replaced by the sugar-sharp caw of rooks rising up from a plantation somewhere below. Swallows, unaware of my presence or casually indifferent to it, scythed the air at ridiculous speeds just inches from my face. Even so, they provided no preparation for the sight of two RAF Tornadoes that went shooting over me in an apparent attempt to clip the hilltop with their undercarriages. The boom of their engines a second or two later fair blasted my body several feet into the hill.

I spent the last couple of hours happily pottering about on the platform. I read some Boethius. I looked across the track and the space where a second track used to be to the remains of Sugar Loaf's other platform – barely visible now beneath a cloak of wild grasses. I had read that there was a wall beyond the platform that marked the place where steam engine drivers exchanged tokens (a fail-safe system that ensured only one train at a time could use a single section of track, thus avoiding collisions), but though I peered long and hard from both ends, I couldn't be sure I'd seen it.

Before I knew it, my five hours were up. Despite my best efforts, they had raced by. The train, however, did not appear. When, ten minutes later, it had still not put in an appearance, I began to fantasise about spending the night there – I was, after all, more than adequately prepared. Although there are only four trains a day each way along the Heart of Wales Line, one of those sets off from Swansea at the alarmingly precocious time of 04.34, reaching Sugar Loaf shortly after six. I was calculating the time I would need to get up at to ensure that I had everything packed away and my teeth cleaned before hailing that particular service when my train chugged apologetically into view.

Breezy's train-management duties had been taken over by a new woman, who shared her blonde ponytailed hairstyle.

'That's only the second time in eight years I've stopped here,' she told me in a voice that suggested she was genuinely excited about this.

I told her what a great time I'd had there and she replied that she should really go and do the same thing herself. People are polite like that.

At the very next station she got out and was replaced by a guard with auburn hair. I like to think she walked straight back down the line to immerse herself in the Sugar Loaf experience. Everyone ought to give it a go once in their lives, if only because the little halt's existence is a triumph of whimsy over cold hard economics.

TO PENHELIG

It's interesting to watch the reaction of animals to the coming of the train you're travelling in. Some flee before it as if the sky were falling in, while others in the very next field take no notice whatsoever of the rumbling tube of metal, or merely cast a contemptuous glance towards the intruder before resuming their scrumptious grassy meal. Of the wild animals such as rabbits and deer, I wonder whether the terrified ones stand more chance of prolonging their lives by conditioning themselves to take flight at the slightest noise, or whether the cool ones are more likely to enjoy longevity by reserving their energy for when the real predators arrive? I'm a bit out of the loop as far as cutting-edge animal behavioural science goes. Is this the sort of thing we know nowadays?

PENHELIG

I'd taken a morning train heading west out of Shrewsbury, cutting Wales in two roughly equal parts on my way to the Cambrian coast. It was a wonderful late spring day. The sun was out and something between a zephyr and a breeze passed through the boughs of the row of Scots pines that guarded the western end of Penhelig station. The only let-down was that this line of trees, in cahoots with a terrace of slate-roofed houses, blocked what would be a terrific view from the platform of the sandy Dyfi estuary.

If getting off at Sugar Loaf was like being dropped into a crater, then Penhelig felt like the physical representation of that cheery Vladimir Nabokov expression: 'The cradle rocks above an abyss, and common sense tells us that our existence is but a brief crack of light between two eternities of darkness.'*

The station, you see, is squeezed into a section of track barely 300 yards long between two quite substantial tunnels. Admittedly, neither of the tunnels takes an eternity to pass through, but passengers aren't to know that when they enter them for the first time.

It got me thinking about the Boethius that I'd read at Sugar Loaf – he was, after all, expecting to enter a period of eternal darkness when he wrote his most enduring work. I was particularly struck by the opening lines.

---

* I know, you're worried about the baby. Let me reassure you that I saw no actual cradles rocking above the abyss, though there was a gazebo up on some very high cliffs. I suppose that might have contained a baby, though on balance I'd say it was unlikely.

Who wrought my studious numbers
Smoothly once in happier days

If someone had read out to me the English version of this couplet without telling me who the poet was I'd probably have guessed Wilfred Owen. I can imagine the diminutive second lieutenant huddled over a candle in some frosty dugout in Savy Wood or Fresnoy scratching these words in his untidy hand. His own brief crack of light was brought to a sudden end on the banks of the Oise–Sambre Canal a week before the Armistice was signed. He was just 25 years and 231 days old. I know this because when I was 25 years and 231 days old I gave an ill-attended and maladroit performance of his work. I felt very young and far too much a fledgling to consider the possibility of my death, let alone dying there and then. Also, unlike Owen, I hadn't really done anything up to that point. I hadn't fought in a war, I hadn't met Siegfried Sassoon. I hadn't even ticked anything off the definitive modern-day checklist 'Plant a tree, have a child and write a book', as prescribed by Cuban revolutionary poet José Martí. I had merely been a child, abandoned two novels after scribbling a few desultory pages, and climbed a tree or two. All I really had to show for a quarter-century's existence was a failed attempt to become a pop star.

Actually, 'failed attempt' is rather too generous a description of a nine-year quest that began full of hope on the day I formed Nigel Golfclub and the Modern Existentialists at the age of 15. The musicianship and song-writing improved a little with each new band I was involved with, but it says all you need to know if I tell you that the greatest fame any of them ever achieved was when one of them, Narsh, made a post-split appearance as an entry in the *Urban Dictionary*, and only then as 'a combination of nasty and harsh'. Which is a bit nasty and, though I say it myself, a bit harsh.

If any song I wrote did have a redeeming feature it was usually its lyrical content. I enjoyed playing with words and telling little stories and coming up with unlikely rhymes. Words, I decided, would save me from a life of mediocrity. They would prevent my sojourn on the planet from passing completely unnoticed. I would become An Author. Chaucer-Shakespeare-Dickens-Wills – it seemed a natural progression. Yet here I was, quite content to be standing on a platform on my own on a sunny day with the prospect of a fortnight or more of interesting travel ahead of me, but at the same time prey to an undeniable state of unease and generalised dissatisfaction with life.

Dysphoria, the feeling is called. I stumbled across the word in a thesaurus once and was so pleased with it I looked it up in the dictionary to find out what it meant. If you're not the sort of person who has ever felt dysphoric and you're struggling to grasp what it might be like, it's not really the opposite of euphoria, as you might think, and it's not depression as such, but a gnawing sense that life should be so much more than it is – something akin to Thoreau's dictum about most of us living 'lives of quiet desperation'.

I imagine it can turn into quite a paralysing condition but I prefer to see it in a positive light – it's like an alarm clock going off at all times, day and night, to remind those who experience it not to make it to their death beds without ever having lived first. All they need to do is answer that hoary old question of what it means to live.

But here I was on the platform with my back to a jaunty little wooden waiting room decked out in green and white and adorned within by artworks from local schoolchildren. Penhelig station was built as part of the Aberystwith and Welsh Coast Railway* that ran from Aberystwyth along the coast to Pwllheli on the Llyn Peninsula. The line opened in various stages over the 1860s, during which time it was incorporated into a larger company (Cambrian Railways), as was the way of railway enterprises in mid-Victorian times. Although it serves the tiny seaside village whose name it bears, an accident of history also means that Penhelig station is closer to the centre of the neighbouring small town of Aberdyfi (Aberdovey) than Aberdyfi station is itself. This came about because Aberdyfi station was built on the main line a little to the west of the community while a tiny and somewhat bizarre branch line slipped back east to Aberdyfi harbour, behind which the town was built. This spur went down onto the beach to mingle rather awkwardly with the ice cream lickers and sandcastle builders – Francis Frith produced a charming postcard of such a scene in the 1950s. When this branch line and station were closed, the vast proportion of the good citizens of Aberdyfi found their closest station was not Aberdyfi but Penhelig. Despite this, while all trains stop at Aberdyfi, passengers must ask to get out at Penhelig.

As far as we know, it was the Romans who first laid on transport links through here, I found out rather by accident. On a map at the entrance of the station I noticed a tiny isle named Picnic Island. Being a bit of a fan of tiny islands, I decided to investigate. No sooner had I reached the side of the estuary than I saw a signpost to 'Picnic Island and Roman Road'. The path along the rocks above the sandy

---

* This was the company's official spelling – the change of the university town's name to Aberystwyth would come later.

beach, which, under other circumstances, I would have assumed had merely been polished by the flip-flops of holidaymakers, had in fact first been worn smooth by the sandals of our capable Italian guests. The irregular steps that lifted the path up and over the trickier obstacles had been cut by some unknown indentured or forced labourers who would doubtless have been encouraged to know that their handiwork would still be appreciated over a millennium and a half later.

Oxeye daisies – surely the cheeriest of all Britain's wild flowers – flanked the path as it rose to snuggle against the railway line, space beneath the cliffs being at a premium. The daisies gave way to gorse and thrift until finally I came upon my prize. Picnic Island, however, turned out to be a bit of a disappointment. Not because it wasn't gorgeous – who couldn't fall in love with a teardrop of rock topped with a few trees and shrubs and a little low tower that had 'folly' written all over it? It was because Picnic Island is only an island for picnicking if you happen to own the island or be invited as a guest. It is attached to its mother house on the mainland via a causeway and a bridge and has its own little tidal pool just deep enough for swimming. Being a man versed in high-mindedness and purity of spirit, I refused to feel envious of the woman I saw doing a bit of light gardening in the sunshine at the back of the house. I was sure that the look of complete serenity she possessed as she pruned and trimmed masked a whirlpool of existential angst and secret suffering beneath.*

On the way back to the station I passed a memorial to the members of 3 Troop 10 (IA) Commando. Since

---

* Still, if you're that lady and happen to be reading this, do get in touch – I'd love to picnic on your island. And I'm sorry about all the angst and suffering.

inadvertently having passed myself off as a commando down at Lympstone I naturally felt a kinship with the outfit and stopped to have a read. This troop apparently trained in Aberdyfi in 1942–43 for 'special duties in battle'. They were rather a remarkable collection of commandos (if any group of commandos can ever be described as unremarkable) and I was surprised, once I'd read their story as told on a plaque on the sea wall, that it was not better known:

> *This British Army Commando Troop initially consisted of eighty-six German-speaking refugees from Nazi oppression who were given fictitious names and identities as British nationals for their own protection and effectiveness. Commanded by Major Hilton-Jones MC, their special duties were reconnaissance, interrogation and intelligence. Deployed singly or in small groups, they rendered distinguished service in the defeat of Hitler's Germany.*

Twenty of them were killed in action, sacrificing their lives so that idlewilds like me could wander about musing on the point of existence. I felt a bit ashamed. And then it occurred to me that they might actually have been pleased that their selflessness had won me a life so free of other cares that I had time to reflect upon its meaning. Although the reality of being a refugee fleeing from an oppressive power is doubtless more terrifying than I can possibly imagine, part of me envied the members of 3 Troop 10 (IA) Commando their lives and their courage. I know the Chinese intend it as a curse when they say, 'May you live in interesting times,' but I wonder whether being born into times that are intrinsically tranquil somehow fails to bring out the best in us?

TO TONFANAU

And though I didn't know it at the time, it was on this 18-minute journey that disaster struck and the interesting times began.

TONFANAU

One of the scariest true stories I have ever heard concerns Ernest Hemingway and his first wife, Hadley Richardson. In 1922, the still unpublished Hemingway was working in Lausanne as a correspondent for the *Toronto Daily Star* while Richardson was living at their home in Paris. Hemingway showed some of his writing to an editor he had met called Lincoln Steffens. Impressed, Steffens asked Hemingway to show him some more. Richardson dutifully hunted around their flat for every scrap she could find of her husband's work. She packed the originals and the carbon copies into a suitcase and set off for the Gare de Lyon to take the train down to Switzerland. While waiting for the train to depart, she hopped off to buy a bottle of water, leaving the suitcase on board. When she returned, it was gone. It has never been seen since.

It's a tale that has always sent a shiver up my spine. It pains me when my laptop seizes up and I lose a single paragraph of work: what the loss of practically everything you've ever written must feel like is beyond my comprehension. So it was a not altogether pleasant experience to be standing on the platform at Tonfanau station delving around in my rucksack with increasing degrees of agitation in search of my notebook. I checked once, twice, thrice – each time with greater thoroughness and each time with greater certainty that I would not find it. I did not check a fourth time, for there is never any point in checking something for a fourth time. If there were, the English language would have acknowledged the fact by providing us with the word 'fourice' or possibly 'frice'.

I calculated that my notebook contained about 10,000 scribbled words that faithfully chronicled my journey thus far. As any of my former girlfriends will tell you,* I possess a memory that makes a concussed goldfish a more reliable pub quiz team mate than I am, so this was a loss I felt keenly: if I did not get the notebook back I would have to begin the journey all over again. Also, it contained Verena's email address – a piece of information I had stored nowhere else.

Summoning all my meagre powers of recollection, I made myself picture where I had last seen the notebook. I had definitely had it in my hand when I got on the train at Penhelig. I had sat down, popped my rucksack by a seat and, mindful of Hadley Richardson's fatal error, taken the precious document to the loo with me rather than leave it at the mercy of my fellow passengers. Try as I might, I couldn't picture the notebook from that moment onwards. I had to face reality – I had left my notebook on the train. Worse still, *I might well have left it in the loo*. What would Dr Freud have made of that, I wonder? Did I subconsciously believe that my career as a writer was going down the pan? Worse still, did I secretly consider that the best thing to do with my output was put it in a place where effluence was flushed out of sight forever? It was a nest of ferrets I really didn't want to explore.

---

* I realise that this might make it sound as if a legion could be formed of my ex-girlfriends. This is not actually the case, though there are now enough of them to form their own support group.

Calling upon the stores of Zen I had built up at Sugar Loaf, I determined to quash the panic welling within me and not admit that the universe had imploded until I was certain that the book was as irretrievably lost as Hemingway's hoard. Then I would take it calmly, dispassionately and stoically. And then I would cry night and day for a week.

Though I think we can take it as read that, when seen against the loss of Hemingway's suitcase, the disappearance of my notebook would be judged a far crueller blow to World Literature, my situation was perhaps more comparable with that suffered by the travel writer Patrick Leigh Fermor. As a fresh-faced 18-year-old in the 1930s he set off to walk from the Hook of Holland to Constantinople, as you do. In Munich, his rucksack was stolen from the youth hostel in which he was staying and he lost not only his sleeping bag, money and passport but also all the notes and sketches he had made up to that point. It says much about his character that he saw this as a blessing in disguise, because it meant he could travel even lighter than he was already doing. Furthermore, when he came to write up this section of his mammoth walk 40 years later for the volume that became the classic *A Time of Gifts*, he was somehow able to recall his experiences in astonishing detail. Unless, of course, you believe the commonly held suspicion that his ability to fill in the blanks owed less to memory and more to the imagination.

So I finished the meal I had been cooking before I made the unwelcome discovery of the non-presence of my notebook and I hatched a plan. I had no mobile – I bought my first one a few years ago but I've never liked them so I barely use it – and there was no telephone hereabouts.

Indeed, there really wasn't anything much at all at Tonfanau. The only thing to do was to hightail it back to Tywyn, the small town whose station my train had passed through immediately before reaching Tonfanau, find somewhere that would lend me some WiFi in exchange for the purchase of a cup of tea and send a tweet from my laptop to Arriva Trains Wales, the train operator whose toilet was transporting my magnum opus up the western shore of Wales and on to possible oblivion.

I guessed it was about two or three miles back along the coast, so I picked up my heels and started walking, then running, then walking again when I realised that my rucksack was really quite heavy and I was not, as has been previously advertised, a bona fide commando, or indeed any other sort of commando. I had no map, but I could see Tywyn across a swathe of low-lying pasture. I cut across fields, eyed by cows not quite bored enough to bother chasing me, and trit-trotted over a beautiful brand-new footbridge wide enough to admit a London Marathon's worth of pedestrian traffic. From here a dusty road looked as if it might eventually lead me into town. Unexpectedly, for the road reached a dead end at the beautiful brand-new bridge, a car came up behind me. For no other reason than that it seemed like the right thing to do if you were someone in a hurry to get somewhere, which I clearly was, I stuck my thumb out. The car stopped.

'You should go to the police,' suggested one of the elderly good Samaritans in the front seat as her husband drove us into Tywyn.

I confess I'm not a great fan of the police – I've got too much first-hand experience of their attitude and actions at otherwise peaceful demonstrations to regard them with much fondness. So to seek them out now had never crossed my mind. Apart from anything else, it seemed too trivial a matter, notwithstanding the cruel blow to World Literature and all that. Nobody except you reads books now, anyway.

However, my knights in shining hatchback would not be gainsaid – 'The railway station is unstaffed, so there'd be no point in you going there' – and insisted on dropping me outside the police station.

'There's only one policeman in Tywyn, so if he's out on a call the station will be closed. It'll be your best chance of getting your notebook back, though,' repeated my driver as I clambered out, hauling my rucksack after me. I thanked them, wished them well for the remainder of their holiday and approached the front entrance of the police station, summarily unconvinced.

More to please my chauffeurs than out of any conviction, I rang the bell. Silence. I was on the verge of turning away and heading for the nearest WiFi-positive café when a voice crackled through the intercom asking my business.

'Erm, I suspect this is rather too trivial for you to bother with,' I began, 'but I may or may not have left a notebook in a loo on a train and the future of literature as we know it depends on its recovery.'

At least, that's how I would have finished my opening gambit if the voice hadn't already told me that he'd come round after he heard the word 'train'.

'You're lucky, I've just this minute got back in,' began a young police officer called Gareth Edwards (not the rugby player of the same name – he's now a television pundit). He asked me to explain my problem in full. I know I should have been thinking about the loss to World Literature and everything, and more pertinently the loss to my bank account when I didn't get the slice of my advance dependent on me delivering a manuscript, but all I could think of was that he must be awfully hot in his full uniform and stab vest. Who would think to stab a sweaty policeman in Tywyn anyway? This was a town whose most recent convicted criminal had to do time in Botany Bay.

Anyway, within five minutes PC Edwards had secured the services of a hundred Interpol officers who dropped their collective croissant/bratwurst/schnitzel and began scanning Europe for my notebook. Or at least, he'd done the next best thing, which was to put me in touch with a helpful woman at Machynlleth railway station who said she'd try to get hold of the guard on the train whose loo was probably hosting my precious scribblings.

There then followed a very long 20 minutes in which there were no developments to speak of. I made small talk with PC Edwards. He didn't seem at all put out to be spending his afternoon on a matter that he must have thought inordinately inconsequential. To keep my mind from dwelling on the book, I asked him about his job. As I suspected, the crime rate was very low in Tywyn, a town that, with a little more effort, might even have aspired to the status of resort.

'Burglaries and car theft are almost unheard of here,' he admitted. I asked if anything exciting – by which of course I meant very *very* illegal – had taken place here during his time.

'Just once,' he replied. 'A huge consignment of drugs got washed up on a local beach – it was too big to move.'

Despite my pressing him for details, he could not remember precisely when this had happened or the street value of the immovable drugs or even what they had been. This is, obviously, an unsatisfactory state of affairs, so in my head I concocted a headline for the local paper: 'WHAT A LOAD OF JUNK! DOG WALKER IN £35M HEROIN HAUL'. I have no idea whether it was a dog walker who made the discovery but it usually is, isn't it? I worried whether the junk/heroin rib-tickler would prove too subtle for the small proportion of the readership without a serious smack addiction. No matter – I ploughed on to the sub-heading: '300kg of Class-A drug washed up on Tywyn beach'. This would give heroin a street price of £116,666.66 a kilo at the time of the beaching. Call me naïve but I really don't have a clue how much my local dealer charges for heroin, though I admit that the best part of £117k a kilo does sound an awful lot, especially when you compare it with the street price of tea, which I've been told is equally refreshing.

I later turned to the all-seeing eye of cyberspace to try to ferret out some information about the story and discovered that in my excitement I had put a few too many legs on the mule. According to the *Western Mail*, which reported on the event in May 2008, the Tywyn package was one of three that fetched up around the Welsh coast at that time, each one containing cocaine weighing about 30kg (that's around 4st 10lb in real money) and each worth roughly £1.6 million on the street. It was thought that the consignments may have belonged to a Colombian drugs cartel, in which case one rather fears for the future of whoever messed up. That said, I can't imagine drugs cartels from any other nation looking terribly kindly on a member of the organisation who, for whatever reason, jettisoned £5 million worth of product. But then again, what do I know? Perhaps £5 million is the sort of trifling sum that gets laughed off nowadays in whatever exclusive bars the top bananas of drugs cartels infest.

Anyway, I'm not all that good at small talk and after a bit I began to dry. The one question I was burning to ask Gareth was, of course, 'Why do you have to wear a stab vest?' but it's not the sort of thing you can ask someone on first acquaintance. He went away to make some more calls on my behalf. The sound of dropping croissants, bratwurst and schnitzels was almost audible. Still no news, however. We couldn't even be sure that the helpful woman from Machynlleth had been able to contact my train, which I calculated couldn't now be far from its journey's end at Pwllheli.

Then, all of sudden, the phone rang. Gareth leapt to pick it up.* The only word I managed to catch him saying was 'Oh', which didn't sound overly hopeful. There was a pause for about five years and then he said, 'So where can he pick it up?'

Which is how I came to be skipping off along the road to Tywyn station with a heart considerably lighter than it had been for some while. Alerted by the helpful woman in Machynlleth, the guard on my train had found my notebook, which – Freud scholars take note – was indeed in the loo. In order to get it back to me, the book had been given to a cleaner who was heading down south.

'If you get along to the station now,' Gareth had advised me moments before I started pumping his hand, 'the

---

* Correction: he walked across to the phone and picked it up without any undue haste but in the film version of these events, for which rights are being negotiated even as you read, he's *definitely* going to leap.

cleaner will hand you your notebook.' I thanked him about 50 times, told him, 'You're as much a legend as the other Gareth Edwards,' and thanked him another 50 times.

I went hot foot down to the station where, in a scene worthy of the big screen, the cleaner jumped out from the back of the train waving my notebook at the dozen or so passengers on the platform in a frantic attempt to discover which of them was me. Since he was the only person on the platform running about with my notebook in his hand, my task in identifying him was rather easier. He gave me the book and I said 'thank you' about a hundred times – this is my standard level of gratitude for people involved in hauling my sorry frame from the jaws of misadventure – while attempting to wrench his arm off with my handshake. With a despairing lunge he finally broke free and scrambled back on board the train.

The notebook, which barely a couple of hours earlier had been merely an object, albeit a useful one, had become an object of veneration. My joy in being reunited with it was, like all proper joy, unbounded.

It made me consider how things might have been had the incident not occurred – if, like an averagely observant person, I had happened to notice that I'd put my notebook down and had simply picked it up again. Certainly I would have avoided some less than cherishable moments of heart-sinking horror. I'd have spared myself ten minutes in which I really *really* wanted to punch myself in the face, and would have done so if I'd had any assurance that I wouldn't have missed. I'd have also gone without an hour or two of doleful resignation during which all my actions were undergirded by the knowledge that I was really only going through the motions just so that I could reassure myself later that I'd done all I could to get the notebook back.

On the other hand, though, I would have missed out on quite a bit: I wouldn't have enjoyed the kindness of the friendly couple who gave me the lift; I wouldn't have had my attitudes challenged by spending time with a police officer who didn't see himself as a natural successor to the Black Shirts; and I wouldn't have had a role in the dramatic handover scene with the cleaner. Perhaps more pertinently for someone as self-sufficient as I am, I wouldn't have experienced the vulnerability and humility that come from having to put your fate into the hands of others. I should try it more often really – I'm sure I used to be a much more open, slightly less self-contained human being when I lived in Latin America and put my life into the hands of psychotically unhinged bus drivers on an almost daily basis. Indeed, when I thought about it, so manifold were the blessings that broke upon my head as a consequence of mislaying my notebook that I immediately resolved to leave it in the loo on the next train as well.

I've given a name to this resolution to pick the nuggets of gold from the torrents of excreta that flow everyone's way sometime in their lives. It's The Philosophy of Redemption™. I fully intend to write a self-help book about it, the sales of which will make J K Rowling look like Will Self.

So, here's a thing. What you have to decide for yourself now is this: is my story of the lost-and-found notebook just a little too good to be true? Did I really recover it or did it disappear for good like Fermor's jottings in his stolen rucksack? I mean, it's a bit *deus ex machina* that a car happens to be coming along a deserted road just at the time I need it and that its occupants give me a lift to exactly where I want to go. Then there's PC Gareth Edwards. Gareth Edwards? *Really?* How timely that he should turn up at the police station just seconds before I do. And do the boys and girls in blue really help trace 99p notebooks nowadays, when even crime-free towns throw up £1.6 million drug seizures to be getting on with? Then there's the cleaner who conveniently happened to be on his way south at just the right time to deliver the book. The whole thing smells incredibly fishy. Unfortunately, if it turns out that the notebook did go permanently AWOL, then I've clearly had to invent everything you've read so far. But would that really matter?*

As for Tonfanau (pronounced *ton-van-eye*), it's really rather appropriate that it was overlooked in the flap over the errant notebook, because it's a station that has only briefly had any sort of purpose since the local anti-aircraft training camp was closed after the end of World War II. Trainees were brought here during the conflict to practise hitting markers in the sea or targets trailed behind aeroplanes. Very little now remains of what was then a substantial camp that spread out on both sides of the railway line. Indeed, I imagine most passengers scooting through on the little diesel trains that ply this line have no idea that an army base existed here at all. Most of the area has been converted back to farmland, with the only evidence of Tonfanau's part in the war effort being a small clutch of very decrepit buildings, a tumbledown Nissen hut, a butt for a firing

---

* Yes, of course it would. Have we come so far together that you can still happily contemplate the possibility that I'm telling you a pack of lies? Shame on you.

range, the remains of some concrete tracks and the occasional post or wall that defies the elements.

The camp's near disappearance seems extraordinary considering that just over 40 years ago, in 1972, it was more or less extant and party to an event that gripped the news at the time. It was on a miserably wet and windy night in the autumn of that year that a special train pulled into Tonfanau station carrying the first group of around 1,300 Ugandan Asian refugees given shelter at the former army camp. The train apparently had to stop and shuffle along four times in order that all the passengers could get out onto the short platform. It's difficult to believe that they can have taken much comfort from their first view of the camp. Footage taken at the time shows it was more or less unchanged from its wartime utilitarian glory – all high fences and barrack blocks.

There was a good deal of demurring by locals regarding the sudden influx. For some, the refugees were the first people of Asian origin they had ever seen and no doubt this played a part in their objections. However, a good many inhabitants of Tywyn and neighbouring communities did make an effort to spruce up the camp as best they could. They were also at Tonfanau to welcome the disorientated newcomers who had fled with few belongings after Idi Amin had given them just 90 days to leave Uganda or face almost certain death. (Forty years later, some of the friendships forged between the refugees and local volunteers are still going strong, a fact that makes one feel a bit better about the human race.)

A medical centre and canteen were hastily organised and the children placed in local schools. The station came back into its own, providing the refugees with a valuable means of getting to and from their isolated new home. However, most of the Ugandans were at the camp for only a few months before being rehoused elsewhere in Britain. When they left, the station fell all but silent again.

Tonfanau has had just the one moment in the national spotlight since. On 8 January 1982 a train was trapped in the snow here, leaving four passengers and three crew members stranded on board overnight. The next day an RAF helicopter from Valley on Anglesey was sent down to rescue them. Even in the summer the station feels exposed and rather bleak, so when ravaged by the exceptional blizzard that visited in the winter of 1982 it must have seemed a benighted place indeed.

By the mid-1990s the number of trains stopping here had been reduced to a daily ration of four (one northbound and three southbound – an imbalance that was hardly designed to attract new passengers) and British Rail made an unsuccessful appeal to the government for permission to close the station. That close shave behind it, Tonfanau has pottered on, the nearest station to nowhere in particular. Even so, around 40 times a week someone stands on this platform and waylays a train or asks a guard to let them alight. It's a figure that is as cheering as it is remarkable.

TO LLANDANWG

It's frankly astonishing that more is not made of the Cambrian Coast Line, for it must rank among the most picturesque rail journeys in Europe. It's glued to the shore for the greater part of the trip north to Pwllheli, and on a calm cloudless summer day the sea becomes a cloth of azure so redolent of the South Pacific that you could almost swear those Snowdonian mountains were a ring of volcanoes. Even parochial Barmouth looks exotic from the train window as you approach from the south.

The illusion begins to blur with the sighting of sheep grazing the greensward between the line and the cliffs, and the spectacle of a huge grey heron lumbering across the beach, its undercarriage all but grazing the sand as it makes its heavy-winged way out to the tide line.

The previous evening I had broken my journey along the Cambrian coast at Llanbedr, another request stop, to walk along the road over the causeway to Shell Island. At 300 acres, it forms what is reputedly the largest campsite in Europe. Given that I'm a fan of tiny campsites, spending a night at such a monolith wouldn't usually be my thing, but it's so famous that I felt it my duty to go there at least once in my life. I ended up pitching at a lovely spot right on the edge of a low cliff, beyond which the sun gave a barnstorming display of horizon-crashing. With so few other campers about – the school holidays being still six weeks away – it felt almost as good as wild camping, which made me glad that that was precisely what I would be doing for most of the rest of the trip.

Llandanwg is two stops (or just one if no one asks to get on or off at Pensarn) and less than two miles north of Llanbedr. This makes a trip between the two something of a hazardous journey, because those attempting it have roughly three minutes to contact the guard to ask that the train come to a halt. It lends the expedition a very mild *Mission Impossible* flavour – a *Mission Just About Possible But Something Could Feasibly Go Wrong If You Were Unlucky* sort of show. I was well aware of the potential risks involved – people or luggage blocking the aisle and preventing me from reaching the guard; a sudden attack of aphonia rendering me physically incapable of expressing my request; an armed maniac taking control of the train and threatening to shoot hostages if the driver did not take us non-stop to Harlech – so when the train pulled up bang on time at 08.00, I checked my watch and steeled myself for 180 seconds of heart-pumping action.

It was a pity, therefore, that I got on right next to where the guard happened to be.

'Llandanwg, please,' I said as I passed her.

'Right you are,' she replied, and a few minutes later we pulled in.

LLANDANWG

The little single-platform halt at Llandanwg with its aquamarine shed-like shelter and matching bench gives the appearance of a Hornby model railway station that woke up one morning and found to its delight that it was a real-life full-size one. This may explain why no one has yet got around to building a proper village to which it can be a station.

The settlement at Llandanwg, such as it is, is a half-hearted linear affair that stretches to a few houses – mainly bungalows – a site for static caravans and a road up the hill to the more substantial community of Llanfair. However, things get better if you turn left at the station entrance and go down the slope to where the road peters out near the beach. Here you will come across a café, a little church and a small plot of National Trust land called Y Maes.

The church is a simple stone construction that dates from early medieval times, though it's been heavily restored since. It is said to have been built on the site of a place of worship founded by St Tanwg as early as the fifth century. One end is all but rammed up against the dunes, so it's no wonder that when the roof collapsed in 1883 the building quickly filled up with sand. In its churchyard lies the body of the poet Sion Phillips, who lived on Shell Island and who had the misfortune to drown in 1620 while venturing to cross the water to Llandanwg.

However, it was not the church that thrilled me (it was locked anyway) but the small patch of grassy land and sand dunes called Y Maes. Indeed, it was not even the small patch of grassy land and sand dunes that thrilled me – for all its undoubted importance as a habitat for rare plants, insects and animals – but rather its name.

Allow me to explain. I'm not Welsh and to the best of my knowledge I never have been. I confess I wouldn't mind if I were, though. A Welsh identity seems magnificently chic if you hail from an insignificant town at the scrubby end of Surrey whose only claim to fame when you were growing up was that the IRA exploded a bomb there. What's more, you don't have to go back many generations to discover my Welsh roots, a fact highlighted by my mother's maiden name (Thomas). Sadly, I am still too indistinctly Welsh to play for any of their national teams, for most of which I would otherwise be a shoo-in. I make up for this by having felt an affinity with the Welsh language since the time when I was just a *mab*. Mere affinity, however, doesn't get you very far with language, which is good news for the purveyors of language-learning systems but a bit irritating if you want to understand someone who speaks a different one to you. I mean, I've travelled more miles in Wales on a bicycle and on foot than is possibly prudent in one lifetime and yet up until about ten years ago, not only was I unable to pronounce the place names I came across, I had no idea what any of them meant.

So it came to pass that, one day, determined to put an end to this state of affairs, I asked someone in Penmaenmawr what Penmaenmawr meant. Little did I know I had inadvertently hit the jackpot. Penmaenmawr, if not quite the Rosetta Stone of the Welsh language, is at least a fragment chipped off it, for it contains three words that are very common in Welsh place names. *Pen* means 'head' or 'end', *maen* is 'stone' and *mawr* is 'big'. Put them all together and you've got 'big stone head', which suddenly makes sense if you've ever been there. Excited by my haul, I purchased a tiny Welsh dictionary and began to squirrel away any other words that came up repeatedly on signposts.

Porth ('port') and *Aber* ('mouth', e.g. of a river) are popular coastal prefixes (see Porthmadog, Porthcawl, Aberystwyth and Aberporth). *Isaf* and *Uchaf* ('lowest' and 'highest') and their variants are as ubiquitous as one might expect in a country largely consisting of mountains and valleys. *Du* ('black') describes almost everything in Wales, from those same mountains and valleys to the humour. *Maes* ('field') pops its head up wherever there is farmland – so our National Trust plot, Y Maes, is simply 'the field'. I know I shouldn't have been quite so excited about knowing this when I came across the sign, but this is how I take my pleasures nowadays. It may also explain to a certain degree how I have remained unmarried. *Llan* ('church'), meanwhile, is all pervasive (accounting for 430-odd place names across the country) and is often followed by the name of a saint. So Llandanwg means 'the church of St Tanwg'.*

Over the last decade I have built up a concise list of words that, in my experience, have proved the most useful when deciphering Welsh place names. It is in a spirit of public service that I share this list with you now:

---

* Now, I am aware that that 'd' in Llandanwg has cheekily changed into a 't' in Tanwg. It's due to a process called mutation and it's quite common in Welsh and all the other Celtic languages. Life is too fleeting to get uptight about it though, so unless you plan to learn Welsh properly, just accept it and move on.

**Dixe's Guide to the Fifty-One Welsh Words
You Need to Master in order to Translate
Hundreds of Welsh Place Names and
consequently Feel Better about Yourself as a
Person which will not only Mask the Fact
that the Way Your Life Is Going You Are
Heading Towards a Sad and Lonely Death
and an Untended Grave but also Hamper
You from Doing Anything Much About It
because You Feel Good Right Now
Having just Worked Out that Bryncoch
Means 'The Red Hill' (which It Does)**

(Patents pending)

Aber	Mouth
Afon	River (hence the River Avon means 'river river')
Allt	Hill
Bach	Small
Betws	Sanctuary
Bryn	Hill
Bwlch	Gap or pass
Cae	Field or hedge
Capel	Chapel
Castell	Castle
Coch	Red
Coed	Wood
Craig	Rock or crag
Cwm	Narrow valley
Du	Black
Ffordd	Road
Garth	Hill or enclosure

Glan	Bank or shore
Glas	Blue (confusingly, can also mean green in older Welsh)
Gwyn	White
Hafod	Shieling (i.e. summer pastures)
Hen	Old
Isa/isaf	Lower/lowest
Llan	Church
Llyn	Lake
Maes	Field
Mawr	Big or great
Melin	Mill
Moel	Bare hill
Môr	Sea
Morfa	Marsh (usually coastal)
Newydd	New
Pant	Hollow
Pen	Head, end, top or chief
Penrhyn	Promontory or cape
Pentref	Village
Plas	Mansion or hall
Porth	Port
Pwll	Pool or pit
Rhiw	Hill or rise
Rhos	Moor or heath
Sant	Saint
Sarn	Roman road
Tal	Tall, high or lofty
Tan	Under
Traeth	Beach or shore
Tŷ	House (*tŷ bach* is the loo, literally the 'little house')

Tyn	Tight
Ucha/uchaf	Higher/highest
Y/yr/'r	The or in the, on the, by the, etc
Ynys	Island

Got those? Excellent. But remember, this is all well and good if you're happy merely knowing what the place names mean. If you want to speak them out loud as well, you're entering a minefield, my friend. Let's not fool ourselves, when it comes to pronunciation, if you're not Welsh you're never going to kid any of the locals that you're one of them, however many hours you put into perfecting an accent that doesn't board a plane bound for Bangladesh after the first three words. However, you can at least stop yourself from making the sort of pronunciation errors that scream: 'I'm not from around here.' Here are three basic rules to get you started:

i. Only a double ff is sounded like an 'f': a single f sounds like a 'v'.

ii. *—au* at the end (as in *Blaenau*, *toiledau*) sounds a bit like the English word 'eye'.

iii. A 'y' is often pronounced like a 'u' and vice versa, and depends to a certain extent on whether you're in North or South Wales – fudge if at all possible.

Back at the station, there was a rather officious notice by the entrance to the shelter. It listed nine activities prohibited on stations at which Arriva Trains Wales operated. The notice was somewhat in the manner of the classic 'no bombing, no petting' posters you still sometimes see at swimming pools, though lacked the comic drawings that leaven the message of the latter. The list outlawed smoking, swearing, the putting of feet on seats and the consumption of alcohol, along with more serious misdemeanours such as vandalism and the abuse of railway staff. However, there was one proscribed pursuit that really stood out: there was to be no loitering.

Now, I don't know how you stand on the issue, if you'll excuse the pun, but I'd say the line between waiting about and loitering is not one that is always obvious. And of course as soon as I knew that I was not to loiter I felt unconscionably self-conscious about the manner in which I was waiting. Up to the point when I read the notice, I had been leaning against the shelter, but that seemed *exactly* the sort of thing a loiterer would do. I swiftly straightened my back. This, I felt, moved me more into respectable 'waiting' territory. There was no denying, however, that I was still on my feet and as a general rule loiterers are folk who like to stand about. I took a seat on the aquamarine bench. Unfortunately, this seemed the sort of a manœuvre a loiterer would perform in order to shake off suspicion. I stood up again. *Exactly* what a real loiterer would do! The sad truth was that the more effort I put into not appearing like a loiterer, the more like a loiterer I felt I became. Perhaps if I looked impatiently at my watch? There, no loiterer ever does that, because the nature of their louche pastime requires that time is of no essence whatsoever. Sadly, I had forgotten that the strap had broken and I'd put my watch in my pocket. I was staring at an empty wrist. I was banged to rights. I looked at the poster again to see if there was an address at which I could hand myself in and free myself from the unbearable existence of the inadvertent loiterer. There wasn't. There was a phone number, but of course I had no phone.

Then I had a brainwave. What Would Verena Do?

I'm happy to say that there was nothing on the Arriva Trains Wales 'Passenger Codes of Conduct' poster that prohibited its passengers from being upside down. Much to my surprise it turned out to be quite relaxing too. And people complain that art these days is out of touch with ordinary life.

TALSARNAU

Begin a discussion on tsunamis and you can be pretty confident that it will go on for some time before anybody mentions Wales. That wasn't always the case, however. If you'd been living in Talsarnau in 1927 (I make the bold assumption here that you weren't) you'd probably have spoken of little else, for that was the year the tsunami struck. Sweeping in from the Irish Sea up the Dwyryd estuary on 28 October, the freak wave piled across the low-lying grassland and smashed into the unsuspecting village. Although the event is very little documented, photographs taken in the aftermath depict scenes of devastation. Flood waters cover the 1,200 yards or so that normally separate the village from the estuary, and in the village itself one road has been completely stripped away, as if it had never existed. It's a wonder no one was killed.

The main line was damaged and large sections of another line were horribly mangled. This latter track, along which Snowdonian slate was transported to local quays, was nearer the shore. Despite running along the top of an embankment, it was swept away as if its rails were mere pipe cleaners.

The local people stoically rebuilt their village. It even went on to become a popular seaside resort for a little while before it faded back into the obscurity with which it cloaks itself today.

The station is built on land that was actually part of the sea until the early 19th century, when the creation of a number of embankments claimed it from the waves. Back then, Talsarnau consisted of a single farm. The railway line from Machynlleth up to Pwllheli was opened in 1867 and a village grew up around the station. Wool from the hill farms came through here. Pit props for the slate mines made a journey in the opposite direction. The hustle and bustle that once characterised the station has long since hustled and bustled off elsewhere though, leaving a forlorn little platform – whose one station building is now a private residence – gazing up at far Snowdon and mulling over more extraordinary days than these.

Talsarnau really has only one attraction as such, and that is the tidal island of Ynys Gifftan ('Anne's gift island'), a dollop of rock resting in the same sandy estuary up which the tsunami surged. The island was a gift from Queen Anne in the early 1700s to an ancestor of the sixth Baron Harlech, who owns the island today. Until around the end of the 20th century it was occupied on and off by perennially unprosperous tenants, but there's nothing on it now except for its one house, which has embarked on that senescent journey from derelict to ruin. The views from the island across the sands to Portmeirion are great, though, so I set off from the station on a little pilgrimage, crossing the embankment of the doomed slate line on my way.

The grass here is of such good quality that from 1953 to 1962, a briefly successful turfing industry was established. Watch a video of any FA Cup final or England home international from that era and the Wembley monochrome grass you'll see under the boots of Stanley Matthews or

Johnny Haynes was grown on this sward between Talsarnau station and the Dwyryd estuary. It was even deemed good enough to grace the courts at Wimbledon. This was certainly a step up from being trampled by soldiers, which was largely its fate during World War II, when the area was used as a rifle range.

Serendipitously, I had arrived at low tide. I'd been here a couple of times before, so, after crossing the grass, I knew I would have to remove my boots and socks and roll my trousers up in preparation for fording the River Dwyryd, whose low-tide channel passes right next to the shore. Except that this time it simply wasn't there. At some point in the 12 months since my last visit it had moved a couple of hundred yards west to cross the sands much nearer the island. I liked the fact that the river had fooled me, but I also took pleasure in the fact that I knew where it ought to have been.

We go back, that little peripatetic channel and I. I find it rather comforting that after years of exploring Britain I now know hundreds of places around it really quite well, thanks to the inscrutable Hand of Happenstance™ directing me back to them time and time again. Although it was only my third visit to Talsarnau, I could pass the workmen beavering away inside its former post office and general store and recall a time when it was still a going concern and I'd popped in to have a friendly chat with the postmistress. I was sad that it had closed − though that had already happened by the last time I was here − but there was something strangely satisfying in having a memory locked up there, just waiting for chance to drop by with a key. It's like having a whole set of little homes dotted around the country that I can slip into when I'm away from my actual home. Since I travel around Britain for roughly four months every year, that's quite a boon. Don't get me wrong, I love roaming about. It's just that from time to time I can sympathise with the line David Byrne of Talking Heads sings in 'The Big Country': 'I'm tired of travelling/I want to be somewhere.'

TO PENYCHAIN

I was pulled up on my pronunciation of Penychain by the guard. This may seem like a matter of no consequence – an incident that most people wouldn't even dwell on for the time it takes to say the word. To me, in the admittedly less than perfect world I inhabit, it was nothing short of a disaster. In getting Penychain wrong I broke a promise I had made to myself many years ago. Taking the train from Pwllheli with a friend, I had confidently asked the guard for a ticket to 'Penny-chain'. When I had subsequently heard him calling out the name of the station over the train's PA, I had been so mortified at the sheer gross Englishness of my pronunciation that after alighting I walked the length of the train to apologise to him. I made a mental note of the way the name should be spoken and resolved that I would never make that mistake again, that next time I would get it right, the world would be set back on its axis and I would be at peace.

Fast forward to the present and my train is heading past Llandecwyn ('Tecwyn's church' – another request stop) and Penrhyndeudraeth ('promontory with two beaches') before turning left to follow the shore of the Llyn Peninsula.

'Pen-ee-choin, Pen-ee-choin,' I repeat to myself.

That 'ch' is pronounced like the 'ch' in loch and so concerned am I that nothing approaching the 'ch' in church should escape my lips that by the time we reach Minffordd ('roadside') I'm barely aspirating it at all. I decide not to risk it and drop the 'c' altogether.

'Pen-ee-hoin.' That's better.

Porthmadog swings into view.

'Pen-ee-hoin.'

I can hear the guard passing down the train.

'Pen-ee-hoin.'

'Tickets, please!'

'Pen-ee-hoin.'

She's right up behind me.

'Pen-ee-hoin.'

I'm definitely next.

'Pen-ee-hoin.'

It's me! I proffer my rover ticket.

'Hello, I'd like to get off at Pen-ee-hoin, please.'

'Pen-ee-*hine*? Sure, that's fine.'

She passes on.

I get off the train a broken man.

PENYCHAIN

My strongest impression from the week I spent in the Butlin's holiday camp at Penychain all those years ago is of never being quite warm. To be fair to the place, it wasn't really built to withstand the rigours of a freezing North Welsh April, but that still didn't excuse the huge gap under the front door of our chalet, nor the entirely inadequate heating which sent the electricity meter spinning faster than a prime minister's press officer.

I was an impoverished student earning an all too tiny sum of money selling magazine subscriptions at a conference. My two fellow students and I spent the week wrapped in thin blankets. I think we used every single one we could find in the chalet's plywood cupboards and covetously eyed the two we had to use as a bung beneath the front door to keep the wind off the Irish Sea from turning us into pathetic student-sized blocks of ice. It was a relief to be on duty in the conference hall – the only room in which we could not see our breath – but I don't remember ever fully thawing out.

The other memory I have of that time was that everything in the chalet that wasn't brown was orange. The place was a little time capsule in which everything from the 1970s that was slightly shoddy or disappointing or in dubious taste had been preserved. Woefully thin curtains, narrow uncomfortable settees (nailed to the wall, I seem to recall), drawers that fell to pieces when you opened them, and a bathroom that even we students, supposedly inured to such horrors, found so heart-sinkingly sad and cold that we restricted our visits to the absolute minimum necessary to maintain a level of hygiene that wouldn't expose us to scabies. It would not have surprised us if we'd opened one of the wardrobes to find Rod Hull and Emu in there.

And then there was that smell. At first it seemed as if it must come from the kitchen (or 'brown-and-orange kitchen-style kitchenette' in our chalet's case) because the odour had a rancid fatty quality to it laced with notes of congealed fish matter. However, as the week progressed we realised that over the years countless oleaginous molecules had risen up from the seething pinguid accretion of hundreds of early-evening family fried dinners and penetrated everything – the woefully thin curtains, the narrow uncomfortable settees, the very plywood of the collapsible drawers. Lord love us – even the thin blankets we pulled tight around our blue-tinged bodies smelled of stale cooking oil and shattered dreams.

After the initial shock that such a place could still exist in the thrusting go-getting nineties, we spent our week fluctuating between two states: hilarity that all the jokes told about Butlin's and its copycat rivals were in reality mere statements of fact, and sheer grim determination to get through the week without losing any limbs to frostbite.

That said, I was rather looking forward to renewing my acquaintance with the Pwllheli holiday camp (as it was always known despite Pwllheli being four miles away), even though it had been run by Butlin's sister company

Haven since 1997 and had changed its name to Hafan-y-Môr ('haven by the sea'). I was to discover that that was by no means the only thing that had been altered in the intervening years.

The camp is built on both sides of the railway line with a bridge connecting the two parts and Penychain station positioned at its far western end. In this respect, nothing has changed since the camp was constructed by Billy Butlin during World War II. However, it was built not as a holiday camp but as HMS *Glendower*, a training centre for the navy. The government of the day asked Billy to set it up somewhere on the coast of North Wales after he had successfully converted the holiday camp he was building at Filey in Yorkshire into a base for use by the RAF. It's no surprise that, with so much overlap between these militarised encampments and the holiday camps they became, a holiday in the latter developed a reputation for aping the regimented life in the former.

Butlin chose 150 acres of farmland at Penychain, which conveniently already had its own underused station. Within three weeks of the work starting, 8,000 servicemen were sleeping here in tents while buildings were hastily constructed around them. After the war, Butlin was allowed to buy the camp; he opened it to holidaymakers in 1947 in the teeth of a great deal of local opposition and a public inquiry.

The heyday of Penychain station came in the summers of the fifties and early sixties when the vast majority of the weekly intake of 8,000 holidaymakers made their way to the camp by train. In 1960 and 1961 they were entertained by acts that included Rory Storm and the Hurricanes, who did two 13-week engagements at the Pwllheli camp. The band is now best known as 'the one that had Richard Starkey drumming for it before he joined The Beatles and became better known as Ringo Starr'. It's difficult now to imagine The Beatles without Ringo. Take the two Ringo-penned songs 'Octopus's Garden' and 'Don't Pass Me By' from The Beatles' canon and their cupboard is bare indeed.

With the advent of cheaper air travel, holidaying in Britain became markedly less popular and Butlin's Pwllheli went into decline. The company attempted to forestall this by introducing funfair rides such as the Vekoma Boomerang rollercoaster, which arrived in 1987 and threw riders' stomachs into their mouths for the next ten years. In 1990, somewhat more comprehensive changes were made, when £30 million was invested to turn the camp into a subtropical water paradise called Starcoast World.

Even then, some old-fashioned fixtures gamely struggled on. The camp's own railway line, which had run since 1953 and took guests three-quarters of a mile from the centre of the complex to the beach, was shut down as recently as 1996. However, it wasn't until the following year, when Haven took over, that the chalet in which my fellow students and I had held our noses and shivered was finally pulled down.

Nowadays the camp (or rather 'park', which is now the preferred term) is awash with static caravans. But I was pleased to see that there are still some chalets here, albeit turned out to a significantly higher standard than the one my friends and I endured.

I walked from the station along the sheltered lane that skirts the perimeter of the camp all the way to the A497 where the main entrance can be found off a roundabout. I chatted with a friendly old guy who was manning the barrier, but I confess I didn't cough up to go into the park as a day visitor. I'm not sure I exactly represent their target market and, to be honest, I would have felt uncomfortable in a setting where families are the norm and where lone males wandering around are, I suspect, treated with some suspicion.

Though the camp was open and it was early summer, no one else got off the train with me when I arrived, and no one got on the train with me when I left. Perhaps there is the occasional Saturday in the high season when the huge barn of a building that sits on the platform and could easily shelter a few hundred departing fun-seekers or host an impromptu rave finds itself filled to the gunwales, but I somehow doubt it. I looked up the figures later and found that only around 3,000 passengers a year jump on or hop off here. To put that into context, that's almost 2,000 fewer than the number of people who stay at the park *in a single week* when it's at full capacity. I know that the car has lorded it over the train for decades now, but for anyone who's more a fan of the latter than the former that still makes for a dispiriting statistic.

TO PONT RHUFEINIG (ROMAN BRIDGE)

My journey to Roman Bridge involved taking a steam train on the Ffestiniog Railway from Porthmadog up into Snowdonia. If this were a television programme you might be forgiven for imagining that I had somehow crowbarred this jaunt into my itinerary to suit the demands of the director. 'Who cares if it doesn't make sense, Dixe? Think of the fantastic shots of you in a train pretending to get a smut in your eye as you point at some mountains. It'll be a high-altitude *Brief Encounter*.'

Thankfully, you have chosen to immerse yourself in the world of the book, where we don't do that sort of thing. It turned out that it was just the easiest way – when combined with a couple of normal trains – to get from Penychain to Roman Bridge, my next port of call.

There's only one class of ticket on the Ffestiniog Railway but several classes of carriage from which to choose. From what I saw of it as I walked along the platform, my particular train comprised first class, third class, and some sort of sub-third cattle class compartments. Did nobody travel second class back in the day? I've always thought it a bit of a mystery that in old films the toffs sit decorously in first class, the peasantry bundles into third , but there's no second class at all. This seems a bit tough on the bourgeoisie. Did no one who was middle class travel by train until the railways were nationalised? Or did they have to disguise themselves with a top hat and tails and sneak into first, or a titfer and faceful of grime and slum it in third, hoping no one blew their cover in either? You can imagine the agonies this would entail – either sweating over whether the gent behind *The Times* would notice that your cummerbund wasn't from Jermyn Street; or fretting that you weren't dropping enough aitches when conversing with the colourful Cockney sparra across the aisle. Neither scenario is exactly a breeding ground for a serene and equable journey. Why oh why must it always be the middle classes who suffer?

Of course, there's no second class on British railways nowadays either – just first and standard. This long-standing prejudice against the second as a class is something I hope to write my doctoral thesis on some day.

The second-classless Ffestiniog Railway was opened in 1836 to ferry slate from the quarries around Blaenau Ffestiniog down to Porthmadog, where it could be shipped to a waiting roofless world. Initially the line consisted of a mere trackway. Horses hauled empty wagons up to the mines and the power of gravity was harnessed to push the full wagons back down the mountain. Steam locomotives arrived in 1863, and two years later a passenger service was started, with stations at various points along the line. Special four-wheel carriages were designed for the purpose. They had a very low centre of gravity and short wheel base in order to prevent them from toppling down the mountain at any of the line's extremely tight bends (the track even performs a complete spiral near the top). It was the third-class versions of these unique conveyances that I had rather cruelly dismissed as sub-third cattle class. I only hope I look as good when I hit 150.

A great deal of the rolling stock on the Ffestiniog is Victorian and made of wood you can see your face in. I was struck by how every carriage I passed, no matter how humble its status, was more inviting than its characterless modern cousins. Since it didn't seem to matter where one sat, I opted for the luxury of a first-class carriage – one of those with the corridor down the side, snug little four-seater compartments off it and a table on which to spread out. The other carriages had begun to fill up but I noticed that mine was completely empty. This started to make me feel a little edgy. I got my ticket out and looked at it again. There was nothing on it to indicate that I had purchased a third-class ticket. I decided to sit tight and, if challenged by the guard, assert the totality of my ignorance, apologise profusely, gather up my possessions and trail off in abject shame to a class more of my standing. As it happened, when the guard came along she checked my ticket, gave me a nice smile and told me that I could order refreshments if I wanted to. I did. I ordered a whole bottle of Welsh cider to celebrate the fact that I had not been humiliated.

I suspect it says something rather uplifting about the British on holiday that when faced with the choice of first, third or cattle class they pile into the latter two, regardless of the fact that all three cost the same. I'm only sorry I let the side down on this occasion.

The journey was great,* not least because it afforded me the chance to gasp at the size of the two luggage racks in my compartment: they were just about large enough to

---

* 13½ miles climbing 700ft, my fact-loving chums.

hold a Homburg each, as long as the wearer didn't possess a prodigiously large head. It made me a bit ashamed of my rucksack, which in comparison had taken on Brobdingnagian proportions. Indeed, it was difficult not to feel a bit like Gulliver, what with the slender corridor and the petite seats. It drove me to wonder if feeding ourselves to the point of gluttony and beyond and having so much more stuff has made us one iota happier than our forebears.

But I was happy all the same. The views were fantastic, the request stop at Campbell's Platform was a little marvel – just a lawn and a minute waiting room built of slate – and I could point at mountains to my heart's delight. Best of all, I even managed to get a smut in my eye, thereby saving myself the bother of pretending. There was no *Brief Encounter*, but then I think what I could do with right now is more of a lengthy encounter than a brief one, so perhaps it was no great loss.

PONT RHUFEINIG (ROMAN BRIDGE)

One word that didn't make my list of *Fifty-One Welsh Words You Need to Master* was Rhufeinig ('Roman'). The Romans, polite to a fault, made sure they had a good old root around Wales when they came over to Britain in the first century. They brought a bottle or two of wine, only making their excuses and leaving in AD 383 when all the canapés had run out. However, they didn't leave much behind them by which they could be remembered, except for the aqueducts, sanitation, roads, irrigation, medicine, education, etc.* As a consequence, in contrast to England with her interminable –chesters and –cesters, Wales is not riddled with names harking back to the occupation.

It's a pity, then, that when a place name does recall the Romans' presence in the principality, its local station can't be bothered to spell it correctly. The station's name boards manage 'Roman Bridge' without error, but the Welsh equivalent 'Pont Rhufeinig' they render as 'Pont Rufenig'.

Now, I'll grant you that, according to the 2011 census, only 27 per cent of people in the Conwy County Borough claim to be able to speak Welsh, but just over the border in Gwynedd that rises to 65 per cent. In Blaenau Ffestiniog they even run ten-week Welsh language courses for newborn babies. Yet less than four miles away, there's a

* And an amphitheatre, fort and practice camp a few miles away at Llyn Trawsfynydd (a reservoir created in the 1920s to supply water for a hydroelectric power station).

railway station that has been blithely spelling its own Welsh name wrong for years, missing out not just one letter but two. Can you imagine the hoo-ha if all the name boards at Portsmouth station said Potsmoth or the capital's principal terminus for trains to the northwest announced itself as Loon Euston?

It's bad enough that, while most request stops have enjoyed some sort of heyday, Pont Rhufeinig (I'm going to refer to it by this name for the rest of all time, by the way, in a vain and almost certainly pointless bid to redress the balance) has only ever been moderately patronised and has spent extended periods of its life as a lowly, underused request stop. As long ago as 1904, 26 years after it came into being, traffic was described as 'extremely sparse' and trains were already 'calling as required'.

There was once a goods yard, though. In the February 1939 edition of that evergreen classic the *London Midland Scottish Country Lorry Services* booklet, Pont Rhufeinig is noted as the scene of 'Deliveries of Grain, Flour, Oilcake, Feeding Meals, Manures and Basic Slag'.

This came as news to me because I had no idea that slag could be anything *but* basic. No doubt posher stations further north like Betws-y-Coed and Llandudno were getting deliveries of fancy slag or slag *à l'orange* or similar. Anyway, the Pont Rhufeinig siding was removed in the late 1950s, ending all hopes of even basic slag going in or out of the place.

The station's indignities were passed on to what few passengers haunted this isolated spot 'twixt moorland, farmland and hills. Gents had a urinal – but nothing more – to the east of the station building. If members of the distaff side of the species were caught short, they enjoyed the delights of a small wooden hut which served as both toilet and ladies' waiting room.

Visitors to the station today would look upon even these meagre facilities as luxurious, for nowadays Pont Rhufeinig runs only to a bus-stop-style shelter. If you've the best part of half a million pounds to spare, however, you can snap up the station house, which is currently for sale. It's been converted into a three-bedroom private residence and includes a bathroom that I imagine knocks spots off the former conveniences laid on here. You get nearly ten acres of land thrown in, too, on which you could set up the import/export business for fancy slag of which the area has been deprived for too long.

What you won't get, unfortunately, is a Roman bridge. I know, because I went in search of it. For such an apparently remote area, it has what might almost be described as a surfeit of bridges, all of which looked suspiciously modern to me until I spread my net to the west. There, underneath a road so important that it grinds to a halt at a farm about a mile away, was an unmistakably elderly looking bridge. To cross the Lledr, a river of no great girth, it relies on seven or eight oblong stone pillars holding up a decidedly wonky set of lintels on which sit layers of jerkily undulating bricks. The comic effect is spoiled only by the addition on both sides of cheap and nasty metal barriers.

Inspired by my sudden proximity to the work of Romans, I tucked into some more Boethius. Philosophy, in the guise of a woman, has come to visit the author in his cell and begins to recite a poem about his 'confusion of mind':

Alas! in what abyss his mind
Is plunged, how wildly tossed!
Still, still towards the outer night
She sinks, her true light lost,
As oft as, lashed tumultuously
By earth-born blasts, care's waves rise high.

Which reminded me that dusk would soon be upon me and that I had a train to catch down the line to North Llanrwst before I could pitch my tent for the night.

It wasn't until much later that I discovered that the Roman bridge was almost certainly built some time after the Romans had packed up their togas and upped sticks for warmer, drier climes. It's likely that they did throw up a bridge here at one time, for one of their roads, Sarn Helen, ran through this valley on its 160-mile journey from Aberconwy to Carmarthen and would have had to cross the Lledr somehow. This current bridge, for all its antiquity, was most assuredly not the means, though.

It rather adds insult to injury that the Roman bridge after which Pont Rhufeinig station is misspelled does not actually exist and is, indeed, a mere supposition. Given this lamentable circumstance I can't help feeling it would be as well to scrap the Roman association entirely and rename the station Llaes Ceuffordd ('long tunnel') in recognition of the fact that it lies close to the 3,726-yard Ffestiniog Tunnel, the longest single-track tunnel in Britain. I passed through it on my brief journey from Blaenau Ffestiniog. The station would then at least be named after something that exists. And if 'Ceuffordd' proves beyond the wit of the name-board writers, they can always plump for the other Welsh word for tunnel and call it 'Llaes Twnnel'. If they spell that wrong, there's really no hope for humankind.

DOLGARROG

While a number of the stations featured within these pages experienced a few years or sometimes even a few decades in the sun before fading to request-stop status, Dolgarrog may be the only one whose future looks so bright that it might actually become a fully fledged compulsory stop again. I have it on good authority that whenever this happens an angel gets its wings, so I expect there are a fair few members of the lowest order of the nine-fold celestial hierarchy looking down on events in the village with more than a tingle of anticipation.

By contrast, my arrival at Dolgarrog had been somewhat downbeat. Things had looked much more promising the previous night at my campsite in the village of Trefriw. Famous, if famous at all, for its woollen mills (which are still very much in business), Trefriw is a mile from North Llanrwst station – one of seven request stops on the 13-station Conwy Valley Line – and I'd walked to the latter by way of the squeaky Gower footbridge, which took me over the Afon Conwy in a series of exhilarating bounces.

Come the morning, my rare good fortune with the weather thus far seemed to have run out. A sky dark with intent filled the air with sporadic bursts of drizzle that were clearly mere teasing curtain-raisers building up to the main event. I was keen not to be outside when that particular show started because sometimes I feel as if I have spent my entire adult life walking in the rain in Snowdonia. I'm not sure if there is a rota system in operation, but if so, it's definitely someone else's turn now. I wouldn't mind so much but Snowdonian rain is just *so* wet. It has a quality of dampness above and beyond any other rain I've ever known. Even Latin America's diluvial downpours* never made me as wet as I've been while trudging across Snowdonia's mountains. I swear that on occasion it has permeated my skin and diluted my blood. If you ever catch the late-night extended weather forecast on Radio 4, do listen out for the words, 'And the wettest place today was Capel Curig in Snowdonia.' It's such a common occurrence that I imagine they have the sentence pre-recorded and the forecaster just hits a button to play it. It's a set of words that brings back a welter of sodden memories, but I love hearing it at the end of a day when I haven't been there.

You can perhaps imagine, then, with what trepidation I shouldered my rucksack and stepped out along the road to Dolgarrog. If the original plans for the line along the Conwy Valley had materialised, the railway would have run along the side of the river I was walking down. As it was, when it opened in 1863 it missed out both Trefriw and Dolgarrog, whose doughty citizens were forced to walk a mile or so and cross the Conwy to get to the stations that bore the names of their respective villages ('Llanrwst and Trefriw' in the former's case before it became North Llanrwst).

Some way out of the village I arrived at the Trefriw Wells Spa. I'd come across this while reading the 1937 edition of the *Llanrwst & District Official Guide*, which was

---

* The Spanish for these is *aguacero*, which always used to amuse me because it comprises the words meaning 'water' and 'zero' – the exact opposite of what they were.

a surprisingly fascinating document. Apparently, the deep cave the spa waters come from was discovered by soldiers from the XX Roman Legion stationed at nearby Canovium. As with the woollen mill, I hadn't expected the spa to have survived into our brave new millennium, but then again, we do not live in an age of reason. I am quite willing to believe that some of the minerals in Trefriw's spa water may be of some benefit to the imbiber, but I'm of the opinion that the anonymous writer of the *Llanrwst & District Official Guide* was slightly over-egging the pudding with his description of its restorative powers:

> *Trefriw possesses two chalybeate springs. In these waters four most powerful stimulants – iron, sulphur, alum and silica – exist in their most powerful form; iron as proto-sulphate and sulphur as sulphuric acid … The value and efficacy of the waters in all cases of rheumatism cannot be too strongly emphasised, but even then there are hundreds of other ailments which they have been known to cure, most definitely those resulting from torpidity of the digestive and blood-forming processes.*

Like most people, I hate torpidity of any kind and torpidity of the digestive and blood-forming processes is the very worst sort, so naturally I was excited at the possibilities of the chalybeate springs. But stone me if there wasn't more to come, as revealed in an advert for the spa waters on page 27:

They are wonderfully efficacious in cases of Rheumatism, Arthritis, Sciatica, Neuritis, Neurasthenia, Anaemia and various other classes of ailments. Many very remarkable and striking results are obtained in cases of severe and chronic Rheumatism and Rheumatoid-Arthritis – even in bedridden cases of long standing – from an extended course of home treatment.

Now, I don't know about you, but although I can see how iron might help those suffering from anaemia, this advert looks suspiciously like the work of a copywriter who was bored with his job. How else do you explain the hilarious horizontalist-verticalist joke about 'bedridden cases of long standing'? It almost made me want to catch a bit of neurasthenia just so that I could be cured of it, but I couldn't work up the energy to do so. Sadly, although the water is still for sale, the spa itself closed to the public in 2011, so I was unable to stock up on my new favourite cure-all. Beneath a sky that had turned the colour of slate, I pressed on towards Dolgarrog, feeling decidedly low on alum.

My deficiencies in the bauxite-derivatives area were as nothing, though, when compared with Dolgarrog's. The immense aluminium works that dominate the village and had been going for exactly a hundred years were as definitively shut as a place could be. Despite an injection of cash from the Welsh Assembly in 2002, the complex closed for good in 2007 and demolition of the site began two years later. The works were a major source of employment in the valley, and when Dolgarrog Aluminium called in administrators to wind up the company, 170 much-needed jobs were lost. I pressed myself up against the locked steel gates and peered through a fresh salvo of drizzle. Just one large factory-like building now stands amid a sea of destruction. Piles of bricks sprawl across an expanse of concrete like ranges of ragged hills. Weeds and shrubs have begun to cover the newly derelict spaces like a moth-eaten shroud. Traffic cones attempt to bring order by plotting a way across the wasteland to a distant Portakabin. The speed limit in force on this hundred yards or so of makeshift road is 9mph. I couldn't help but admire the mind of whoever it was who set that speed limit. He was a man (I was sure) of commendable precision.

I turned away and sought directions to the station from a middle-aged gentleman who was passing by.

'You can turn down this road immediately on the left,' he informed me. 'That will take you all the way to a bridge. The station is the other side of it. It's a long way though: three-quarters of a mile.'

I thanked him. But there was more.

'The next train is the 09.27 heading for the coast. If you walk at an average pace it should take you 18 minutes.'

I thanked him again, forcing myself not to raise an eyebrow at his assertion that 2.5mph constituted an 'average pace'. He took out a key and began to open the gate I had just been peering through. All of a sudden I had a feeling I knew who had set the speed limit at 9mph.

Keen to take advantage of whatever inside knowledge he might have of the works, I called back to him, 'Are they going to do anything with the site?'

'Yes,' he called back. I expected him to give me a fastidiously accurate rendering of all the proposals for the site up to the last planning meeting. I was disappointed, for he chose not to expand on his answer.

'What?' I persisted as he clunked the padlock behind him.

'Read the leaflet in the window of that shop over there,' he replied and walked away at 2.5mph.

I followed the direction of his pointing hand and crossed the road to the shop, which turned out to be a post office, tiny general store and one-table café. As had been promised, there in the window was a leaflet heralding the advent of something called Surf Snowdonia. I sat down at the one table, ordered a black tea and asked the friendly woman who served me if she knew anything about the project.

'I'm going to a meeting tonight, as it happens,' she told me. 'Fingers crossed it all comes off.'

According to the blurb, what may be about to come off is a 'multi-million pound scheme to regenerate Dolgarrog and the surrounding area by developing the old aluminium works into Europe's first Wave Garden'. This will apparently take the form of an artificial lagoon on which waves up to 1.9m will be generated for the benefit of those who wish to surf without troubling the sea.

I had a go at surfing once. A newspaper asked me to go down to Cornwall in February to try out a new surfing-and-volunteering holiday organised by the National Trust. It bucketed with rain nearly the whole time I was in the sea. You might think that getting thrown repeatedly off a plank of wood into the Atlantic in the pouring rain on a cold winter's day wouldn't be all that much fun, but I fell in love with it instantly. I promised myself that I would book some more lessons and learn how to stay up on a board for longer than two and a half seconds. Three years later I've yet to keep that promise, but that hasn't held me back from being a surfing evangelist. I therefore hope Dolgarrog gets its Wave Garden. It may not quite make the list of the thousand most useful things to build on a vacant aluminium works site, but it should give a lot of people a lot of harmless pleasure. And it's not as if they're short of water around here.

They were even less short of it a few minutes later when the sky fell in. I made my tea last half an hour until I calculated that my train was 18 minutes away from Dolgarrog station. At which point, the rain obligingly stopped. Walking down the attractive tree-lined track, I passed the place where the aluminium works had had its first siding installed in 1916. It was lifted in 1963 but the Dolgarrog Railway Society is in the process of putting some of it back again. If you want to see the original tracks and sleepers – and no one at all will think you odd if you do – you'll have to scour the Welsh Highland Railway. They've apparently been put to good use somewhere around Beddgelert.

Dolgarrog station – no more than a flimsy wooden platform, a token shelter and a bench – looked exactly like the sort of halt that was more likely to drift out of existence than become a thriving transport hub again. Opened in 1917 as part of the war effort, it closed in 1964 and all its buildings were removed. This proved a little premature because, after a change of heart, the station opened again in June the following year. No one could quite bring themselves to restore the station buildings, though, and Dolgarrog's lowly status was guaranteed.

But then again, who knows? If Surf Snowdonia gets built and (hem hem) rides a wave of popularity, Dolgarrog station may well find itself becoming so fashionable that it is made a compulsory stop once more and deserving of a few facilities. Indeed, it seems to be heading that way before even a single Jan and Dean song has graced the would-be leisure centre's speakers. Burrow around in the latest spreadsheet of official user statistics for Britain's railway stations and you'll come across an intriguing line written alongside Dolgarrog's figures. It notes: 'Continues high growth from previous year.' The sleeping giant awakes. My advice is to visit the village now before everything goes really crazy and the café has to get another table in.

CONWY

I must have passed through Conwy station dozens of times. I'd even got off once or twice before. It means I'm in a position to inform you that the platforms are so close to the castle walls that if the citadel's garderobes were still in use you'd have to watch yourself when waiting for a train.

Which makes it all the more remarkable that when my train glided gently to a stop next to platform 2, I found I was nowhere near the castle at all. True, there was a medieval town wall at the eastern end of the station. The castle, however, was about 300 yards away. There would have to be something extraordinarily amiss with the plumbing at the ancient fortress – possibly combined with a freak weather event – to put anyone waiting on the platform in danger of an unsavoury soaking.

It goes to show how unreliable memory is. Or at least how unreliable *my* memory is. It's a blessing in some ways, of course. Can you imagine being able to recall every single regrettable thing you had ever said, done or even thought? Every insult, snub or slight you had received? Every moment of grief, despair, heartache? So on balance I'm glad that I thought Conwy station was right beneath the walls of the castle. Ask me again in a year or two and I'll probably be back to swearing blind that it is.

The town's walls are almost wholly intact and their elevated walkways can be ambled along at will, so I needed no second invitation to renew my acquaintance with them. They're my favourite town walls in the whole of Britain, since you ask. Yes, even better than York's or Chester's. Berwick-upon-Tweed's are good too, but they haven't quite got the shazam of Conwy's ramparts.

In defence of my preference, which might seem perverse at first glance, I should like to call Witness A: the town's information boards by the old harbour – both an objective and an impartial source.

'Conwy is one of the World's most cherished manmade places,' they begin. I don't think there can be any arguing with that. I used to visit remote jungle communities in Guatemala and as soon as the inhabitants discovered that I was from Britain it would be nothing but, 'Tell us about Conwy. Is it as magnificent as they say?' and, 'Breathe on us, señor, so that we may inhale air from lungs that have breathed in Conwy.'

The information board continues: 'As a World Heritage Site, [Conwy] is amongst the planet's greatest built structures, equal to Stonehenge and The Pyramids as an example of mankind's most inspired creativity.'

So excited was I by this claim that I was moved to write a univocal poem* about Conwy, its station and its place in the pantheon of the world's all-time greats.

Conwy

Conwy
Stop of joy
Stop for folk who stop locos
For strolls on lofty stony blocks
To do long slow loops of old town

---

* Univocalism was invented in the 1960s by a group of French poets called the OULIPO – it requires the writer to forsake four of the five vowels for the entire length of a poem.

On top of crops
On top of shops
By long lost port
By old school fort
London's stronghold
Crown's bold foothold
Lordly symbol of control
Rock to brook no row, no oppo

Conwy, o town not blown down by pot shots
Holds own on roll of Old World's hot spots
Sphynx? No monopoly of good looks now
For Conwy's nobody's fool. How cool, how
Strong, how boldly grown, how oblong (mostly)
By Ynys Môn, Conwy's not snooty nor ghostly
Nor posh, nor forlorn, oh look how crowds do flock
To look on Old Glory, so now do not mock

It's astonishing, when you think of it, that a place on a par with the Great Pyramid of Giza, the only surviving Wonder of the Seven Wonders of the World, does not run to a station at which every train can trouble itself to stop. Indeed, there are many trains that pass through here each day that will not stop even if requested. This is surely indicative of some imbalance or other in the cosmos.

The station's glaring lack of importance is compensated for by the impressiveness of the approach to it from the east. Passengers hurtle straight towards Edward I's belligerent statement along a narrow spit that thrusts out into the Conwy estuary and ends with no fewer than three bridges jostling for space. To the right is the functional but dull road crossing, while in the middle is Thomas Telford's elegant suspension bridge, now used only by pedestrians and camouflaged by the addition of turrets imitating those of the castle immediately behind. The wrought-iron tubular railway bridge was built by Robert Stephenson* as a trial run for the much larger one (since burnt down) he threw up over the Menai Strait. It too has attempted to disguise itself as an extension of the castle by means of two substantial fake keeps – one at either end of the bridge. Made of a similar stone to the castle, they would blend in very well if it were not for the fact that they are oblong while all the towers behind them are round. Even so, the effect is a powerful one: sitting on the train you get the impression that you are being driven straight into a castle. Without making too many excuses for myself, this may go some way to explaining my own mis-memory of the castle's relationship with the station.

Just before entering the station, the double-track line passes through a convenient arch in the town wall. It is like no arch you will have ever seen in a medieval town wall: a whole army lifting banners aloft could pass through this one. I did wonder, as I stood on platform 2 awaiting a train to take me further west, how Master James of St George, the architect of Conwy Castle, could have allowed such a thing.

The truth is, of course, that he didn't – it's an astonishingly clever fraud. Nowadays, you would hope that a major railway line wouldn't go crashing through the centuries-old wall of one of the world's most cherished manmade places. However, in the 1840s when Robert Stephenson was beavering away at the construction of the Chester and

* Whose father, George Stephenson, was also known as the 'Father of the Railways', which makes Robert the 'Half-Brother of the Railways', assuming the Mother of the Railways was The Muse or something and not Frances Henderson, Robert's own mother.

Holyhead Railway, less store was put on the past. After all, back in those days, the walls were only a little over 550 years old and so could practically be considered new build.

To mitigate the damage caused, Stephenson had this huge Gothic crenellated archway erected. It followed the line of the wall and gave the impression that in days of yore troops defending the town would have crossed this arch along its elevated walkway. Over the last 170 years the stone has weathered to match that of the town walls, making the illusion complete. The only imperfection is a notch on the northern side of the arch which had to be hacked out in order to allow larger trains to use this curved stretch of track without their coach roofs colliding with the stonework.

The station itself shares a common heritage with Dolgarrog – it, too, like Lazarus, was summoned from the dead, though it spent rather more time in that unenviable state. It was closed on Valentine's Day 1966 after 118 years of service but then reopened, though only as a request stop, in June 1987. It also underwent another change. In its first incarnation it had been known as Conway, but by the time it sprang back to life the town was becoming more widely known by its Welsh rather than its Anglicised name. Seeing which way the wind was blowing, it dropped the 'a'.

It seems a bit of an anomaly that a station used 38,000 times a year should be a request stop, and indeed it was one of very few on my trip at which I was neither the only passenger getting off when I arrived nor alone in getting on when I left. It's a bit of a scandal really. In Guatemala, I can tell you, they talk of little else.

PENMAENMAWR

Travel west of Conwy and you get the impression that the North Welsh coast here is simply marking time. It's as if it's used up most of its creative energy in producing the mighty peninsula of Great Orme's Head at Llandudno and what little it had left it exhausted on the Conwy estuary. From Conwy to the eastern end of the Menai Strait it's just coasting – it's not ugly per se but there are no particularly interesting features, nothing to catch the eye or raise the pulse.

The little settlements along the way have clearly picked up on this topographical languor and sought to reflect it. Two of them, Penmaenmawr and Llanfairfechan, have stations (both request stops). Neither have remarkable histories but I felt drawn to get off for a couple of hours at Penmaenmawr for old times' sake – I had spent several summers at camps here as a teenager and it was, famously, the scene of my first Welsh lesson. Some places you should not go back to, though, and Penmaenmawr is one. There's nothing terrible about the village itself, aside from the fact that it does the double trick of feeling more like a town than a village in scale, but more like a morgue than anything else. Its station is large but mostly shut up and its long platforms are exposed and unwelcoming. Express trains clatter through at a rate of knots, taking advantage of a section of straight track. Their evident eagerness to pass through as quickly as possible lends the station an even more desolate air. It would be easy to imagine that no train was likely to come to a stop here ever again.

The area is dominated by the noise of a dual carriageway that, while taking a huge quantity of traffic out of the village, effectively cuts it off from the sea, which used to be its saving grace. If it has one now it's The Lazy Dollar, an American-style ice-cream parlour-cum-diner, which, rather improbably, is entirely vegetarian. Its chrome and coloured glass interior gleamed with such intensity that I had the feeling I was their very first customer – I was certainly their only one for the hour or so I was there. What it was doing in Penmaenmawr was a bit of a mystery: it seemed completely out of place, as if an ice-cream van had turned up at a funeral. I'm not a great fan of Americana but I do hope it succeeds, for it is a rare vital sign in a village that otherwise seems to have given up the ghost. I paid my bill, slipped quietly along the silent streets back down to the station and whispered a goodbye as the train pulled away.

I discovered later that, ironically, Penmaenmawr was once touted as a place to come to if you wanted to put off the evil day of your demise. In the second half of the 19th century it styled itself a 'Health, Rest and Holiday Resort' and attracted some high-profile visitors including (serial) Prime Minister William Gladstone, the Dukes of Westminster and Rutland, the poet Tennyson, the actor Sir Henry Irving and even Mark Twain.

It seems there was some foundation to the health-giving claims made about the compact resort. In a book published in 1905 with the heroically self-effacing title *The Switzerland of Wales: Penmaenmawr and Dwygyfylchi*, one M H Parry notes with pride that, 'The particularly mild and dry climate of Penmaenmawr makes it exceptionally favourable for winter residence. The rate of mortality is far below the average, being for 1903 13.5 per 1000, and the zymotic death-rate* 0.54 per 1000.' I wonder what Mr Parry and his fellow members of the Penmaenmawr Town Improvement Association would make of the place today?

* Death caused by alien abduction.

LLANFAIR PG

Slipping over Robert Stephenson's rebuilt Britannia Bridge (the original tubular construction was inadvertently burnt down when two local boys set fire to it one night in 1970 while playing inside it with a burning torch, as you did back then), and thinking of anything other than zymotic death rates, I soon found myself at Llanfair PG, better known to extrovert types as Llanfairpwllgwyngyllgogery-chwyrndrobwllllantysiliogogogoch. You can't not have a nose round at a station that possesses the longest place name in Europe, so I duly asked the guard to drop me off there, using its shortened appellation.

Unlike the science behind the theory of man-made climate change, the history of this sesquipedalian name is unsettled. The village's own website claims that when the railway from Chester to Holyhead was built in the 1850s, a local committee of what was then the small village of Llanfair Pwllgwyngyll discussed how train travellers could be inveigled into stopping there a while and spending some money. A cobbler from neighbouring Menai Bridge is credited with coming up with the elongated name, which he hoped would put the village on the map. He famously did so by dragging in two churches and a clutch of local landmarks to come up with a confection that means 'St Mary's church in the hollow of the white hazel near a rapid whirlpool and the church of St Tysilio of the red cave'. However, Welsh grammarian John Morris-Jones contended that it was not a Menai Bridge cobbler but a tailor from Llanfair Pwllgwyngyll who was the source of the convoluted new name. Whoever it was, the ruse proved extremely successful and the village bucked the trend on Anglesey by growing in both population and prosperity right up to the outbreak of World War I.

I pray forgiveness from the current locals for saying this, but Llanfair PG is a forgettable little squib. Encircled by those highways of romance the A5 and A55, its sole purpose nowadays is to serve as a fine early example of the triumph of marketing over substance. Even the Marquess of Anglesey looks down his nose at it from the top of his 89ft column at the edge of the village. If you're into tourist-priced woven goods, though, you'll love it here.

Y FALI (VALLEY)

Every station on Anglesey (or Ynys Môn, as the island is also known) is a request stop except for Holyhead, which, being the end of the line, will forever be compulsory, even should the population of the town dwindle to nothing. My little train passed through Bodorgan, Tŷ Croes and Rhosneigr without stopping and I sensed a certain reluctance on its part to come to a rest at Y Fali. I was soon to become very glad it did, though, because it was here that I realised an ambition.

Y Fali station's main claim to fame nowadays is that it shares its name – in its anglicised form – with the nearby RAF Valley (although, confusingly, Rhosneigr station is closer to the aerodrome). However, it had already enjoyed almost a century of quietly productive life before World War II brought the RAF to town. Opening in 1849, it had a small goods yard with one siding serving a corn mill. The station gradually grew in importance: its buildings were improved in 1870 and the platforms lengthened in 1889.

It was the coming of the airfield that provided the most thrilling years of its existence, though. Britain's air defences were naturally concentrated in the south and east of the nation, where they faced the foe. The Germans, sneakily, were getting around this by flying along and up the coast and conducting air raids on Merseyside from the west. This was clearly not cricket and merely added to the reasons why it was thought better if the Nazis were defeated. One of the measures deemed necessary to achieve this was the construction of an airfield in northwest Wales. The mountains of Snowdonia were obviously unsuitable for such a project, so attention was turned to Anglesey, whose largely flat terrain was far more promising. As it happened, the location decided upon – right next to the huge dunes that backed onto Cymyran and Crigyll beaches and on top of more sand at Tywyn Trewan Common – turned out to be a rather unfortunate choice.

Work on the airfield began in 1940 with the flattening of part of the common, for which much of the supplies and equipment arrived by train. RAF Valley came into operation the next year, with Belgian, Polish and Czech pilots all distinguishing themselves in the Allied cause, and this disparate group was joined by American flyers later in the war.

Unfortunately, the airfield's four-and-a-half-year wartime record is peppered with accidents. The decision to build the runway so close to the dunes meant that aircraft engines were forever being fouled by sand. This seems a rather predictable disadvantage to plopping an airfield on a windy spot next to an area of sand, but if anyone at the War Office did raise any concerns beforehand they were clearly disregarded. It's perhaps a little surprising, then, to discover that RAF Valley is still very much a going concern: fast jet aircrew are trained here, as are search and rescue pilots. Search and rescue missions launched from Valley continue to save lives.

The 1960s proved something of a rollercoaster period for the railway station. In 1962, sidings were installed to help supply materials for the building of the Wylfa nuclear power station, which began the following year, and later to allow spent fuel from the plant to join the main line. In 1966, however, the station itself was closed down as part of the Beeching cuts, only to be reinstated in 1982. The Wylfa nuclear power station, meanwhile, had come on line by 1971. It was due to cease generating in 2012 but was asked to soldier on for two more years. That's not to say it will be disappearing any time soon. The Nuclear Decommissioning Authority's plan for Wylfa foresees 'final site clearance' occurring sometime between 2091 and 2101.

I had a wander around the stretched-out and sadly anonymous village that Y Fali station serves. Its main point of interest was a butcher's shop in a building whose raised red-brick lettering declared it was once a police court (the old-fangled name for a magistrates' court).

And what of the valley suggested by its name? Well, that takes a leap of the imagination, for the whole area looks as flat as a mat. Inspecting a map, you can see that the village is ever so slightly lower than some of the ground around but that's it. If it were called Slight Depression it would be a lot more understandable. For this is a village that cries out, 'Forget me – there is nothing for you here but a sense that you wish you were elsewhere.' It's a very persuasive message. I visited several times when my friend Chris was training at the RAF base and yet not a single atom of Y Fali or its station had lodged itself in my memory. All I remember is that Chris would whizz about the skies during the day in a Hawk – the standard training plane for fighter pilots –

while his wife Helen and I amused ourselves as best we could visiting the sights of northwest Anglesey and stopping off at Y Fali for provisions. More often than not, though, the airfield would be enveloped in fog or sea mist or be quietly drowning beneath a typhoon, a weather event that is a particular speciality of the area. Chris's plane would be grounded, allowing all three of us to amuse ourselves as best we could visiting the sights of northwest Anglesey, none of which we could actually see on account of the fog, sea mist or typhoon. They were good times.

Chris never got to live out his dream of strafing innocent civilians. Although he became a fully fledged Tornado pilot, his squadron was always next in line to be sent to war when each conflict of the nineties ended, so he passed his time carrying out interminable peace-keeping duties. This was obviously no fun at all, so he eventually left. He and Helen went on to have three children. And a series of cats. I always used to envy them the latter but not the former (lovely though their children are). Standing now in a queue at one of Y Fali's two convenience stores behind a woman cradling a sleeping baby, I experienced a pang that I cannot say was one of paternal longing exactly but which certainly betrayed a fear that I had taken a wrong turn and had missed out in some way.

Finding nothing to detain me, I returned to the station early to await my train back to the mainland and it was while idling there that I noticed a man in the signal box. Furthermore, there was a path leading off the end of the platform to said signal box. Now, of all the myriad places I've been in my life, a signal box is not one of them. I wasn't sure if members of the public were even allowed in.

But here I was, with ten minutes to kill and a working signal box just 20 yards away. 'The worst that can happen,' I thought to myself as I climbed the steps leading up to the door, 'is that the signalman kidnaps me and threatens to kill me and/or derail the 17.36 to Chester unless his list of exacting and arcane demands is met. Frankly, that's the sort of excitement I could do with in my life right now.'

The signal box was one of those classic wooden affairs with a flight of steps leading to the upper of two floors. This storey comprised mainly windows behind which blinds shut out the late spring sunshine. I noticed the building also had a tiny shed-like appendage at the top of the steps that looked for all the world like a privy and, for all I knew, probably was.

I knocked gingerly at the door. After a few seconds a well-built man in a royal blue short-sleeved polo shirt and multiple tattoos answered it. I hesitantly asked him if I could come in and have a look around, expecting some variation or other on the theme of 'more than my job's worth' as a reply. Much to my delight, however, he instantly invited me in. And there they were, all lined up along the front of the box: a score or more of numbered levers, each with a little release handle at the end. To cap it all, above them there was one of those circuit-diagram whatsits showing the layout of the line with lights to indicate where the trains were. We live in a restless world where that which does not change is not only left behind but devoured. This rule does not apply to signal boxes.

My reaction to seeing all this was evidently too wide-eyed and joyful, because the signalman was swift to bring me down to earth a little.

'It's a good job, but the shifts do you in,' he said, before counting on his fingers the number of days straight he had done and announcing the total. I can't remember exactly, but it was a lot.

The training is tough too, he assured me. 'It lasts six weeks and there are tests every Friday. If you fail any of them you're out immediately – they just send you straight home.'

It still sounded pretty good to me. It takes seven long years to qualify as a doctor, so six weeks didn't seem too onerous. I began to wonder whether I hadn't missed my vocation. Think of all the splendid staring out of the window I could do if I were a signalman. I might even knock out the odd novel between trains – perhaps found a whole new literary genre called something like 'box lit' or 'lever fiction'. In my head I was already inhabiting some remote bucolic signal box with four trains through a day and none at all at the weekend.

'They say they're going to get rid of them all soon. It'll all be controlled from Nottingham then.'

'What, the whole system?' I protested, my dream bursting like a bubble.

'Looks like it,' he confirmed.

So much for progress not devouring the signal box.

'It's all computerised already,' he continued. 'They know everything I'm doing here. My boss told me, "If you make a mistake, put your hand up and admit it, because they'll find out anyway."'

So much for the romance of the signal box. Big Brother was watching us even here.

Presumably content that he had dashed any fanciful ideas I might have had regarding my future career path, the signalman talked me through the system. He couldn't let a train through before the people down the line had given him the all-clear. This ensured that there was only ever one train on a section at any given time. Also, it was physically impossible to signal a train through if the level-crossing gates were not shut to traffic. He only very rarely had to change points. Occasionally a movement of waste nuclear material from the power station necessitated this, but by and large it was signals that were being raised and lowered from this box.

I yearned, of course, to see him pull a few levers around, the way they do in every black-and-white film of any class, but with the unseen overlords observing his every move, I knew he was unlikely to give me a quick demo.

It was my own train that came to the rescue. Its imminent approach stung the signalman into action. He squeezed the release handle and hauled a lever towards him.

'Do they take much physical effort to move?' I asked him as he reached for another one.

'No. They used to back in the day, but not any more,' he replied, whisking a third lever into position.

I thanked him for letting me realise what was, if I'm honest, a fairly minor ambition. I didn't mention the bit about it being minor, though.

Suddenly realising that his signals wouldn't actually stop my train and that there was no one on the platform to stick out an arm, I hurried away, silently cursing myself for forgetting to ask him if the privy outside his door was actually a privy.

REDDISH SOUTH

I said goodbye to Wales with an all too brief early morning stroll along the prom at Llandudno and wished I were the sort of person who got up to have early morning strolls when not driven to do so by the exigencies of a train timetable. Three trains and one abandoned ship later* and I was on the platform at Stockport boarding what is jocularly known as the Denton Flyer.

If you wish to travel to Denton station, the 10.13 on Friday from Stockport to Stalybridge is definitely the train to catch — not just because it will speed you there in a lightning 11 minutes, but because it is the only one. Not just the only one all day but the only one all week. Miss this one and you're in for a 168-hour wait. Yes, that's right: every week just one train has Denton in its sights. And if you wish to approach Denton from the north, then I'm afraid you're out of luck, chum, for trains there are none.

To add insult to infrequency, Denton does not even merit its own line in the railway timetable: it appears merely as an item in footnote F to Table 78. Was there ever a more overlooked destination?

Well, actually yes, and its name is Reddish South.

Aside from Denton and the compulsory stop at Guide Bridge, Reddish South is the only other possible halt

---

* What's going on with that ship? It's an ex-British Rail passenger ferry called the *Duke of Lancaster* and it's been beached and mouldering at lonely Mostyn Quay for aeons. Can someone either renovate it or break it up, please? When I pass it on the train between Fflint and Prestatyn it always gives me the shivers.

185

during the Denton Flyer's epic eight-mile journey north to Stalybridge. Like Denton, Reddish South is served by this single solitary train. Yet while Denton is accorded immortality in the naming of this weekly service, poor old Reddish South finds itself comprehensively disregarded. I freely admit, therefore, that my journey that day was driven by one emotion alone: pity.

If I had hoped for the guard to raise an eyebrow when I asked to be put off at Reddish South I was to be disappointed. Indeed, he actually yawned when I told him of my chosen destination. A minute or so later, as he ambled back through the carriage, he yawned again. A couple of passengers noticed this and smiled.

'It's not very interesting, this route,' he joked.

The chagrin I felt at his studied ennui was assuaged somewhat by a group of a dozen track-maintenance men* in fluorescent jackets who waved at me en masse soon after we pulled out. It pains me to say it, but the guard's estimation of the trip was, if anything, a little generous. The train takes a tree-lined route through a drab suburbia leavened only by the occasional light industrial concern. In mitigation, the journey takes just seven minutes, so it's hard to work up too much of a lather about it and start chuntering, 'Well, that's seven minutes of my life I won't get back.'

Anyway, it was all worth it because I got papped at Reddish South. A man who had been travelling in my carriage brazenly pointed his big camera out of the window to capture me standing on the platform. In order to give him a more dramatic photograph I held my right arm aloft

---

* In railway parlance, these people are known as a 'permanent way gang'. I didn't use the term here on the grounds that I spent almost my entire childhood and all of my adolescence knowing that my stepfather had a job in 'permanent way' without ever grasping what that actually meant.

in a salute of triumph. He smiled. Let nobody say that my fame has made me forgetful of my fans.

As you might well imagine, there wasn't much at Reddish South station, though I was pleasantly surprised at how well kept it was. There was nowhere to shelter or sit but there were newly planted flowers, shrubs and trees that did battle with wild grasses on the bank that runs the length of the station's one platform, and the plentiful notice boards were kept spick and span ('Sometimes engineering works will affect how trains run from this station'). I suppose the 56 people who typically use Reddish South every year don't cause it all that much wear and tear, but I was expecting something more akin to wilderness and found instead a station acting as though having just the one train a week was standard practice on the railways. 'Nothing strange about me,' it said, hands behind its back and breaking into a tuneless whistle. 'Everything is perfectly normal here, oh yes.'

Though on closer inspection it clearly wasn't. For one thing, the station's other platform, a relic of the halcyon days when this line was important enough to warrant two tracks, was completely covered with a mound of ballast at one end while the rest of it was smothered by a layer of sand a good 18 inches thick.

But attached to the wall that runs along the top of the bank at the back of the platform was the crowning glory of Reddish South station – a bright and bold mural in five parts. This quintych (let's roll with it and pretend this word exists) represented the gallery of the Friends of Reddish South Station, which also explained the flower planting and the generally scrubbed appearance of the place. Four of the panels incorporated life-affirming aphorisms, which, for the good of humankind, I shall reproduce here:

There is no passion to be found playing small, in settling for a life that is less than the one you are capable of living.

Life is the sum of your choices. Every moment is a chance to positively direct your life.

Be the change you want to see in the world. We can't go back in time and undo past decisions or events that we may now regret. That is why having a second chance is so important to us all.

The greatest glory in living lies not in never falling but in rising every time we fall.

I know I should have found this all deeply inspiring. Believe me, I really wanted to jump up and cry, 'Yes, I ain't gonna play small no more! I'm through with small! Small sucks!' but when it comes down to it I'm just not American enough.

I'd come across the third and fourth maxims before. 'Be the change' is a Buddhist idea, if I'm not mistaken (if I am mistaken, then my second guess is JFK). I have some friends who are vaguely Buddhist and I think I've seen this injunction in fridge-magnet form at their house, which on reflection is probably not the best way to lend words of wisdom gravitas.

The sentiment undergirding the fourth is derived not so much from Ancient Athens as from Modern-day Athena. I can't read it without imagining the words appearing on a poster beneath an image of a kitten trying to get out of a basket. Now, I love kittens – probably rather more than the next man – but I rarely look to them for life-coaching.

The second saying includes a split infinitive, a misdemeanour that someone possessed of a more mature and tolerant mindset than mine would be able to overlook. That person doubtless already chooses to direct their life positively at every moment. I think the rest of us all know deep down that a grammatical error as elementary as that entirely undermines whatever message it's attempting to convey, rendering it null and void.

However, there was one last word of counsel to be seen at the station, even if it was rather less official. Moseying down to the southern end of the platform, I saw that someone had taken it upon themselves to walk underneath the road bridge that crosses the tracks there and had written in large white letters the words, 'Question everything.' [full-stop mine]

And therein lies the nub of my restlessness – it's not that I take too much at face value but that when it comes to the big issues in life I'm guilty of questioning everything a bit too much. The result is that I never really settle on anything. After all, if you only ever see shifting sands, you never stir yourself to putting in foundations. Now *that* would make a great poster slogan. Perhaps beneath a kitten trying to get out of a basket.

In a normal world, I would have had to wait an hour or two for the next train in order to visit the celebrated station at Denton, a four-minute rail journey away. As we know, though, the world of the Stockport to Stalybridge line is not normal. Since I was determined to visit the Denton Flyer's eponymous destination, I considered pitching my tent on the platform and waiting seven days in a Zen-like trance for the next train, devoting the remainder of this book to an hour-by-hour account of that week.

But in the end I decided instead to leave the station and walk a mile to Reddish North through what proved to be an unremarkable slice of suburban Greater Manchester. Reddish North is on a loop off the rather more popular Sheffield to Manchester Piccadilly line and enjoys the relative bounty of two trains an hour in each direction during the week. Admittedly, it makes getting to Stockport or Stalybridge from Reddish a little more involved, but I imagine that most people attempting to make either of those journeys by public transport hop on a bus (or two, in the case of Stalybridge).

Which raises the question, 'What on Earth is going on with the Stockport to Stalybridge line?' It's difficult to envisage that there are hosts of people in Stockport thinking, 'I'd very much like to go to Reddish South/ Denton/Guide Bridge/Stalybridge [delete as applicable] but only want to go just after ten on a Friday morning and never need to come back.' So why doesn't Northern Rail either run a lot more trains here or abandon the station altogether? Why continue paying lip service to a service that clearly doesn't pay?

Rest assured that I had not given up on Denton. I simply carried on my tour around the request stops of the nation knowing that I must return to Stockport in seven days' time to repeat my journey, albeit getting off four minutes later, like a man trapped in some obscure rail-based Groundhog Week. In fact, if I *am* a man trapped in some obscure rail-based Groundhog Week, you can be pretty certain that I'm still catching that train every Friday until I succeed in saving someone's life (I seem to recall that's how the film goes) and magically break out of the time loop.

THE LAKES

Underwhelming. That was my first impression of the lakes that give The Lakes its name. I had marched down the poker-straight road from the station full of wide-eyed anticipation. After all, weren't these the lakes that had exerted such pulling power among the populace that a station had had to be built specially for them? Even the spectacle of houses that had been torn straight from the pages of *The Stepford Wives* did little to dampen my expectation.

But when the houses ended and Earlswood Lakes were suddenly on both sides of me – the road splitting two of them down the middle – they just seemed a bit grey and a bit dull, a pair of enormous paddling pools rather than oases of life and beauty. Unless things around here have taken a nose-dive since the 1930s, I fear the fact that this was such a popular day-tripper destination back then may say something rather telling about Britain at that time.

It had been something of a convoluted four-train journey down to this anonymous patch of North Warwickshire. Along the way I had taken in the sights of Manchester, Wolverhampton and Smethwick Galton Bridge. The platform on which I waited at this last station soared high above a broad canal in a deep cutting with a wood covering one bank and occasional trees or healthy-looking shrubs guarding the towpath on the other. It was such an Arcadian scene that I was astonished, when glancing at a map a few days later, to discover that immediately behind the canal's northern bank there lay a major industrial estate and, immediately behind that, the M5. You don't have to be a tree-hugger to sigh at the contrast between the disfigurement brought upon the landscape of Britain by motorways and the beauty bestowed upon it by our first go at a mass transport system.

It was the need to supply another waterway – the Stratford–upon–Avon Canal – that led to the creation of Earlswood Lakes (aka 'The Lakes') in the early 1820s. The increasing number of barges flitting up and down it as the Industrial Revolution continued apace meant that the canal required extra water to keep it topped up. The solution was to construct an earth dam across the valley at Earlswood to form three lakes – Windmill Pool, Engine Pool and Terry's Pool. An engine house was built with a pump that drove water down a half-mile-long ditch from the lakes to the canal. Laboriously dug out by hand, it was five years before the lakes were ready to play their part in speeding the wheels of industry.

By the turn of the century, Earlswood Lakes had become a sanctuary for workers from the surrounding industrialised towns. They flocked here in droves to escape for an afternoon the smog and dirt of their everyday existence. Boating, fishing and ambling about were the main pursuits they indulged in. Some came by horse and cart, others by bus, and those from further afield by train to Earlswood station. 'Scarborough of the Midlands' they called Earlswood Lakes, without irony. It wasn't until 1935, however, that

The Lakes Halt was opened (the 'Halt' was dropped in 1968). A mile down the track from Earlswood station, and considerably nearer the lakes themselves, this unstaffed halt with almost laughably short platforms was to save a great deal of shoe leather over the years.

Aside from the station and the lakes themselves, not a great deal is left to remind us of what a happening place this once was. However, The Reservoir Inn, which flourished as a hotel during this period, is still with us. It's not a ravishing beauty but rather resembles an attempt by some giant to tidy the street up by squashing a cottage, two houses and a bungalow together. Now just called The Reservoir, it no longer offers accommodation. The owners style it a 'very large destination food house', which is about as dispiriting a description of a pub as might possibly be dreamt up, but is perhaps the only way to keep it a going concern. The only other survivor from the heyday of Earlswood Lakes is a red-brick engine house built to pump water to the canal.

I hacked along the road between Engine Pool and Windmill Pool, passing a large dead bream in the gutter. It managed the impressive trick of staring balefully at me despite having lost the eye with which I fancied it fixed me. I was also exposed to a fearsome gale that whipped wild waves against the distant banks, spewing foamy water high into the air. To evade this battery and the onset of showers, I wove my way around the shore, passing stony-faced anglers dressed in their customary army-style camouflage, huddled under those oversized umbrellas anglers have and looking as if they were having a really great time. I was finally able to take shelter in some woods by Terry's Pool, where in a glade I hauled out my stove and cooked myself a lunch so late that by the time it was ready it was my tea. Naturally, I contrived to leave myself far too little time to get back for the train I had to catch, but was saved by a couple walking their dog who, in reassuringly local accents, gave me directions along a shortcut.

I'm sure it's a more inviting place on a day when the weather is less inclement, but the mass appeal Earlswood Lakes once had has sadly dissipated. It's not entirely moribund – angling competitions are held here with special prizes for those catching the lakes' most baleful bream, and there's a sailing club too. But there's a slightly sterile, municipal feel to the place, for all its information-board promises of kingfishers and stoats (some swifts and a lonely-looking coot were all I came up with). This ersatz atmosphere is understandable, I suppose, since they are not natural lakes and their primary function has always been a practical one. It made me wonder whether they would have had a golden age at all if it hadn't been for the pollution dealt upon Midlanders by the arrival of the factories and the mills (and, indeed, the railways). As I jumped on a train bound for Stratford-upon-Avon I thus resolved to settle on a cheerier reading of the relative tranquillity that now rests upon the lakes, viz. that urban-dwellers in the vicinity no longer have to flee here to experience the privilege of breathing fresh air. In light of this more optimistic perspective I decided that my verdict on the place should be ramped up by a notch. I'm happy to say, Earlswood Lakes now officially leave me whelmed.

TO BERNEY ARMS

The journey south to Stratford-upon-Avon took me through three more request stops. Although no one troubled the guard with a desire to explore either Wood End or Danzey, I was pleased that we came to a halt at Wootton Wawen. The name harks back to the dying days of Saxon rule in England. It means 'farm near a wood, belonging to Wagen' – the Wagen in question having been the last Saxon thane to hold sway in these parts before the coming of the Normans. The local priory was dissolved on the orders of Henry VIII and little seems to have happened here since, save the building of Wootton Hall in 1637, and the shortening of the station's name from Wootton Wawen Platform 337 years later. Who cares about events, though, when your village has such a fun-sounding name? I defy anyone who finds themselves pulling up at Wootton Wawen not to give their mouth a little pleasure by saying it out loud:

'Wootton Wawen. Wootton Wawen. Wootton Waaaaawen.'

Admittedly, this may make you look a bit of a simpleton. I caught a woman smiling slyly at my gleeful repeated enunciation of the name, which I had mistakenly thought was inaudible to anyone but me. But I bet if I said it 20 times every day it would make me a better kisser, so who's the winner there, eh?

My journey onwards from Stratford-upon-Avon to London recreated the one Shakespeare made several times between his home and the Globe Theatre, except for the fact that I was finishing at Marylebone and wasn't travelling via Shipston-on-Stour, Chipping Norton, Woodstock, Oxford or Marlow, or indeed any of the places he'd probably have passed through. Furthermore, I was on a train, whereas he had had to walk the 120-odd miles. Nonetheless I felt a deep and wonderful kinship with the playwright and had a thrilling sense that his fortitude in overcoming rain, mud and ne'er-do-wells was mirrored by my stoic patience at the slight delay my train experienced at Banbury, albeit that we had made it up by the time we reached London.

The next day found me hurtling towards Norwich and I felt a deep and wonderful kinship with Queen Boudicca of the Iceni, who had made this journey in reverse the best part of two millennia beforehand. Unlike her, though, I was at pains to ensure that I did not burn London and Colchester to the ground on my way, which forbearance I hold up as a sign of my growing maturity. Instead, I contented myself with a quick change of trains at Norwich and the destruction of a sandwich as we struck out east along the River Yare towards Berney Arms.

BERNEY ARMS

The smell of the coal fire hit me before I even had a chance to take in my surroundings. The silence, too, seemed to assail my ears before my eyes had become accustomed to the gloom. The Silence enveloped everything. It was like an extra character in the room, an unseen and resentful host. When The Silence spoke, we all slouched about glumly beneath the dark brown carapace of the ceiling and listened. Welcome to the Berney Arms, pub of joy.

I'm being a little harsh here, for these were merely my first, second and third impressions. Hours later, when the place filled up with gaggles of pleasure boaters and families out for a stroll along the River Yare, it attained an atmosphere that all but bordered on normality. But that was in some far and distant future.

A man with a fabulous walrus moustache and wild hair stood behind the bar. A woman sat mutely staring into space. Another man so taciturn that I felt he had to be the owner stood near the fire, hoarding up all the words he wasn't letting pass his lips. For something to say while my cider was being pulled, I asked him if there were any plans to keep the pub open all year rather than just through the season.

'I'm thinking about it,' he replied, with an air of suspicion and a whole pitchfork of Norfolk vowels. 'We're living here, so we might as well open the pub.' Then The Silence intervened and neither of us could get a word in edgeways.

I sat down and started to take some notes – not so much because I needed to write any but to have something to excuse my further participation in the quick-fire badinage. Two middle-aged couples came in, and although they had wisely prepared a topic of conversation beforehand – they were holding some sort of do in the pub in September – they too were cowed into wordlessness by The Silence. One of them, driven to distraction, said the first idiotic thing that came into his head:

'It's a pity the pub isn't accessible by road.'

'Noooo!' I wanted to scream. 'The brilliance behind the Berney Arms is that you can only get here by train, boat or on foot (or by bicycle at a pinch).'

'If there was a road outside it would lose its character,' replied the owner. 'It would be nothing.'

I wanted to cheer, but that's the sort of behaviour The Silence probably punishes by death.

It was unfortunate that an hour or so later – before the gaggles had arrived with their exuberant food orders and idle chatter – I attempted The Humour.

A punter – in his late forties, if I had to hazard a guess – approached my table and announced that he was from Loddon, a place I knew from youthful holidays to be on some bend of the Norfolk Broads. His accent was even deeper Norfolk than that of the taciturn owner, which is a thing I would not have deemed possible. He was deeply interested in my tablet. Despite my misgivings about mobile phones, I'm not a complete technophobe and I had just bought a tablet to save myself from dragging my heavy and bulky laptop around with me. Loddon asked me question after question about it, as if it were some mystical alien technology that had fallen to Earth from Outer Space. It was then that I made the fatal decision to deploy The Humour. My chosen theme was how modern technology, and some functions of the tablet in particular, had a whiff of *The Emperor's New Clothes* about them.

'I don't always write myself notes on this tablet. Sometimes, I use this thing called Paper,' I began hilariously. Detecting that The Humour hadn't yet hit its mark, I continued, 'I get this thing called a Pen and move it across the Paper and it leaves a decipherable trail they call Ink.'

I was expecting a little smile from Loddon at this point to indicate that my amusing observation regarding the overlooked merits of an ancient technology had been grasped. None came. At this juncture, of course, I should have given it up as a bad job. Naturally, I ploughed on.

'Look, I'll show you,' I said, reaching inside my bag and rooting around. I pulled out my notebook and flourished it with a punchlinetastic, 'There!'

There was a pause.

'Tha's just a book,' Loddon replied, not attempting to conceal his disappointment.

I was in deep here and, as I always advise, if you're in a hole, keep digging: at least then you're getting some exercise while committing social suicide.

I affected an attitude of mock horror. 'Is it?' I squealed. 'I paid £200 for this. They've ripped me off.'

A pause. Then came the unmistakable clink of a penny dropping.

'Oh, are you joking about?' Loddon asked.

I had to admit, shamefacedly, that I was.

The Silence swarmed over us.

For me, Berney Arms will always be The Original Request Stop. I came across it first as a child – my stepfather took our family to the Norfolk Broads every summer for about a thousand years when I was growing up. It is often claimed to be the smallest railway station in Britain and, since just 26 paces took me from one end of its makeshift cinder platform to the other, I suspect this is true. There have been shelters here from time to time – the latest erected in 2003 – but they tend to get torn to pieces by the wind that careens across the marshes and there was no trace of one now. With its roughly painted sleepers marking the edge of the platform and its cast-iron name board, it would be easy to imagine you had been sucked back to the 1840s, when the halt opened, if it weren't for the miniature help point and the cycle stands. En route from The Lakes I'd picked up my bicycle from my flat and it was mildly thrilling to note that if I had wanted to leave it here I could have done so.

On weekdays there are just two trains a day each way here – to Norwich or Great Yarmouth. Only on Sundays does it explode into life with five trains in either direction, presumably catering for walkers tramping the Weavers' Way or the Wherryman's Way, though the fact that fewer than 30 people get on or off here in an average week suggests that not many of those trains are packed with prospective ramblers.

However, Berney Arms didn't begin life as a request stop. The establishment 'in perpetuity' of a halt in the midst

of a great deal of nothingness was forced upon the Yarmouth
and Norwich Railway (YNR) by one Thomas Trench
Berney as a condition of him selling them the land they
needed in order to lay the line through here (the engineer,
by the way, was our old friend Robert Stephenson, who
presumably never slept). This was not an uncommon
stipulation in the 19th century, though it was more
frequently wealthy landed gentry who insisted on the
building of a halt and often for their exclusive use. Tellingly,
Berney Arms station was missed out of the first YNR
timetable in 1844. Its existence was only admitted two
years later when a timetable alteration was published.

By 1850, the board of the Norfolk Railway, which had
gobbled up the YNR five years previously, was discussing
what to do about the paucity of passengers using Berney
Arms Halt. Contractually restrained from closing the
station, they came up with the novel ruse of keeping it
open but not actually scheduling any trains at all to stop
there. As Sheila Hutchinson notes in her excellent *Berney
Arms Remembered*, 'A legal confrontation ensued.'

The battle of the lawyers dragged on until 1860, when
the board relented and generously announced that one
train each way would halt at the station on Mondays,
Wednesdays and Saturdays. They also paid Berney £200 in
compensation, which was a tidy sum in those days, being
about double the asking price of Scotland.

By all accounts, life at Berney Arms in the intervening
years could not be described as hectic. There was the inn,
of course, after which the station was named, and a windmill
which is still a famous landmark for those negotiating
the Broads by boat. Two semi-detached station cottages of

red brick and slate roof were built at the same time as the railway, but had neither electricity nor running water. Combine this with the sheer isolation of the wannabe hamlet and the constant wind blasting over the marshes and it's a wonder that any tenants were found for them at all. Furthermore, a room of one of the houses had to be preserved as a ticket office, waiting room and post office (the postman came once a week by train from Great Yarmouth).

In the 1950s the couple then renting the cottages, Bob and Violet Mace, were given the option of buying them for £50. They turned it down and moved away. In the 1960s, the same offer was made to the new tenants, the Hunts, but at the price of £250. They too found it within themselves to turn it down and they moved away in 1969. I expected to learn that nowadays the cottages are worth £550,000 apiece, because that's usually how such stories end. I'd quite forgotten, however, that there are no cottages at Berney Arms. They were demolished with the help of a local tractor shortly after the Hunts moved out. Their footings can apparently still be seen, but if so I missed them.

Berney Arms is not the only station in Britain with no road access – step forward Corrour in the Cairngorms and Dovey Junction in Wales – but it does feel like one of the most desolate. A half-mile or more from the excitement of the mill and the pub and the river, it sits amid marshes and the flattest of farmland beside a single track that runs as straight as a ruler as far as the eye can see in either direction. It is all rather strange and beautiful, but it's difficult to get away from the feeling that you're on the set of a moody indie film in which the lead character (I'm thinking a mute and friendless teenage girl who spends her days cutting paper into those strings of people holding hands) has hopes that cannot be dashed because to be dashed they must first have existed.

The sheer unwavering flatness of the place is eerie, especially if you're on your own. A bench near the mill bears the legend, 'Vast skies/How small I am,' and I suspect that this lies at the heart of it. The big skies make us feel small and insignificant. Our newly diminished self then feels extra vulnerable in a landscape where there is nowhere to hide and which affords us no protection from the wind or from anything else more sinister that might sweep across the plain. No wonder we feel unsettled in such places.

At the end of the afternoon, I sat waiting beneath the Berney Arms name board for a train to take me west, but the scraps of shrubs behind it were no match for the fierce northerly wind that turned this sunny early summer afternoon into bleak midwinter.

BUCKENHAM

They say you haven't lived until you've seen a grey heron and two lapwings fighting over a headless rat. At Buckenham – three stops west of Berney Arms – my luck was in. I'd walked straight down the track from the station to the River Yare, a quarter of a mile away, where I found an RSPB hide, or 'wildlife watchpoint' as they'd clumsily put it, as if English were German. It looked out over marshland and a pool that was alive with the high-pitched remorseless dots of oystercatchers and the more melodious dashes of lapwings.

However, it wasn't until I left the hide that I noticed the life-goal-fulfilling fracas taking place on the other side of it, away from prying eyes. A heron was loping along the marshes, daintily holding a head-free and necessarily lifeless rat by its shoulders. Even without its head it was an exceptionally large rat, so large in fact that the heron was clearly unable to take off with it in its bill. The sight of a loping heron attracted the attention of a couple of opportunist lapwings who dive-bombed the bird repeatedly for five minutes. The heron flinched each time the lapwings made a pass; on one occasion, it dropped its benighted prey, but otherwise stood firm and the aggressors eventually gave up and went off to hunt elsewhere.

This scene had been played out to the accompaniment of a fair organ whose jaunty notes wafted from some unseen steam fair far across the fields. It gave the mêlée the air of a comic dance, which I'm sure was not how any of the parties felt about it, particularly the rat.

Just as I was about to walk back towards the station, the lapwings returned to re-engage their victim. Clearly the hunting had not gone well elsewhere. They were even bolder this time, all but making contact with the heron's head. The heron, no doubt weary of holding the enormous headless rat, let it drop by its feet and flew off, ratless, pursued by one of the lapwings until it was out of their airspace. At this point I expected the lapwings to swoop down and feast upon the lovely tasty rat meat, ready de-headed like you buy in the supermarket. However, they showed no interest at all in the prospective meal, flying off without giving it so much as a backward glance. It occurred to me then that perhaps they had a nest nearby and had merely been protecting their young. So perhaps this wasn't a fight over a headless rat at all, but one over territory. There are so many lessons to be drawn from this episode that you could probably base a whole new school of philosophy on it.

You probably wouldn't want to base the school at Buckenham, though, because you'd get no devotees turning up to your lectures during the week. Not if they were planning to come by rail, anyway, for not a single train stops here on a weekday, on either of its platforms (excitingly skewed so that one is 150 yards up the track from the other). You can plead with the guard or stand on the platform waving a red flag as large as a cricket pitch, but it will all be in vain. Things look rosier on Saturdays – indeed, as far as stopping trains go, they show an infinitely improved percentage in that one will take you to Lowestoft and one will take you to Norwich. On Sunday, Lowestoft falls off the map for some reason, to be replaced by Great Yarmouth and a veritable feast of three and sometimes even four trains each way, depending on the time of year.

If you're not keen on establishing a school of philosophy and you're not into octagonal towers (the one that graces St Nicholas' church is visible from the platform), there's not much else to detain you in Buckenham, it being a hamlet of a few houses and the odd farm. This, along with the general dearth of trains, explains how in 2011–12 it notched up a mere (and suspiciously tidy) 100 patrons, securing for itself ninth place in the league of least used stations, just one above Sugar Loaf.

Having checked out the church I cycled to Brundall, where I experienced a bit of light time travel. Standing alongside an elderly man in a purple pin-stripe blazer, white fedora, white trousers, white shoes and silver mutton chops, I heard a bell ring out three times. This drew a man from a minuscule brick cottage who strode towards a level crossing and pushed the four gates one at a time until the railway was closed off to road users. The train arrived some five minutes later. It should really have been a steam train filled with soldiers back from the Boer War. If the universe were truly chaotic, that sort of thing could definitely happen. Among the benefits we enjoy from living in an ordered universe is that there is little danger of our grandmother suddenly becoming our grandson or our bones spontaneously turning to napalm. Consolation indeed.

SHIPPEA HILL

I love the Cambridgeshire idea of a hill. I had a girlfriend who hailed from the county and one day she took me on a tour of the sights she had known as a child.

'Look!' she cried out at one point. 'The Gog Magog Hills!'

I looked in the direction I thought she had pointed. Seeing nothing, I realised I must have somehow got my bearings wrong.

'Um, where?' I asked.

'*There!*' she insisted, pointing again in the same direction.

I peered. I even narrowed my eyes and peered, which is the most effective sort of peering a human can do. All I could see was a group of trees that didn't appear to be much higher than another group of trees that didn't appear to be any higher than us.

'The Gog Magog Hills.'

'What? That slight incline?'

'That's not an incline,' she protested, now sounding not a little defensive, 'that's *hills*, that is – the finest in Cambridgeshire.'

I laughed. It wasn't an unkindly laugh – I come from Surrey, which is not a county that can look down on the topographical eminences of others, either figuratively or literally. However, one of the myriad unwritten rules of romance is that you laugh at your girlfriend's favourite hills at your peril. The trip turned a shade frosty from that moment on and I took care not to mention the Gog Magog Hills ever again. I'm not saying the relationship foundered exclusively because of the Gog Magog incident and its fallout, but it was undoubtedly a factor.

I'm therefore understandably hesitant to ridicule another of Cambridgeshire's mighty peaks. It's just that a moment's glance at Shippea Hill would confirm that Shippea Plain would be a more honest description of it, for here on Burnt Fen there is no hill at the station, nor anything that could be described as a hill, mound, mount, knoll, hummock, bluff or even hillock without bringing forth a torrent of scornful laughter from one's hearers. In fact, it's worse than that, for this must surely be the only railway station in the world that includes the word 'hill' in its name while actually standing below sea level. It's as if the universe had demanded some sort of counterbalance to Y Fali/ Valley not being in a proper valley.

The mystery of how the hill-less Shippea Hill came by its misnomer lies in the final two letters of its first name. 'Ea' is a suffix used locally to indicate islands that stood slightly proud of the surrounding fen, and dates from the days when this part of the world was far more marshy than it is today. Over the centuries, as Burnt Fen has been drained and made fit for agriculture, the former island of Shippea has almost assumed the level of the land around it. Take a look on a map at nearby Shippea Hill Farm, after which the station is named, and you'll notice it's exactly at sea level, whereas most of the area around it — including the station two miles away — is three feet or so below.

Nowadays, the highest vantage points in the district are almost certainly the two platforms at Shippea Hill station, which must rise several inches above sea level. This allows those who climb to their table-top summits breath-taking vistas of the surrounding farmland.

It should be said that the station didn't begin life as Shippea Hill. When it opened in 1845 it was called Mildenhall Road. The shame of not serving anywhere in particular condemned many a Victorian country station to a name that ended with the word 'Road', even when they were nowhere near the place on whose road they happened to lie. In the case of Mildenhall Road, the eponymous town was (and still is) eight miles distant. In 1885, perhaps in a bid to avoid confusing passengers, the station became Burnt Fen, which seems fair enough since that's the fen it's on. It was sometime around 1904 that someone in authority decided that this was not a precise enough designation and renamed it Shippea Hill after the nearby (but by no means closest) farm.

It's a pity, really, that whoever made this final change didn't opt for the almost equidistant Letter F Farm instead. I suspect there are a lot of people in this country who would pay good money to visit a station called Letter F.

Earlier this century, the station recorded just 11 passengers in an entire year, which is a poor showing even among the realms of little-used stations. It has rallied somewhat since – last year it clocked up 378 punters, though it's unclear how – and Shippea Hill looks likely to remain a so-called 'ghost station' for the foreseeable future. In common with South Reddish, Denton, Buckenham and a number of others dotted around Britain, it has to put up with a skeleton service laid on merely to keep up the appearance that the station is operational. Just one Norwich-bound train a day stops here (if requested), with none at all bothering to halt on Sundays. Head the other way, to Cambridge, and you'll have to make do with just one train a week. This superannuated state was succinctly summed up a few seconds after a train had rushed through. The gates opened again, peace returned, and a hare walked confidently over the line – using the level crossing, of course.

In light of this, it's not unreasonable to ask why Shippea Hill, Reddish South, Denton and a slew of others with nonsensically pared-down timetables are kept open at all. It would seem far more rational either to shut them down or to put on a service worthy of the name that might attract more passengers and make the stations viable. Sadly, rationality and the nation's railways have rarely been soul mates, and there are a host of reasons that have nothing to do with reason as to why stations are kept open but starved of any possible means of generating meaningful income.

I came upon an interesting theory on a rail forum (it happens) as to why Shippea Hill has remained at large despite hosting a maximum of seven trains a week. The story told is that although the entire station now falls just inside Cambridgeshire, back in 1975 Shippea Hill became a 'disputed zone' as a result of the redrawing of local government boundaries. The signal box was in Suffolk, the northern platform was controlled by Norfolk, while the southern platform was under the aegis of Cambridgeshire. The closure of the station needed the ratification of all three county councils and Norfolk always dug in its heels.

This scenario seems all too likely except for the fact that – as a later poster to the forum pointed out – during the period when the railways were nationalised (what halcyon days they seem now), the procedure was for the British Railways Board to present possible station closures to the relevant Secretary of State of the day; he or she then gave an aye or a nay, depending on which way the political wind was blowing.

However, we can be sure of an event that occurred the following year and that has saddled Shippea Hill with an unwelcome claim to fame. On 3 December 1976, at the Chivers No.1 level crossing not far from the station, a passenger train collided with a lorry loaded with carrots, causing the death of the train driver. According to the Rail Accident Investigation Branch report, this was the last time in Britain that a member of staff on a train was killed due to a collision at a 'user worked crossing'.

While standing on Shippea Hill station I found myself pondering not the dangers of self-operated level crossings, one of which I had used just the day before, or even the fact that it had been as long as 37 years since an accident of this kind had accounted for the death of a member of staff on a train, but the mention of the carrots. It felt inappropriate that a tragic affair such as this should involve anything as Laurel and Hardy-esque as a lorryload of carrots. Had the lorry been empty or filled with hay, say, or coal or bricks or car parts, there would have been no question of having to stifle a snigger. But *carrots*? It just seemed a little ludicrous.

Such is the inherent narcissism of the human race (or perhaps I'm just projecting here) that this almost immediately got me thinking about my own death and whether that too would involve root vegetables in some way, or include some other not-sufficiently-serious element. Perhaps I'll end up on regional news after being crushed by a crate of bubble bath or having had my neck broken by an enraged koala, thus causing the newsreader to be censured for not having kept a straight face. That would be unfortunate. I'm not an unreasonable man – I don't want my death to blight a newsreader's otherwise promising career.

Perhaps it's best not to speculate. After all, goalkeeper-turned-philosopher Albert Camus once famously proclaimed that the most absurd way to die would be in a car crash, and then he was killed in a car crash. (Worse still, he had planned to take that particular journey by train, but his publisher, Michel Gallimard, had persuaded him to come with him in his car. An unused train ticket was found on Camus' body.) For the record, in case Fate is listening, the most absurd way to die would be in comfort, with all one's marbles but nothing terrible to regret, at a ripe old age, surrounded by loved ones.

TO NEW CLEE

On the train from Ely to Peterborough the electronic dot matrix sign in my carriage made a bid for self-determination. It began with small steps – the adding of a randomly placed green dot here and there among its standard orange fare as it announced that we were homing in on Manea, March and then Whittlesea. Having tested the waters, it went for broke, suddenly turning on every single dot in a long block on its lower line, obliterating the larger part of whatever had been meant to appear there. As a result, when we came into Peterborough the sign announced:

Now approaching
ugh

I don't want to worry you unduly but not only have The Machines begun to think, they have also developed a sense of humour. Anyone who has been to Peterborough will know what this particular Machine was getting at. The cathedral precincts are very pleasant indeed, but the rest of the city looks as if it were designed by someone who spends his days biting the heads off kittens.

I braced myself for the 25 minutes that I would have to spend there awaiting a train to Newark. 'Just as well I'm a commando,' I thought. 'Lesser men might buckle.'

It was a pity, then, to discover that the train I was due to catch had broken down on its way to Peterborough, though we were never told whether this was physically or mentally. This being a bank holiday, I would have to wait a further two hours for the next one.

It was a sunny morning, so I sat on the platform and got out my Boethius, intending to have a good old read. It was no use though: I simply stared at the pages. To be fair to Peterborough, it wasn't entirely its fault. I'd read *The Consolation of Philosophy* – or at least the first 50 pages or so – when I was about 14 or 15 and had found it more of a page-turner than I'd imagined a 1,500-year-old philosophical work by a man on death row would be (at least up to the point where I abandoned it). I had therefore assumed that, as an adult who had been exposed to far more challenging high-brow culture than my early-teen self had experienced, I would take *The Consolation* in my stride this time around.

I plopped myself down on the platform, with my back against a pannier and Peterborough spread out all around me like Despair in concrete form, and read the same line over and over. In it, Boethius asks Philosophy to explain why she has descended from the heavens to visit him in his forsaken state.

In other, not unrelated news, I had sent an email to Verena but it had bounced back. She had written her address in my notebook, but when I had come to look at it later I'd had difficulty making out a couple of the letters. I had thus hedged my bets by sending three emails to what I thought were the most likely spellings. Seconds later they had all returned to me.

NEW CLEE

This is not a place you come to by chance. Even from Peterborough, which is in the county next door to Lincolnshire, I had had to take a train to Newark North Gate, then another to Grimsby Town. I'd planned to catch one of the infrequent services from here to New Clee, but I was forced to cycle the last leg of the journey to make up a little of the time lost by the earlier Peterboroughphobic train. It wasn't exactly a hardship, though: it was only two miles and it's always fun to become acquainted with new streets when the sun's shining.

Fish Dock, which backs onto New Clee station, seemed to have been entirely colonised by Young's (part of the all-encompassing Findus Group). Everything seemed to bear their name: processing plants, an 11-storey office block, some buildings whose use I could only guess at. I fell in with dribs and drabs of young Eastern Europeans cycling to or from a bank holiday Monday shift. I wondered if they knew that everyone else was enjoying a day off. I could see New Clee station behind some mesh fencing but, like the hero in Kafka's *The Castle*, no matter which way I went I couldn't actually get to it. Eventually, I realised that there was no access to it at all from the docks side of the railway and the solution was to make my way to an old bridge I could see crossing the track. It possessed unusually high brick-built sides, as if it harboured illusions of one day becoming a walled garden.

The only difficulty was in getting to this bridge. With the shift workers gone, the back streets became as deserted as they were labyrinthine. I kept ending up at the place I'd started, only to wonder if it really *was* the place I'd started or just somewhere that looked like it because of its nondescript buildings. I eventually got there by accidentally going the wrong way down a one-way street. The driver of a car coming the other way kindly let me know of my error. There's a magic in the stillness being shaken awake by the blare of a car horn belting off hard brick and prefab metal sheets.

The docks had seen better days, but to have seen better days is the natural state of docks everywhere, as far as I can tell. One small warehouse had evidently suffered a serious fire recently – charred debris was scattered everywhere but had yet to acquire a patina of dust. There was no one about, so I had a little nose around, at once drawn in by the thrill of destruction and repelled by the ugliness of it all. Broken roll-up metal doors clanked and shrieked in the wind; blue plastic crates – the only objects to have been spared the flames – lay as if tossed around by an explosion; a false ceiling had been reduced to a matrix of scorched metal. The place smelled of fish and chemicals and Bonfire Night. Across the road, an empty wasteland the size of a football pitch took up the desolate chorus, but, winking, added a jaunty note when it thought no one was listening: wild grasses grew along the cracks between each uniform concrete patch, and was that ragwort and Aaron's rod on the far side? Come back in ten years and this will be a field full of rabbits, mice, fallow deer, a waterfall or two, and probably some nymphs, though only the Saturday-night homeward drunks will see them.

In the background, soaring over the masts of three dozen little yachts, is something else the drunks will swear blind they saw – a 300ft tower plucked from Venice and planted on the Grimsby shore to spear unwary passing clouds. They'll be wrong, though. While the Grimsby Dock Tower is of the Venetian School, it's actually modelled on the Palazzo Pubblico in Siena, and a finer water tower you will not see in the whole of Britain. It took a million bricks to drive its elegantly tapering form skyward. The 30,000 gallons of water inside it produced pressure at 100lb per square inch to drive the huge hydraulic gates of the docks. When completed in 1852, it was the tallest secular building on the planet. Queen Victoria came to open it and still had a year to live when it fell out of use, made redundant by the very first fruits of 20th-century technology. It has been a pure adornment to the docks for twice as long as it was an integral working part of them. The tower stands today both as a testament to what can be done with a little vision and a reproach to the thousand and one architects who have thrown up buildings that neither please the eye nor serve their particular function well. I suspect most of those citizens who call Rome their capital would also point out that it reinforces what they've known all along – that Italians really *do* do it better.

The railway made it to Grimsby three years before the tower went up. The Great Grimsby and Sheffield Junction Railway laid tracks from the town to New Holland, further up the coast. They were quickly subsumed by the Manchester, Sheffield and Lincolnshire Railway, which 15 years later extended the line through the docks and along to Cleethorpes, linking the area to Yorkshire and Lancashire. However, it wasn't until 1875 that a station was opened at New Clee ('clee' being an earlier local form of the word 'clay'). A middle-class neighbourhood of terraced villas grew up around the station and in 1889 the area was incorporated into Grimsby.

New Clee, being so close to the docks, was knocked about a lot during World War II, with German bombers making 37 raids on Grimsby, killing 196 people.* The Albert, Alexandra, Humber, Sunderland, Trinity and Victoria Terraces have all been erased from the face of the town, and its housing nowadays is as drab as you could possibly wish for.

That which did not kill Grimsby made it pong more – by the 1950s it boasted the world's busiest fishing port. However, the advent of factory ships and the calamitous overfishing of the North Sea they helped bring about have resulted in there being just two fishing vessels at the docks today.

New Clee station has mirrored this decline. Inaccessible from the docks and hidden on a back street behind the car park of a home furnishings store, the one remaining platform has already lost a third of its length to nature. A second, completely abandoned platform on the far side of what were once two tracks is fast disappearing beneath wild grasses and is ablaze with yellow wildflowers. The paucity of trains scheduled to stop here if requested

* The Grimsby Dock Tower owes its continued existence to the fact that Luftwaffe pilots found it such a useful navigational aid and so left it alone. For this reason the British government gave serious consideration to demolishing it themselves but thankfully refrained from doing so.

has pushed locals towards Grimsby Docks or Grimsby Town stations, leaving New Clee station an unloved husk of a place.

The late afternoon sun found a young man and a very much older man slouched on the station's one bench smoking away, heedless of regulations. I said a cheery good afternoon to them as I passed. A momentary dismissive glance was their only acknowledgement of my existence. A few minutes later I put my hand out to stop the train and began the tricky business of getting my pannier-widened bike through the door. I noticed the two men didn't get aboard themselves – the station was just a place to come and sit and smoke.

The train was pregnant with day-trippers heading back from Cleethorpes. By his silver hair and lived-in body, I put the guard in his late fifties. He was sighing.

'Long shift?' I asked.

'Just started,' he replied, 'and I'm on until 11 tonight. After eight the bank holiday crowds will have gone though and it'll just be like a normal shift again.'

I nodded sympathetically. It's an action I think I've mastered now. I do this thing with my mouth as well which lifts my chin and puffs my cheeks out in a 'Huh! Sorry to hear that' kind of way. Though I say so myself, the overall effect is quite convincing. I should add that the feeling behind it is genuine too.

'But it's all right,' he continued, 'I don't get stressed, I just plod on. I'm a plodder, that's what I do. Other people might get stressed, but I don't.'

He did sigh and sigh again, though, as he went about his work and I'm pretty sure he didn't realise how deep or audible those heart-sick exhalations were. As I hauled my bike off at Grimsby Town I wished him as good a shift as was possible.

'Thank you,' he said. 'I'm living the dream, I am.'

TO DENTON, A LOVE STORY
OR THE SIGHING CONTINUES

As the train waits to pull out of Grimsby Town, there is a man in his late forties in the seat in front of me and a woman of about the same age standing on the platform. They start kissing through the window. The window can't be opened, so they are kissing their respective sides of the windowpane. I suspect this is less satisfying than Hollywood would have us believe.

I get the distinct impression – not wholly based on the fact that they are kissing through a pane of glass – that they aren't married, at least not to each other. They disengage and I look over at the woman and see that she has tears in her eyes. To cover this, she is bravely making a fake sobbing face – pouting her lips and exaggerating the wobbling of her chin.

The train draws away and she waves until we slip out of her view (though it's quite possible that she continues long afterwards). I can't see his reaction to this, but a few seconds later he flops backwards against his seat and sighs. It's a strange sort of a sigh and a strange sort of a flop. I can't deduce from them whether he's just as sorrowful as she is at their parting or relieved to have finally got away. It isn't the sort of thing you can ask a stranger though.

DENTON

A young man who was clearly on the autistic spectrum (there's no shame in it – I suspect most men appear on it somewhere, including me) was very excited about being on this train. He had short blond hair, was wearing too many layers for this warm morning and looked as if he might be looking forward impatiently to hitting 20. He was busily texting as we pulled out of Stockport station. I knew what he was typing with his flying thumbs because he read it out loud repeatedly while he nodded his head in time.

'Only one train a week. Only one train a week. I'm on the train that only goes once a week. Only one train a week. I'm on the train that only goes once a week.'

And he was, for a week after travelling to Reddish South I was back on this, the Denton Flyer, and bound for Denton itself. The sun had come out, which was gallant of it, and I would have been happy, too, if it hadn't been for the accidental ingestion of prodigious quantities of caffeine the previous night which resulted in me getting rather less than two hours' sleep. My heart, which loves a bit of caffeine, was still racing along at a pace that might even have matched Flying Thumb Boy's.

I envied him his unabashed excitement. I was perfectly content to be here, sitting on a train, the sunshine bouncing around the shiny surfaces of our carriage whose low-backed seats left so much space inside that it felt cathedral-like. I wasn't thrilled to my very marrow, though, nor had I lain awake last night imagining this moment over and over again. So, he was a winner. This morning anyway.

We stopped at Reddish South by mistake. There was no one on the platform and no one got off. All the same, it was nice to have a quick look at the old place again, just to see how the flowers were getting on. When I informed the guard – not last week's bored employee, I noticed – that I wanted to get off at Denton, he asked me whether I was actually getting off or just getting out to take a photo. When I told him I was getting off for good he raised an eyebrow. He must have raised the other one shortly afterwards, because another man further up the train stepped down when we arrived at the station. This avalanche of action at Denton was almost too much for Flying Thumb Boy, who had thrown himself across the carriage and against the window to stare out at us with a look of sheer amazement. I couldn't blame him – here was over 6 per cent of Denton's annual custom on the platform at the same time in front of his very eyes. It pleased me that just by our presence we had helped to make his day. The texts would be racing from his phone. I hoped they were to friends who would send enthusiastic replies. I made a mental note to try to make people's days more often.

Inevitably, even Englishmen will end up talking to each other if they're both on an otherwise deserted platform and both taking photographs of arcane corners of it. My co-Dentoneer introduced himself as Mark Smith. He was not, however, Mark E Smith, *enfant terrible* of Manchester post-punk legends The Fall, or Mark Smith of Britain's premier rail information website The Man in Seat 61, but Mark Smith, freelance electronics engineer, currently enjoying a rest between contracts.

I told him my excuse for being there and he gamely proffered his own. He lived not far from Stockport station, so he had come out for the ride. He would do some shopping now and then wander back home again. I didn't ask if he was single, but this is what single men do. It's a way of getting by. It's what married men envy.

We took it in turns to photograph each other holding a hand out to halt an imaginary Denton Flyer (it's what you do there) and, after discussing the various merits of the station, we said friendly goodbyes and he walked off up the steps to do some shopping and wander back home. I was left in a little self-contained world. Sitting in a dip, with a bridge at the southern end of the platform, another bridge further down the line at the other end and embankments down both sides that were high enough to mask whatever lay beyond (the Audenshaw Reservoirs on one side, Denton on the other, I discovered), the only intrusion from outside came from trucks lumbering over the southern bridge on their way to the M67. It was Sugar Loaf come to Greater Manchester.

Half the length of the island platform had been fenced off. The half no longer in use had become a bonus sliver of countryside. Lupins had leaped over the track from the embankments and now flourished in the thin soil that had accrued on the platform's concrete surface.

Pipping Reddish South to third spot in the least used station charts, in 2011–12 Denton suffered a mere 30 people to soil its spartan but clean platform (the Friends of Denton Station also maintain its two raised flower beds). Only Teesside Airport, with 14 punters, attracted a smaller clientele (the second-place station, Dorking West, was credited with only 16, but that's because of a weird way of collating the statistics – the true figure was far higher). Which brings us to the vexed question of why this state of affairs is allowed to continue.

It boils down to one thing: economics. The weekly Stockport to Stalybridge service is maintained because a Network Rail report concluded that the cost of closing Denton and Reddish South* and withdrawing the route altogether would be more expensive, once closure notices and objections had been taken into account, than continuing this solitary one-way Friday service. In 2010 someone ran through the sums and calculated that it cost a bargain £96 per run. This works out at just £4,992 per annum (and £96 less than that in years when Christmas Day falls on a Friday), equating roughly to the amount a barrister would charge you to make a photocopy or to think about stapling a document. Suddenly, running one train a week for the benefit of almost nobody seemed like good value for money and the most sensible idea anyone ever had.

And that, in a nutshell, is what is called a parliamentary train – a service kept running at the barest level possible to maintain a legal fiction that a station or stations are still open. There are more than a score of them across Britain

* The other intermediate station, Guide Bridge, would stay open because it's also on the Sheffield–Manchester line.

(all but one of them in England, as far as I can tell) and they operate either for the same reason as the Denton Flyer or because the rail franchisee is contractually bound to run a service and so follows the letter of the law if not the spirit, in the grand tradition of the Norfolk Railway in its dealings with Berney Arms.

The term 'parliamentary train' is derived from a progressive Act of Parliament called the Railway Regulations Act. It was brought in by proto-Communist Prime Minister Sir Robert Peel in 1844 in order that poorer people might be able to afford to travel. It enforced the provision of 'at least one train a day each way at a speed of not less than 12 miles an hour including stops, which were to be made at all stations, and of carriages protected from the weather and provided with seats; for all which luxuries not more than a penny a mile might be charged'. It's instructive that the writers of the Act anticipated that the private railway companies would attempt to get around the new law by running non-stopping seatless, roofless trains that crawled along so slowly that their penny-a-mile fares would still make them unattractive to passengers when compared with normal services. Clearly, the parliamentarians understood the stuff of which the men in these boardrooms were made.

Shamefully, this Act is no longer in force but the derogatory name such trains were given at the time (and which gets an airing in Gilbert and Sullivan's *The Mikado*, no less) got passed on to any train that runs for some other purpose than to provide a service for would-be travellers. Nowadays, parliamentary trains are also sometimes known as 'ghost trains'. Our old friend Shippea Hill is an obvious example of a station 'served' by such trains, as is Teesside Airport, which was made virtually redundant when the entrance to the airport was moved, though it has somehow avoided being made a request stop. Other parliamentary trains are dotted about from Cumbria down to Sussex, from Yorkshire over to Gloucestershire, with a good few chugging around London.

However, there may come a day when both Denton and Reddish South are shorn from this list – not because they have closed down but because a new bona fide service has begun between Stockport and Manchester Victoria that would stop at the two becalmed stations. The combined might of the Friends of Denton Station and the Friends of Reddish South Station is behind a campaign to this end in order to alleviate road traffic congestion in central Manchester. If that were to happen, it would almost certainly mean curtains for the Denton Flyer, and presumably also an end to the request-stop status of Denton and Reddish South. So if you feel as if you might be a fan of parliamentary trains, request stops and suburban sprawl, you should probably get your skates on. It's the Greater Manchester equivalent of visiting Cuba before it goes all Western. Only with more lupins.

ENTWISTLE

Look in the international section of the Guatemalan phone book (don't tell me you haven't got one to hand) and you'll find dialling codes for what the local telecommunications company considers to be the principal towns and cities of Britain. The list, one suspects, has been created by someone who may not have an especially deep working knowledge of our plucky little island nation, but it's nice that they've made the effort. The dialling codes themselves are rather out of date and some of the spellings may have strayed from the generally accepted renderings, but I feel this displays a refreshing openness to the possibilities of non-conventional representations of cognomens rather than mere carelessness on the part of the compiler. Of the non-orthodox spellings, my favourites are 'Bournemonuth', which I feel lends a certain Neolithic air to the slightly less than thrusting seaside resort, and 'Blackbum'.

Poor old Blackbum, or 'Blackburn' as I'm told the locals pronounce it. One of the Industrial Revolution's boom towns now looks more like the Slough of the North, as if the North needed one. Its saving grace is that you really don't have to go very far from it before you can lose yourself in some glorious countryside.

Entwistle station is precisely seven and three-quarter miles to the south of Blackburn, but could easily be on a different planet. I had headed up along the Ribble Valley Line from Manchester to Bolton before taking a local train a little further north to Entwistle. My route was an ancient one, following a section of Watling Street that ran from Manchester to Ribchester – an astonishingly straight road even by Roman standards – and passed just to the east of Entwistle. I stepped out onto the single short platform to find myself 650ft up in the hills of the West Pennine Moors. These are not hills that scream for your attention. Their preference is to sit around mumbling. If you notice them, all well and good; but if you don't, that's fine with them too. To be honest, they aren't immediately obvious from the station anyway, because you have to peer through a row of tall trees whose leaf-laden branches interlace to form a pretty effective screen in summer.

The trees cut a line straight through where the goods yard used to be, for there was once a time when Entwistle station looked almost as much like Blackburn as Blackburn itself. This is not bad going for a stop serving a village that barely exists at all and which today is the epitome of the tranquil unstaffed country station – shelter, cycle stand (singular), planters and more than half the platform abandoned to the ministrations of Mother Nature.

It all began in the second year of the reign of Edward VII.

There had been a station at Entwistle since 1 August 1848, when the halt at Whittlestone Head, just over a mile away at the southern end of the Sough Tunnel (also called the Cranberry Moss Tunnel), was moved here. The building of the railway was incredibly labour intensive, involving the construction not only of the 2,000-yard tunnel but also of several long cuttings, embankments and a viaduct over the Wayoh Reservoir. A camp was set up to accommodate 3,000 men, women and children during the period of the construction, which lasted three years and cost three lives.

Serving a high hamlet with a poor road up to it (then as now), the station remained in a happy state of somnolence from which there was little reason to believe it would ever awaken. Then came 1902, the year commerce arrived. The information board at the station records the upheaval involved in remodelling it: 'The up platform was removed, the down platform became the up platform, and a new line was built round the back forming a new platform for down trains.' A photograph taken that year shows a signal box perched up on a gantry that spans the two fast lines through the station, a latticework footbridge working its way across like a lost strand of a spider's web, a large goods shed with its own five-ton crane, plenty of wagons and trucks in the goods yard and the obligatory advertisement for Pears Soap on the side of a brick-built station building.

Entwistle became a magnet for the movement of goods, livestock, horses, parcels and even prize cattle vans as well as the occasional passenger on their way to Blackburn or Bolton and beyond. The brand new Waltons Sidings, just to the north, served a brickworks, while quarrying activities added to the scrum in later years. What made the station particularly special, however, was a faintly Heath-Robinson overhead pulley-driven ropeway. This allowed the transfer of materials between the railway yard and the curiously named Know Mill Bleachworks, a driving force behind the sudden transformation of the station.

Keen to discover what remained, I marched briskly up the steep path from the platform (when pushing a heavily laden bicycle and climbing a sharp slope you need to achieve exit velocity or it can all go a bit Mao Zedong). Right next to the station I found a pub which, despite its relative remoteness, was thronging with lunchtime punters. It's called the Strawbury Duck nowadays, but used to be the Station Hotel. You can still stay there and their rooms are very smart, but, confusingly, their address is given not as Entwistle but as Turton. I checked a map and it's obvious that the Ordnance Survey is a bit bewildered about this, too. They've fudged the issue by slipping in the word Entwistle half a mile north of the station on the slope of a hill that boasts a single building – a barn or a shed by the looks of it.

Opposite the pub is the wonderful New Hall, built of local stone in 1680. It's a former dower house to Entwistle Hall and looks like a scaled-down version of a grand country house. It was up for sale when I was there, so if you missed out on the station house at Pont Rhufeinig, you could pick this one up for not a great deal more.

The remainder of the hamlet lay along Overshores Road, a rutted track running past the pub that tested the thin wheels of my venerable Falcon Oxford. It dropped down to the Turton and Entwistle Reservoir, which, when it was created in 1832, was the highest in Britain. It is joined by a short waterway to the Wayoh Reservoir and it is this latter lake that played a part in bringing about the downfall of Entwistle station. Its enlargement in 1958 involved the demolishing of the bleachworks. With other traffic through the station also on the wane, by the time Dr

Beeching came along just a few years later, it was obvious that cuts were going to be made. Though the line itself survived, Entwistle was gutted and returned to its original state as a country halt with just a shelter to call its own. A decade later its two tracks were reduced to one and the humbling was complete.

It was while musing on this rags-to-riches-to-rags story and admiring the circular panels on the station fence with their photos of local scenes and birdlife that I was joined by a fellow traveller, a local man called Neil. He let me in on another reason why Entwistle is merely a request stop nowadays: he used to commute to Manchester, he told me, and, like nearly everyone else in the district, rather than getting the train from Entwistle, he would drive the three miles to Bromley Cross station.

'A monthly season ticket from Entwistle to Manchester would set you back £130,' he explained, 'but Bromley Cross was just inside the Greater Manchester area so it only cost £80. It made a lot of sense, therefore, to go a little bit further in the morning to get the train in to work.'

He believed it was this ticket-pricing policy and the subsequent exodus of south-bound passengers from Entwistle station that ultimately cost it its status as a compulsory stop.

'I'm not sure, but I think it's been a request stop for four or five years now,' he said, before hailing his train. 'It's quite fun, though – it always makes me feel like it's my own private station.'

I had one final mosey around in the warm afternoon sunshine and discovered that the busy goods yard I'd seen in the photograph on the information board had taken on a whole new existence as a woodland cemetery. For anyone writing about the slow deaths of obscure railway stations, this was a metaphor that cried out to be used. But I didn't have the heart. To be honest, I was still wondering if I'd overlooked some further possible variations on Verena's email address. I tried a couple more and they both bounced back. It was making me wonder if I might have misinterpreted other parts of the address too. And, yes, I do know what you're thinking.

BURNLEY BARRACKS

Entwistle held the title of East Lancashire's Only Railway Request Stop until May 2012, when it suddenly found itself joined by four others: Huncoat, Hapton, Pleasington and Burnley Barracks, all of which can be found on the line from Colne to Preston. The local operator, Northern Rail, claimed that the decision to downgrade these other stations to request stops had been taken to make the line 'more reliable'. This does sound a little counter-intuitive at first hearing. After all, you wouldn't usually try to make something more reliable by adding uncertainty to it. Whereas beforehand everyone knew that all trains would stop at every station, now they might miss out one, two, three or four stations in any combination (apart from the 'four stations' – that would just have to be all four stations). However, the move did present the possibility of making up a few minutes if a train was running late. Presumably this is what appealed to the board of Northern Rail, since they, like all rail companies, can be fined if enough of their services fail to run on time. They also claimed that there was an environmental benefit to request stops – an angle I confess I had never considered. Trains that don't have to stop at every station are more energy efficient and thus emit less carbon dioxide, which makes sense. Certainly, a lack of interest in the stations on the part of the travelling public cannot have been at the heart of the decision: between them, in 2011–12, the four notched up a creditable 67,000 passengers a year.

It was Burnley Barracks that caught my eye. I was keen to find out how much of the former military establishment was still there, for it began life not as a mere garrison of run-of-the-mill infantry but as a splendid and dashing cavalry barracks. Before I got there, though, I had the pleasure of passing through a Lancashire station whose name, Hall i' th' Wood, invited parody.

Arriving at Burnley Manchester Road station I cycled across town to Burnley Barracks in the hope that I might stumble across the barracks en route and thus experience the pleasure of surprise, if indeed you can be surprised by something you're actively keeping an eye out for. Around each corner, I anticipated being confronted with something barrack-like. Around each corner I was disappointed. It wasn't as if I was expecting some huge complex with a parade ground pitted by the hooves of long departed steeds; I just wanted something to which I could point and say, 'Ah, that must be the old cavalry barracks,' while nodding my head sagely in the manner of a television historian.

It was only when I came around the final corner that I realised I wasn't going to see them, for there was Burnley Barracks station instead. At least there was its station sign propped up like a raised hand trying to attract the attention of drivers tearing past on the A671. Giving up my search for the barracks for the time being, I dropped down a steep cutting to the platform.

Even its most ardent admirers would find it difficult to describe Burnley Barracks station as aesthetically pleasing.

It is dominated by a road bridge that flies low across its sole platform, the riveted girders on its belly as attractive as the beach-exposed paunch of a middle-aged man. The station sported the first graffiti I'd seen on a request stop on this tour – a fan of the English Defence League had evidently passed through on his way to his regular Friday night dog-baiting session. An uncompromising metal fence has been erected on the abandoned platform opposite. The waste ground behind used to be covered with trees, but they were all cut down a couple of years ago and have not been replaced. Hidden from view and unlovely to look at, Burnley Barracks is the sort of place where the arrival of your train is an even more welcome event than usual.

At the time of my visit, nature had attempted some sort of rescue operation. The disused end of the platform had become so thoroughly de-urbanised that there was actually a little winding muddy path through the undergrowth that looked as if it might have been created by foxes, while beside the bridge great bushes of Darwin's barberry distracted the eye with showers of bright orange flowers.

It would be unfair, though, to paint this as a story of a station that had hit the skids. A black-and-white photograph taken in 1962, when Burnley Barracks had two platforms, two tracks, a footbridge and a covered stairway down from a ticket office, shows a station just as unprepossessing as the current one.

To be honest, it's probably glad just to be here. After all, when it was opened on 18 September 1848 under the name Burnley Westgate it was intended to be only a temporary terminus for the East Lancashire Railway's extension from Accrington. Indeed, as soon as the line was extended through to Colne, Burnley Westgate was closed as planned and local duties were taken over by Burnley Central, a station whose possible future expansion would not be stifled by the sheer banks of a cutting.

Burnley Westgate's story could well have ended there, its 137-day life merely a footnote in the annals of railway history. However, these were the busy days of Victorian industry and Empire and the area around the defunct station began to fill with factories, workshops, workers' houses and, most importantly of all, a cavalry barracks. The station was hastily reopened in 1851 and renamed Burnley Barracks to reflect its new-found purpose.

One of the more notable officers to have spent time stationed at the barracks was James Yorke Scarlett. Having begun his military career as a teenage cornet in the 18th Hussars, he rose through the ranks to the point where, in 1854 during the Crimean War, he found himself ordered to lead the Heavy Brigade at the battle of Balaclava. It's often forgotten in the brouhaha surrounding the calamitous Charge of the Light Brigade that there was also a Charge of the Heavy Brigade and that it met with considerably more success. The Heavy Brigade had to go uphill from a standing start and the enemy was barely any distance away, so 'charge' might be something of an exaggeration, but at least it spared them the torturous half a league half a league half a league business. Glorious defeat may make for better poetry, but James Scarlett had the satisfaction not only of surviving the mêlée but of becoming a national hero in the process, with a slew of parents naming their children Scarlett in his honour.

The barracks enjoyed an altogether less illustrious career. It was reported in 1898 that the depot of the East Lancashire Regiment had moved from Burnley to Preston because the barracks at the former were in a poor state of repair. The 20th century ushered in the beginning of mechanised warfare, signalling the end for the cavalrymen (no doubt to the relief of their horses). The last cavalry charge by an entire regiment of the British Army took place in Turkey during the 1920 Chanak crisis, when the 20th Hussars made a successful strike against Turkish infantry. Burnley Barracks was duly converted for use by the infantry, though old habits apparently died hard. Rowland Farrer, who grew up opposite the camp in the 1930s, recalled that, 'The officers in those days wore silver breastplates, helmets and rode horses; they also had a small troop of soldiers dressed the same way.'

The 1960s and '70s brought wholesale destruction to this part of Burnley, with large numbers of the Victorian terraces knocked down and the barracks demolished. Then the M65 motorway cut a swathe through in 1981, further diminishing the local population. This has been supplemented by more recent housing, which has helped keep the station open even if it has not been sufficient to save it from becoming a request stop.

My search for the barracks was not entirely fruitless, though the remnants of them hardly make for an exciting day out. One corner wall still exists at what was the northern extremity of the camp. The land immediately to the south is now part of a dual carriageway called the Westway. The outline can also be traced along the south side of a car park just north of Accrington Road. That's as romantic as it gets. The only other reminders that Burnley was once a barracks town are two street names – Cavalry Way and Barracks Road – and the station.

If a local campaign in 2008 had taken off, the barracks would no longer have been recalled in the name of the station either. In recognition of the election of America's first black president, lobbying took place for the station to be changed from Burnley Barracks to Burnley Barack Obama, which would not have gone down well with one man I stumbled across later that day in a Burnley pub.

He was a fat man, carefully treading that delicate line between clinical and morbid obesity. He was in his fifties, white, and a bigot. I don't usually attend to bigots if I can help it, but this one was so supremely lacking in self-awareness and so wilfully ignorant of history that I felt constrained to order my quicksilver fingers to fly across the page and record the exact wording of his ravings. We never achieved first-name terms, so for the sake of clarity we'll call him Mr Bigot.

Mr Bigot caught my attention not only with his stentorian voice but also with his free use of some ugly, well-worn epithets to describe people of Asian origin. He seemed to know an awful lot about such people – a great many of his sentences began, 'They come over here and ...' Indeed, so often did he use this phrase that I began to wonder if he had studied Asian people in some academic capacity. Mr Bigot had two somewhat cowed drinking companions – a younger couple whose views were rather more conciliatory than his, but who always deferred to him and his evident sagacity. On one occasion the woman from this pairing augmented the results of Mr Bigot's doctoral thesis with an airing of that good old standard, 'They get free housing and free money,' just to show that she too was no slouch when it came to carrying out study in this area.

Mr Bigot nodded gravely and decided it was time to introduce his protégés to his theories on historical restitution:

'If the Commonwealth countries all paid to Britain what they owe us,' he began promisingly, 'we'd be one of the richest countries in the world.'

And there was me thinking it was Britain that had done quite well out of the Empire. I was glad to have been put straight on that one – it wasn't us who had plundered the resources of other nations, forced them into unfair trading agreements and carried off their people as slaves, but quite the reverse. Load of parasites, those Commonwealth countries. No wonder Guyana and Kiribati are doing so well today while we have to make do with being the eighth largest economy in the world.

Naturally, I was beaverly eager to hear Mr Bigot expound on this premise, but his genius mind was already off elsewhere, restlessly pouring forth light upon another subject in order to expose the shamefully unrecognised truths therein. He suffered his erudition to train itself upon a more parochial theme: his inability to land a teaching post. He expanded on the unfairness of his position – or rather lack of one – at some length, his acolytes mournfully shaking their heads and tutting as each injustice was picked over.

'They always go for those *academic* types,' he declaimed, the sneer in his voice lively enough to melt the chairs in the first ten rows of any lecture theatre in the land. I was understandably outraged – how dare those academic institutions employ people who appear academic?

But he wasn't finished there, oh no. With jabbing finger and a spray of spittle only the truly great orator can work up, he brought his epyllion of rhetoric to a climax of irrefutable logic.

'They might have the "qualifications"' – I'm sure he would have expressed the inverted commas with his fingers had one hand not been wrapped around his pint of lager – 'but I've got the *wisdom*.'

And all of a sudden the fog lifted and it struck me why he may have struggled to secure a teaching post. And I was glad. Sore glad.

TO BOOTLE

So entranced had I been by Burnley Barracks station, its missing barracks and Mr Bigot that I ended up catching a later train than I'd planned, which meant having to get a much later train from Preston to Barrow-in-Furness. The very last train, as it turned out, which scuppered my prospects of picking up a service around the Cumbrian coast to Kirkby-in-Furness, where I had hoped to find a quiet spot to pitch my tent.

'Not to worry,' I thought, 'I shall cycle up the coast instead – it's only a dozen miles or so.' I had no map but I was reasonably confident that if I kept the sea – or more properly the Duddon estuary – to my left I couldn't go far wrong. The night was beautifully still, and Cumbria goes to bed well before 11.30, leaving even the major roads all but deserted.

Cycling through the countryside on a bright cool night is such a joy and such a deeply sensual pleasure that I feel sad for anyone who hasn't experienced it. Noises that get lost in the hubbub of the day sing out across a stage emptied of humdrum rivals. The calls of night-flying birds, the cry of a fox, the sudden squabbling squall of a cat fight, the fearful yelps of lambs and the reassuring responses of their mothers, the distant sound of you know not what mysterious thing – they all take their turn in your ears. Smells, scents and aromas rise up out of the ground to launch a sneaky nocturnal assault on your nostrils. On my way up I breathed in newly mown grass, the last of the season's wild garlic and, at one point, detergent, though there seemed to be nothing around to clean but mud. The night cyclist's eyes become the eyes of an owl, pupils dilated, peering into the darkness for hints of movement or, on fast downhill stretches, errant drain covers. You become more aware of the breeze on your face, the breaths you take in as you take on a climb, the reassuring whir of your rubber on tarmac, the squeak of your brakes that you forgot to adjust during the day and daren't now in case you drop a nut and lose it forever. It's like being alive, only a great deal more so.

If it pours with rain, of course, the whole experience can also be a bit rubbish.

Tonight, though, I was in luck, for, as you might have picked up by now, the summer had begun disarmingly well – so well that I suspected it must have been one brought in from abroad while we were all distracted by whatever it is that distracts a whole nation – a Brit winning Wimbledon, perhaps. Following a hunch, I turned off the main road at the village of Soutergate and headed straight towards the estuary along a narrow lane. When that gave out, I followed a public footpath across fields and over the railway line and there, my hunch rewarded, I found a nook in which to pitch my tent while insomniac curlews mewed somewhere beyond me on water too black to distinguish from the sky.

The early-morning sunshine found me at Kirkby-in-Furness station. I was enjoying how terribly sky blue the sky had already become and how warm my bones felt even though it was not yet 7.30. There was nothing in the air to tell me that this would be an extraordinary day – in fact, I was rather looking forward to an unextraordinary but highly pleasurable day hopping on and off trains as I made my way around miles and miles of eye-easing Cumbrian coast before heading over the border into Scotland.

I pottered happily around Kirkby-in-Furness station, which once found fame, if not fortune, as the location of the longest station seat in the world. When the prodigious bench was eventually removed, the station went from the sublime to the ridiculous, going for a spell with no seating at all. It now had a humble little three-seater bench which I imagined sufficed on most days.

What hadn't disappeared, however, was Kirkby's astonishing view. If it hasn't won awards for being the most picturesquely situated station in England, it must signify that such awards do not exist. With The Hill (it's a hill, that's its name) behind it, the fells behind Broughton-in-Furness off to the right and the cricket-pitch flat Angerton Marsh through which Grize Beck patiently carves its circuitous way towards the Duddon Channel, it's the kind of place at which you pray for your train to be delayed so you might wear your eyes out in staring and staring.

I determined to spend my time here in blissful Mindfulness, examining the smartly turned-out station minutely. I was rewarded when, inspecting the graceful seaweed-green latticework footbridge, I noticed it had been embossed with tiny red Lancastrian roses, recalling a time when a large chunk of what is now southern Cumbria was an exclave of Lancashire, though the whole coast from Cartmel round to the Scottish border was firmly Cumberland, including Kirkby-in-Furness.

The station is just one among 15 request stops on the Cumbrian coast line between Barrow-in-Furness and Carlisle* so I spent the day as I had planned – amusing myself by stopping off to explore the best of them. I chose Foxfield and Flimby, which were new to me, and Corkickle and Drigg, which were old friends. I chatted with guards and held out my arm and chatted with guards and held out my arm some more. The sun shone all day and, it being a Saturday, almost everyone was happy. But there was something that I had not planned, and that thing happened at Bootle. It was shocking and then it was traumatic and a little while afterwards I think I was mistaken for a serial killer, but after that it was *great* and I realised it was a day I would remember all my life.

---

* Purists will point out, I know, that one train on weekdays – the 06.14 – stops compulsorily at Kirkby-in-Furness, so the station is a request stop only 97.02 per cent of the time. Call me a man who aims low if you will, but anything in this life that achieves 97.02 per cent should be spared our hair-splitting ways.

BOOTLE

There is nothing on Bootle station commemorating the valiant deeds of those unlikely war heroes Harold Goodall and Herbert Stubbs. There's no blue plaque, no information board, no brass plate dedicating a bench to their memory – no tribute at all to two men who one night risked their lives to save the lives of others and, in Goodall's case, sacrificed his own. If you've never heard of Goodall and Stubbs – and the odds are pretty good that you haven't because obscurity has all but gobbled them up – I shall tell you about them here and the injustice will be undone ever so slightly.

A little after ten on the evening of Thursday 22 March 1945, Harold Goodall was driving a freight train of 57 wagons down the Cumbrian coast from Workington. His fireman that night was Herbert Norman Stubbs, a 22-year-old from Harrington. The report of the official inquiry into the incident notes that as they passed the Bootle station signal box (which is still there) at 10.10pm 'the signalman noticed a white glow coming from inside a wagon near the engine'. The wagon in question was one of seven in Goodall's train that contained explosives – in this case, depth charges destined for anti-U-boat operations. Goodall and Stubbs apparently also noticed the glow reflected in the windows of the station buildings at Bootle, which must have been an unnerving sight.

The signalman set his signal to danger and immediately informed the next box down the line, which was at Silecroft, five miles away. In the meantime, Goodall had brought his train to a standstill at a safe distance from Bootle station. The fire had taken hold by now, but, thinking quickly, the two men managed to uncouple the burning wagon from the ones behind it. Goodall then drove the train forward a short distance and he and Stubbs returned to the burning wagon, this time to uncouple it from the rest of the train. Having successfully isolated what had in effect become a time bomb, they jumped back into the engine and took it and the remaining wagons up the line to safety. Here, the two parted company. Stubbs ran forward to place warning detonators on the track to stop any trains coming north, unaware that the Bootle signalman had already prevented the next train north from leaving Silecroft. With scant regard for his own safety, Goodall returned to the burning wagon for a third time, apparently with the idea of tackling the fire. He was killed instantly at 10.15pm when the depth charges detonated. The explosion was so violent that it left a crater 45ft deep, 45–60ft across and 105ft long. Around 80 yards of track were destroyed on both the up and the down lines, with ballast and rails 'hurled a considerable distance'. The report further noted that, 'The windows in Bootle station and in houses up to a mile and a quarter away were shattered.' Stubbs himself was knocked to the ground by the blast. With his driver dead, he got back into the engine and drove it to Silecroft signal box in order to seek assistance.

Had it not been for Goodall and Stubbs' presence of mind and phenomenal courage, the other six wagons containing munitions would almost certainly have gone up too, turning a destructive incident into a catastrophic one. For his actions that night, Stubbs received both the George Medal and the Order of Industrial Heroism.

Harold Goodall seems to have been a singularly unlucky character. Just the previous year he had been the driver of a 20-wagon munitions train that ran out of control on the Buckhill Colliery Line while negotiating the incline down from Seaton. He was saved only because a signalman heard his desperate whistle blasts and whisked the runaway away from a buffer-stopped siding onto the main line. Here it careered down towards Workington Central station, eventually coming to a halt on a bridge. Had the train crashed, it is said that it would have wiped out half of Workington. As for Goodall's death the following year, it would not have happened at all but for a cruel twist of fate. He was not scheduled to work on the night of 22 March, but had swapped shifts with a driver called Herbert White, who was down to take out the fatal train.

Goodall also missed out on a George Medal (which did not begin to be awarded posthumously until 1977), though I suspect that when you are dead that sort of thing doesn't matter so much.

Astonishingly, just 48 hours after the explosion at Bootle the crater had been filled in, the track repaired and the line reopened. It's amazing what can be done when there's a war on. Naturally, nearly 70 years later, there's no inkling that this section of railway was ever dealt such a devastating blow. The day on which I visited was so beautiful it seemed impossible that anything so dark and terrible could have happened here.

I parked my bicycle against the abnormally large wooden shelter, very smartly painted in white and blue with a sturdy tiled roof and an exquisitely tiled floor that gave it the air of a Tudor mansion. It had survived largely unaltered from the day it opened to the public and was a fine example of a mid-Victorian railway shelter, the vast majority of which we have lost. The only sign of abandonment was at its far end, where two cheeky strands of ivy had penetrated the front wall to enter a small locked waiting room and were now peering soulfully out through the frosted glass of the windows, possibly regretting their adventure. In common with so many of the request stops I had visited, Bootle's platforms had been quite savagely truncated, with the discarded footage left to the twin mercies of time and nature. Intriguingly, the more westerly of these amputated limbs sported a green metal shed. It was evidently still in use, securely padlocked and topped with a solar panel, yet had a sticker on it rather dubiously identifying it as a 'lamp oil store'. Given that the station lighting was electric, as one might expect, I could only conclude that the shed was full of gold ingots and probably pirate treasure too.

In contrast to the abandoned platforms, the substantial station building on the southbound platform had been immaculately kept and was largely unaltered. The tops of the downpipes leading from the guttering were marked '18FR73', which was a bit misleading because the station was opened in 1850, when the line from Whitehaven was completed. This was not a venture of the Furness Railway, as might be supposed by the initials, but the Whitehaven and Furness Junction Railway, which wasn't acquired by the Furness Railway until 1865. Many of the improvements the latter company made to Bootle station in 1873–74 are still with us, including the station buildings, shelter, signal box and goods shed (though the sidings they put in were removed in 1965). The level-crossing gates are still hand-operated, too. Sadly, the station buildings no longer function as such – they've long since been converted into a private residence which is now a holiday let. It was also up for sale when I was there, so if you got bored with your acreage at Pont Rhufeinig or your dowager's house at Entwistle, you could come and live here in four-bedroomed luxury for less than half the price.

In his book on the Furness Railway, W McGowan Gradon gives an interesting insight into the complexities of travel in this part of the world in 1850. Even with the opening of the Whitehaven to Bootle line, an apparently straightforward journey from the port to the major Lancastrian hubs was a complex procedure. On weekdays, four trains ran each way between Whitehaven and Bootle. Of these, the 09.30 from Whitehaven was one of two 'crack' services, taking just 75 minutes to cover the line's 20 miles. Travellers then had to catch a coach from Bootle to Broughton-in-Furness, where they could pick up the Furness Railway to Piel Pier. A steamer would then ferry them from the pier across Morecambe Bay to Fleetwood. At Fleetwood station, the intrepid voyager could take a train that would reach Preston by 6.45pm, Manchester by 8.50pm or Liverpool by 9pm.

In comparison, to make the same journey in today's post-Beeching world, if you take the 09.02 from Whitehaven on a weekday and change at Carlisle, you can be in Preston just before noon. If you change trains there you'll be in Manchester an hour later. Alternatively, change at Carlisle and Wigan and you'll come whistling into Liverpool a minute or two after 1pm. We don't know we're born, we really don't.

Wistfully, I cycled off in the direction of Bootle, the village being just over a mile from the station along a flat road that passed between fields. This had been the second station I'd visited that had its own tale of life-saving courage, after Charles Hawes' swimming exploits down at Lelant. It made my own life seem rather dull. I had neither saved a life nor had my own life saved. What was especially galling was that both of these events run in my family – before I was born my mother rushed into a room to snatch my brother from his cot after a heater had fallen over and caught fire – and yet somehow both had passed me by. Of the two, I'm less inclined to seek out having my life saved but I'll take it if nothing better is on offer, as long as it doesn't involve me stupidly putting myself in danger in the first place: that would rather taint it.

In the Bootle Store was a tall thin man as old as the hills and not quite as fast moving. The shop was small, so to compensate it had very narrow aisles arranged so that you had to pass along all of them, as in a maze, before you reached the till. The elderly man – we'll call him Bill, though that's not the name I came to know him by – had entered just in front of me. Progress was, shall we say, sedate. Foodstuffs that were fresh as he approached them were past their sell-by date by the time he arrived, and yet so constricted were the aisles that squeezing past even this wafer-thin man was out of the question. Aeons later he reached the till and paid for his few purchases. I noted that he then became energised by the chatter of the shop owner, his pace notably quickening to a meander as he shuffled away.

I bought a few bits and pieces for lunch and a packet of Victory Vs as a treat, and began loading them into one of my bike's panniers outside the shop. As we've discussed, memory is a tricksy thing and I cannot say for certain what happened next. I'm pretty sure, however, that it was one of the following three scenarios:

i.   I heard a thud, looked to my left and saw a man collapse onto the pavement.

ii. I heard a thud, looked to my left and saw a man already collapsed on the pavement.

iii. I saw a movement out of the corner of my left eye and caught the final stages of a man collapsing onto the pavement, during which time a thud emanated from his direction.

Half an hour later I gained the impression that I had seen Bill's glasses fly through the air, though this may have been fanciful. They did, however, fly through the air at some point, because they landed some way from his face. I remember being surprised that they hadn't broken.

I hared across to where he lay – he'd made it only about 20 yards from the door of the shop. I knew from the thud that this was more serious than a mere trip in the street.

Thriller writers are fond of forewarning readers that a character is not long for this world by describing a blow to their person as emitting a 'sickening thud'. This was just such a thud. I don't know whether it came about through a collision of head on wall or head on pavement. What I do know is that by the time I got to Bill, which cannot have been more than five or six seconds after the event, there was already a pool of blood on the pavement. Shockingly, it wasn't anywhere near his head. He was trying to sit up, but he was like a newborn giraffe – his limbs were gangling and wouldn't work properly. As I reached down to him I realised why the blood was so far away – it was squirting out of his head like a fountain. With every beat of his heart a further gory gush leaped forth, clearing us both and landing a couple of feet away.

To my shame, I'm not a trained first-aider. The greater part of what I know about the craft of medicine I learned when I was a Cub and at this moment I dearly regretted winning my emergency heart-bypass badge (you use the casing from a Bic biro and a shoelace) at the expense of the one on basic first-aid techniques. However, I had seen enough head injuries from my humble career as an amateur footballer to know that you had to hold the wound together.

I can't remember exactly what I said to Bill in those first moments, but I don't think I bothered asking him if he was all right: if I knew anything about him at all it was that he was not all right. I got him sitting upright, or as upright as he and I could manage, and I told him I needed to hold his wound together. As I stretched out my hand towards the corner of his temple to do so, I saw something I'd never seen while looking at someone who was still alive: the brilliant whiteness of a skull. What worried me most of all was that I couldn't get Bill to say anything to me. He didn't seem to know where he was or understand anything I said to him. I'm not sure if I've ever seen anyone so thoroughly scared. His eyes pleaded with me to make some sense of this bewildering situation.

I was just able to reach his glasses without taking my hand from his head. I slipped them back onto his face in the hope that, if he could see again, he might be able to restore some order to his world. It was a forlorn hope – it merely made his pleading eyes larger. I remembered the other thing that routinely happened on football pitches after there had been a clash of heads. Some member of the team with pretensions to medical expertise would thrust his hand in front of the face of the dazed parties and ask them how many fingers he was holding up. Bill was so far beyond this that I didn't bother. Even if he could see and even if he could count, he wouldn't have understood the question.

It was then that, for the first time in my life, I wished I had a mobile phone on me. Bill evidently needed to go to hospital quick smart. Despite my fingers pinching and staunching for all they were worth, he was still losing blood and would slowly bleed to death in front of my eyes – something that neither of us was keen should happen. However, I knew that if I left him in order to run back into the shop to raise the alarm, he would start spurting blood again. There was no one in the street to call upon and I had nothing on me that I could use as a bandage, so I tried reassuring him that everything was going to be

OK – something I wasn't spectacularly sure of myself – and had a go at lifting his own hand to his head, telling him he should hold the wound together while I raced to the shop and back. It was no good, and anyway he needed both his hands to keep himself from toppling over again. There was nothing for it – telling him I would be back in no time at all, I removed my hand from his head and flew back to the shop. I burst through the door and made a general appeal:

'Somebody please call an ambulance. The old man who was in here just now has hit his head,' I declared, trying to sound like someone whom strangers take to be authoritative and whose requests should be treated as orders. It then occurred to me that the people in the shop might wonder why I had not called for an ambulance myself.

'I haven't got a mobile with me. Please, just call for an ambulance.'

And with that, I was gone, a streak of bottle-green and black, tearing back along the pavement like a superhero whose one superpower was moderately good acceleration.

Bill was still in the position I had left him in, which I took as a good sign, but the crimson fountain had started up again, which was less wonderful. I got into staunching position and told him that an ambulance would soon be on its way, but I could divine nothing from his eyes or incoherent speech to reassure me that he understood. And so there we were: me, on one knee, holding his head as if I were caressing his face while asking him to marry me, and him swaying slightly and staring with terrified eyes into the middle distance, or, more likely, no fixed distance at all. I kept up a one-sided conversation, though I'm glad there's no transcript available. I'm not all that good at small talk with people who *don't* have significant and possibly life-threatening head wounds; my range of chatter with those who do is even more limited, especially when I'm having to fill in the responses as well.

We were there for hours, we two, forming our little tableau of fear and social incompetence. Or at least it felt like hours, but it can only have been a few minutes – five at the absolute most. Eventually, I heard some people behind me emerging from the shop. I turned round to them and was surprised to see the surprise on their faces.

'Oh, Bill!' one cried out. 'What have you done?'

I couldn't believe it. It was as if I hadn't made my dramatic declaration in the shop at all. I wanted to say, 'I told you all just now! He's hit his head!'

Instead, I said, 'He collapsed a few minutes ago and hit his head,' missing out the telltale irritation inherent in the exclamation marks. 'Has someone called an ambulance?'

Nobody had. So now I knew just how authoritative my authoritative voice was.

'Well, can someone do so, please? He needs an ambulance,' I said, in case the point hadn't quite got through. Then, suspecting that nothing I'd originally said had been taken in, I repeated, 'I haven't got a mobile myself, otherwise I'd call.'

A middle-aged woman who proclaimed herself a nurse was sceptical as to whether an ambulance was required.

'Take your hand away,' she said.

I removed my hand and was distressed to see a torrent of blood making its barely coagulated way out of Bill's head.

Perhaps I hadn't been pinching hard enough. It got a reaction, though.

'We need a compress,' the nurse said decisively. 'And an ambulance.' In seconds she was down by Bill's side, soothing him and holding his head together and letting the others who had come out of the shop know what she needed. Someone retrieved a phone from a pocket and began punching in 999. I was suddenly surplus to requirements, which, I have to say, was something of a relief.

'OK then ... I'll leave him in your hands,' I said as I turned to go, but I think the nurse was so intent on the care of her patient that she didn't hear me.

I looked at my watch. I had about five minutes to cover the mile and a bit back to the station if I wanted to catch my train. And then I had to hope that the level crossing had not been closed against me, for there was no footbridge. I tossed into a pannier the bits and bobs of food that I'd dropped in my rush to get to Bill and zipped off up the road. Bill's gift to me of the shot of adrenaline I'd received on seeing his crumpled body gave my bike wings and I was flying through the level crossing before the signalman had even left his box to close it.

I dismounted and walked up the platform with a feeling of triumph – as well I might, for I had just caught a train I had had every chance of missing. As I passed, a teenage girl sitting cross-legged on the floor gave me a look that was somewhere between anxiety and horror. It struck me as a little odd. Teenage girls may sometimes look upon me with pity or contempt, depending on the degree of ineptitude with which I have selected my wardrobe that day, but their eyes don't usually register anything akin to horror. It was only when I leaned my bike up against the shelter that I realised why: my hands were literally dripping with blood. It was a bit of a puzzle as to how my left hand had become so sanguinary – I suppose at some point I must have switched my staunching hand, perhaps when I reached for Bill's glasses.

'I'm not a serial killer!' I wanted to shout to the girl, but this is the sort of sentence that is pretty much guaranteed to have the opposite effect to the one desired by the user, so I said nothing. Her eyes didn't leave me for a moment. I expect she was probably surreptitiously attempting to locate her phone, too.

I had to do something about my hands. If nothing else, it would have been unhygienic to eat my lunch with Bill on me. I slipped my water bottle from its holder on my bicycle and, noticing a small drain below the downpipe from the shelter, began to wash them.

I can now testify that there is nothing on God's Earth more likely to impress upon onlookers that you are a serial killer than using a water bottle to wash blood off your hands into a drain. Even I began to suspect me. I'd probably just done that thing where your mind blocks out the memory of a crime because it's too horrific for your psyche to cope with. This was not comforting.

It was a strange libation. The blood was sticky and I had to use a lot of water to get it all off. I had some weird thoughts about this little oblation being in honour of the sacrifice made by Harold Goodall in lieu of a plaque, and then I had some even weirder thoughts about Macbeth. I studied the play at school for English Lit. and the only lines

from it I ever got off pat were the ones he says just after he's
murdered Duncan:

> Will all great Neptune's ocean wash this blood
> Clean from my hand? No; this my hand will rather
> The multitudinous sea incarnadine,
> Making the green one red.

In the exam I brilliantly managed to attribute these words
to Lady Macbeth. I scraped a C.

Back in the less psychotic world, I noticed with some
satisfaction that the blood I'd dripped onto the platform
did indeed look like beetroot juice, as I had surmised back
on Umberleigh station. With this in mind, I wondered if I
should tell the girl that it wasn't blood on my hands at all,
only beetroot juice, but something told me that this was
unlikely to lessen her nervous hold on her mobile.

The coming of the train proved our mutual salvation. I
hauled my bike on at one end and she scurried away to get
on at the other.

So, the adventure was over. If he wasn't already, Bill
would soon be in the hands of some brilliant paramedics
speeding towards a hospital.

I don't blame the people in the shop for not acting
sooner – I'm sure if I'd been in there and someone else had
careened in and made a similar announcement I too would
have done nothing. There's a well-researched phenomenon
called the Bystander Effect whereby everybody leaves it to
someone else to act in a certain situation and so no one
does. If you're being beaten up in the street, you've got
much more chance of a stranger coming to your aid if
they're the only one around than if a whole crowd of

people see you're in trouble. Remember that and try to make sure that the next time you're beaten up it's in front of a very select audience, preferably of someone big, strong and brave.

I can't say for certain that I saved Bill's life. I've little doubt that had no one been around he would have bled to death simply because he was in no position to help himself or get up to find help. However, if I hadn't been there, someone else would have been in the queue behind him and might well have come out in time to take some action. The chances are they'd have had a mobile phone on them too, so Bill was unlucky that he got me, really. Furthermore, I'd only *helped* to save his life. I'm sure that the nurse, with her expertise and whatever ad hoc compress she devised, did far more to keep him in the land of the living, and the ambulance crew probably even more so. Also, unlike Harold Goodall, and Herbert Stubbs, Charles Hawes and, for that matter, my mother, I had not been in danger of losing my own life at any point and I'd done nothing that couldn't have been done by anyone else in that situation. Still, that said, although I was sorry for Bill and wished he hadn't collapsed, it was difficult not to feel a retrospective warm glow about the incident. I might not have grasped the meaning of life on this trip, but at least I'd had the opportunity to help prolong life for someone else. If life were entirely meaningless, what would have been the point of that?

Little did I know then that my mini adventure in Bootle would not be the most extraordinary thing to happen to me on this trip. Not by a long way. Not by ... ooh, about a million miles.

TO LOCHAILORT

Glasgow was friendlier than I'd remembered it. I'd taken an early-evening train up from Carlisle and I walked my bike from Central station to a hostel on the Clyde. The Saturday-night streets thronged with packs of shirt-sleeved, smart-casual men and posses of high-heeled, short-skirted women and everyone was so happy that it was a warm Saturday night that they had left their city faces at home and were smiling and laughing at the least opportunity. It was the perfect hour: too early for all but the most dedicated drinkers to have become drooling, incapacitated halfwits, yet far enough into the evening for most folk to have achieved a state sufficiently uninhibited to be a joy unto others. The space around them was filled with an intoxicating miasma of aftershave, body spray and perfume. It should have made me feel lonely, being alone on a Saturday night among people with partners, friends and lovers, and it did make me feel another twinge of sadness that I'd completely failed in my attempts to get in touch with Verena, but it's much more fun to enjoy other people's joy, so I let their happiness infect me. I even got into the spirit of the evening by searching out the poshest Indian restaurant I could find and ordering a takeaway. People say I don't know how to live, but they're wrong.

The first train to attempt the West Highland Line all the way to Mallaig the next day didn't leave until the dot of noon, which, after a fortnight or so of early mornings, afforded me the pleasure of a lie-in followed by a leisurely stroll along the banks of the Clyde. The journey up to Lochailort was one I had been anticipating with particular fervour, for the West Highland Line is unarguably one of the world's most scenic rail journeys and it had never disappointed me before, even in unaccommodating weather. Heading first along what was once Scotland's great ship-building river, the line turns right along Loch Long and then Loch Lomond, skirts nimbly around a huge crop of mountains that includes Ben Nevis, fearlessly crosses some of the most desolate moorland you could wish for and drops by the unprepossessing Fort William before gaily skipping off to the wonderful west coast, from which Lochailort is a tantalising hop-and-shimmy shy. The whole kit and caboodle from Glasgow to Lochailort involves 148½ miles of track. It would take my train five hours and ten minutes to cover the distance – an average speed that didn't quite make it to 30mph. There was no pesky changing of trains, so I could just sit back, stare out of the window and let Scotland play me an epic film of itself, David Lean style.

The train's electronic message board had 25 stations to announce, of which Lochailort was the 21st. While we sat in Queen Street station waiting for the off, I watched them glide from right to left. Scotland may only ever have produced one poet (I refer, of course, to William McGonagall*) but that's probably because there's so much

---

* I jest – I am, naturally, referring to Ivor Cutler.

poetry inherent in the country itself – it's embedded in every tree, rock and bog, every mountain and waterfall, every midge and every ball of sleet, whether we have ears to hear it or not. If you don't believe me, read aloud the words that scrolled across the narrow screen above my head. I give you ...

The West Highland Line
As told by the 12.00 from Glasgow Queen Street

Dalmuir
Dumbarton Central
Helensburgh Upper
Garelochhead
Arrochar & Tarbet
Ardlui
Crianlarich
Where this train will

Divide

Join the rear two coaches
For Upper Tyndrum
Bridge of Orchy
Rannoch
Corrour
Tulloch
Roy Bridge
Spean Bridge
Fort William
Banavie

Corpach
Loch Eil Outward Bound
Locheilside
Glenfinnan
Lochailort
Beasdale
Arisaig
Morar
Mallaig

Who can fail to sense the lyricism in that?

So rich is this rhapsodic seam that the train feels no need to augment it with stops at Anniesland, Singer or Bowling. For those whose tongues can wrap themselves around the Gaelic language, a further, hidden wellspring of poesy gutters forth. For instance:

An Tulach
Drochaid Ruaidh
Drochaid an Aonachain
An Gearasdan
Banbhaidh
A' Chorpaich
Loch Iall

are the stops from Tulloch to Loch Eil rendered in even more mellifluous form, if that were possible.

And we were off. Out of Glasgow's midday hangover and along the Clyde to the docks near Partick, where a triple-masted ship dried its timbers in the sun. Garelochhead's extraordinary platforms were covered with a thick layer of red gravel that piled itself up like a snowdrift wherever it was interrupted by a building. It was a look that Ardlui had copied, unless it got there first, of course.

I wasn't sure if this was just a Sunday thing, but when we stopped at a station we really stopped at it, as if the driver was uncertain whether or not we'd make it to the next one. After Garelochhead, the hills became more daunting as we climbed slowly but inexorably towards the Highlands. The precipitous slopes that dropped into a loch to our right seemed at first to be a riot of thousands of florets of broccoli, but I'd got the scale all wrong. Gradually the settlements petered out and the cuttings and curves became more frequent as the mountain passes were tackled.

At Crianlarich, while the train shunted back and forth in its efforts to divide itself, a host of passengers jumped out to smoke cigarettes on the platform (it wasn't strictly legal but we were in the countryside now). Here we said goodbye to four of our carriages, which were now bound for Oban. We were left with just two and thus felt like a renegade bunch, for we took the rails less travelled by.

It was early June and yet I could already see pockets of snow on the slopes of the higher mountains. Meanwhile, between Tyndrum and Bridge of Orchy, a group of walkers below us on the West Highland Way was forging along a wide track up the floor of a valley. Three of them waved to us. I know I should just have waved back but instead I began to analyse why it is that fully grown adults in remote areas wave at trains. What drives this need to make some fleeting and wholly inconsequential contact with other humans?

I decided in the end that they were probably just being friendly and I wished I'd waved back.

A single minute house was hunkered down in the humps and bumps of the western slopes of a valley. There was no road. The track to it – a thin white ribbon amid the purple and green tussocks of grass and heather – made for a thin and fragile umbilical cord. Who lived there? And why? And how? I couldn't remember where I had seen the last plantation, and if this was a shieling then where were the summertime sheep? The nearest we had passed were miles and miles away.

But compared with Rannoch Moor, ten minutes further up, the terrain in which the tiny isolated house sat seemed positively urban. Rannoch is beautiful enough if you like your beauty stringent, but it's no place to get caught out when the weather takes sides with the encircling mountains.

It made the sight of a young beach-blond chef bouncing out of the restaurant on Corrour station bearing a dish piled high with steaming food all the more incongruous. The railway provides the only entry and exit to Corrour unless you're willing to slog your way in and out on foot. The station was also the setting for Renton's less than upbeat appraisal of Scottishness in the film of Irvine Welsh's *Trainspotting*. They were not sentiments I've heard shared by any Scot I've ever known, mind you, though one or two have wished that the deep-fried Mars bar had been invented somewhere else.

An ancient corroded signpost let us know when we were passing the Monessie Gorge. It looked fantastic and I made a mental note to visit some day. Then before I knew it we made it at last to Fort William. I'll declare it now, I'm not a fan of Fort William. I admire the fact that they had electric street lighting that ran off hydroelectric power as long ago as 1896, but it is otherwise a town of outstanding ugliness, a town of huge factory outlets but no soul. It's been a wretched woebegone place ever since its conception. The original stockaded camp was established by Cromwell's General Monck to keep the pesky local clans quiet and English soldiers remained to suppress the two Jacobite Rebellions. However, the fort – eventually named after William of Orange – was situated in such damp and marshy terrain that far more troops died sweating feverishly in their beds than were ever killed by the lusty blow of a Highlander's broadsword.

We owe a great debt, however, to the people of Fort William, for without them we might not be travelling along this line at all. Understandably, they had been overlooked when the railways came to Scotland. While Oban had its own line to Glasgow, their nearest station was a full 50 miles away at Kingussie, on the line to Inverness. In 1889, tired of waiting for a railway to find them, they began to build their own. After many a trial and tribulation – bog and moor and mountains not being the easiest terrain over which to lay a railway line – Sir Robert McAlpine finally connected Fort William to Glasgow five years later. The extension of the line for the benefit of the west coast fishing concerns took even longer to build, although it was much shorter. The small harbour at Roshven was initially proposed as the terminus, but a local landowner refused to let the company build on his estate, so Mallaig was chosen instead and the line at last opened in 1901.

We spent 11 long minutes at Fort William. I counted each one.

By Banavie my unhappiness was forgotten. Here they're proud as punch of their swing bridge and Neptune's Staircase, Britain's longest flight of staircase locks, which lifts boats up from Loch Linnhe onto the Caledonian Canal. We flew through Locheilside, the first of only three request stops on the line. However, we did stop atop an enormously high viaduct – 'The Glenfinnan Viaduct,' a fellow passenger remarked with approval. From our eyrie we commanded a view down the length of a small loch with a slender broch (or tower) at its head. You know you're in the Highlands when, in a single glance, you can take in a loch and a broch.

Glenfinnan impressed me, for it was the first station I remembered seeing in a while that could boast two platforms. The reason for this became clear a few minutes later when the train from Mallaig slid in next to us: this is a prized passing place on a line that has just a single track for the majority of its route. As we lingered there I noticed a signpost:

Water tank 2 mins
Circular walk 30 mins

I don't know about you but I've always taken it as an indication that there is not much going on in a place when I see a sign directing me to its water tank.

The Highlands do go on, don't they? This was but one small corner of them, yet the hills, glens, mountains, lochs and streams came and went in a seemingly endless succession, as if Scotland had them to burn, which perhaps it does. At length we came out beside a body of water I knew must be Loch Ailort. I smiled at the multitude of tiny wooded islands upon it and hastily packed my things away.

But no. We passed on by. 'Welcome to the Highlands, laddie – you might find we've squeezed a few more lochs in since you were last here.'

LOCHAILORT

I had six hours in Lochailort until the next train. Excitingly, the day's second and last service north comes through here at just gone 11 at night, which seems daringly late for such a remote spot. What was slightly less exciting was that Lochailort itself appeared to consist of a road junction and a hotel – the Lochailort Inn, as if it could have any other name – and not much else. Knowing the ways of rural Scotland, I was pretty certain that the Lochailort Inn would have a public bar, but I felt that spending six hours in it, assuming it was even open on the Sabbath, would be excessive. I went into my Zen mode and resisted the pull away from the station. I spent the first hour engaged in three pursuits: tracing the adumbrated line of the opposite platform, which had been abandoned in the 1970s and was now drowning under rhododendrons; cooking myself something vaguely nutritious; and being continually coned by two large Scots pines whose aim was, I had to admit, impeccable.

Eventually taking the hint, I moved off into Lochailort and was pleasantly surprised. Shooting down the hill from the pub to the loch which gives the settlement its name, I came across a fabulously spooky Gothic shooting lodge. Inverailort House – also known by the slightly grandiose title of Inverailort Castle – started life hundreds of years ago as a farmhouse, though you'd be a genius to detect that now. It was converted into a shooting lodge in 1875 and has been lowering at people ever since. It looked a bit shabby and sorry for itself, which only heightened the cold, steely menace emanating from the place.

Three things Inverailort House didn't say to me as I gazed half mournfully, half warily upon it were 'string vests', 'David Niven' and 'exploding pens'. Which just proves how extraordinarily deceptive appearances can be, for although the house didn't have a fancy information board explaining what had gone on there, or even a sign on the front lawn with its name on, it spent 50 years of the last century doing things no ordinary Scottish shooting lodge would dream of. It also helped its local station uphold the excellent record among railway request stops for connections with World War II.

The capers began in 1940, when the house was requisitioned and turned into a Combined Operations training centre called HMS *Lochailort* in the wonderful tradition the Royal Navy has for naming things that aren't ships ships. If even the Navy doesn't know what isn't a ship, there can be little hope for the rest of us, one feels. The house was turned over to the Special Operations Executive (SOE), who jokingly renamed it 'The School of Ungentlemanly Warfare' and used it as a headquarters where they trained spies and saboteurs. These would be dropped behind enemy lines to instruct resistance groups and partisans in the ways of sabotage and guerrilla warfare. Churchill's hope was that the occupying Nazis would be weakened from within, thus reducing their ability to fend off more conventional attacks by the Allies.

A pair named Major Bill Fairbairn and Captain Eric Sykes (not *that* Eric Sykes) taught men and women how to handle explosives, carry out guerrilla campaigns, survive in the wild and resist interrogation should they have the misfortune to be caught, as many sadly were. Visiting trainers included the Soviet spy Kim Philby, who spent a few days at Inverailort in 1940. No one suspected he was a spy at the time, of course, because he had such a nice accent and had gone to Cambridge. Had Fairbairn and Sykes known Philby had acquired his cloak-and-dagger skills courtesy of the Comintern, they might have asked him a few blunt questions, possibly at the end of a double-edged commando knife, which the two of them also invented.

It seemed only fitting, since the commandos had been following me about since I first became one on the train to Lympstone, that when the SOE moved their HQ off to Arisaig House (of which more later) the property should have been turned into a commando training school, for it was here that the word 'commando' was first applied to these special forces. Lord Lovat was a fieldcraft instructor at the school whose grandfather had fought with distinction in the Boer War: there, *Kommando* was the word used for a unit of the Boer militia. In honour of his ancestor, he suggested that the then Special Service Battalions be given the far less pedestrian title of 'commandos' (the 'c' presumably employed to avoid making them look like some sort of Johnny Foreigner outfit).

Experiments carried out by the commando trainers at Inverailort led to the invention of such Q-like devices as pens that blew up when their caps were removed and explosives disguised as horse manure for the Maquis and their equivalents to leave about on roads. Other breakthroughs had slightly wider applications. Commander Murray Levick conducted research into the benefits of salt and discovered that the endurance levels of soldiers who were deprived of it dropped dramatically. Also, it's claimed that the string vest was invented here. Little were the officers at Inverailort to know that when this particular item of clothing crossed over into the civilian world, it would be worn mainly by men whose physiques were best left unseen. A notable exception to this rule would be film actor and all-round smoothie David Niven, who may well have worn a string vest, because he was among those soldiers who took a course at the commando school here.

When Inverailort House and estate were returned to the well-to-do Cameron-Head family after the war, Mrs Cameron-Head transformed it into a place of refuge for all comers. A remarkable woman guided by egalitarian principles and drawing from an apparently inexhaustible well of generosity and hospitality, she opened the house up to anyone who wanted to spend time there, regardless of their situation in life, and they could also stay as long as they liked. It sounds too good to be true, but by all accounts it worked. A huge variety of people came to Inverailort: from the lowly and humble to those in the highest offices in the land, mixed in with a goodly splash of artists (a group not known for turning down a free meal and a bed) – all were beneficiaries of Mrs Cameron-Head's bountiful nature and, what is perhaps just as laudable and harder to pull off, treated alike by her. When she died in her late seventies in 1994 she was deeply mourned. I chanced upon a beehive cairn that was placed beside Loch Ailort in her memory. It enjoined passers-by to:

Remember Mrs Cameron Head [sic] of Inverailort
1917–1994
A friend to all agus Cariad do na Gaidheil*

Now that strikes me as the sort of epitaph that anyone would be pleased to be given.

It's a shame that the house is in such poor repair just two decades after the death of Mrs Cameron-Head (who seems never to have been referred to by any less formal name). However, moves are afoot to renovate and redesign the home that once knew so much joy, if about £6 million can be raised. The plans are to turn it into a post office, museum, chapel, youth hostel and 'senior executive residential conference facility', which seems a peculiar mix, particularly the last two.

I decided to investigate a wee kirk on the braeside I had spied from the lochside. I retraced my steps to the pub to turn left along the A830, the mighty road that sweeps through this way. An inn was recorded here as long ago as 1650 and a hundred years later a village called Kinloch Hoylort appeared on maps of the area. It was only in the early 1800s that the first road actually reached the community with the coming of Thomas Telford and his famous 'Road to the Isles' from Fort William. It's ironic that there was a village here for over 50 years but no road to connect it with the rest of the world and now Lochailort has no village as such but two A roads. I wouldn't be

---

* 'and Friend of the Gael' ('the Gael' being the Gaelic-speaking community).

surprised to learn that long, long ago the message of some wandering preacher had found no purchase with the locals and on his departure he had brushed the dust off his feet and cursed them, saying, 'Ye'll ha'e a vullage but nae road or a road but nae vullage, but there'll ne'er come a day when ye ha'e a vullage *an'* a road.'

The church turned out to be a drab Catholic thing built in 1874, a long time after my vindictive preacher had come through here. Its odd position halfway up a hill is explained by the fact that it was paid for by the Chiefs of Clan Cameron, who stipulated that it must be clearly visible from Inverailort. It also explains its name – Our Lady of the Braes. It lasted barely 90 years as a place of worship, though it did nab a part in the classic film *Local Hero*, which probably cheered it up no end.

And with that, I had seen Lochailort. It was a far cry from the scene I would have witnessed had I passed this way in the 1890s, when the construction of the extension to the West Highland Railway was going full pelt. Along with the building of the nearby Gleann Màma Viaduct, no fewer than seven tunnels had to be bored within a few miles of Lochailort. To facilitate this, the village enjoyed a brief life as a township housing 2,000 navvies and whatever family they brought with them. They even had their own hospital set up in an old schoolhouse.

Having exhausted all the possibilities Lochailort offered up to me, I turned my wheels at last towards the hotel, only to find it was really a pub that happened to have rooms. I have spent many happy hours in rural inns in Scotland, sitting in the corner of the bar reading or scribbling away and trying not to notice the tartan carpet while the odd cheery local pops in and out and old men sit dourly eyeing their pints or their drams, silently waiting for Death to overcome them. I had envisaged something similar occurring at the Lochailort Inn. The first indications that this would not be the case came as I swept down the hill from the church to the strains of a ceilidh.

The pub was jumping. It was also packed. There was not a single spare table to be had, or even a chair to be had at any table. And where were the old men waiting for Death? They had been replaced by a crowd whose average age was younger than mine. It simply wasn't on.

Rather than chatting with the patrons and ending the night singing riotous folk standards with the band like a proper travel writer, I took my pint out to the picnic tables by the roadside. I was the only person there. A very good way to make yourself feel like an outcast is to sit outside a packed, noisy pub in which everyone is clearly enjoying themselves, while you hang with the midges and scribble away in an exercise book about what an outcast you feel. If I turned round I could see the six-piece band thrashing away for all they were worth. No bodhrán player, though, I noted with grim satisfaction. I'd more than happily marry a bodhrán player. In fact, I'm sure it's only the general lack of single female bodhrán players in the London area that has kept me from making my marriage vows.

When the time came to wend my way back up to the station, I found myself sharing the platform with people who were quite well oiled and who also would have been my firm friends for life by now if only I'd been a proper travel writer. One young woman kept threatening to leap onto the track, though she gave no coherent reason as to why. She eventually did jump, which was slightly unnerving because the train had already been due a couple of minutes by then and the bend just beyond the platform meant there was very little warning of its coming if you couldn't hear it. After what seemed an age she was eventually dragged back up onto the platform by her friends. In the event, it was not a close call: the train rumbled in 20 minutes late and full of apologies, just when we were beginning to wonder if it would arrive at all.

I didn't really mind that it was late (indeed, given what might have happened, I was delighted that it was), for I'd decided before the start of this trip that I would camp the night on a station – something I'd wanted to do for a while now – and that that station would be Beasdale, which was the next stop and just ten minutes away. Even allowing for blowing up my mattress and cleaning my teeth, I could be tucked up in bed in 15.

BEASDALE

'Whoa! Whassshappeningg?'

I'd never before been awoken by the 06.25 to Glasgow rattling ten feet from my head. It should have been less of a shock than it was, because I live just ten yards from the tracks on which rolling stock thunders in and out of London Liverpool Street from well before dawn, but for a panicked second or two the train seemed so loud I thought it was coming straight for me. It was already clickety-clacking away by the time I came to my senses and realised where I was. I looked around me in a murky light filtered through drizzle. Above my head was a little wooden roof, below my airbed lay a dry concrete floor and I had posters on the walls, one of which for some reason showed a man asleep, which is a state I intended to return to without delay. It did not matter that it was a dreich old day outside, for I was cosy and snug in my sleeping bag in the Beasdale station shelter, which protected me from the outside world like an oversized Wendy house. It was great and with the next train not due until half past nine, the whole station would almost certainly remain my little fiefdom for the next three hours.

It was an unwelcome surprise, therefore, to be re-awoken at seven by the sound of a car pulling up. There are no houses and nothing else at Beasdale to stop for aside from a station building that has been turned into a private holiday cottage by, I'd been told, a lovely couple. However, the shutters over the windows suggested that the cottage had been closed up when I arrived the night before and I thought it unlikely that anyone would be starting a holiday here at seven on a Monday morning. I listened to the station's little wicket gate click open and then heard footsteps coming along the gravel path. The best thing to do in such circumstances was clearly to close my eyes and pretend to be asleep. I heard the footsteps pause by the entrance to my lair. I felt the blood rush to my face as a schoolboy dread of being told off came flooding over me. But no voice broke the silence. Instead, the footsteps continued further up the platform. Then I heard a sound I wasn't expecting at all – that of water being swilled around a big plastic bucket. In a flash I knew what was about to happen. Whoever was out there was going to drench me in morning-cold water fresh from the tap – it was doubtless the Highland way with vagrants. I looked up from my all too vulnerable position. I could see the top of a man's head through one of the shelter windows. I calculated I had about a second before he swung his Bucket of Summary Cold Wet Justice through the shelter entrance.

'Good morning,' I squeaked defensively.

The head appeared around the opening, attached to a body, which is my favourite way for a head to be. The body wore the tabard of officialdom. I braced myself for the telling off.

'Good morning,' the man replied, 'I didn't mean to disturb you. I'm just watering the hanging baskets.'

Of course! What else would someone be doing at seven on a Monday morning in the drizzle but watering hanging baskets? I cursed myself for a fool.

'I'll leave you in peace now,' the constant gardener said in a friendly manner. 'I've got the other stations to do. Cheerio.'

I had a little look after I'd got up and dressed and I discovered that the incident made more sense than I'd imagined. Even though it was raining, the lip of the shelter roof kept the hanging baskets dry.

That left just one Beasdale mystery to clear up. The previous night, when I'd shown my ticket to the guard, he told me that he and the driver already knew that I was going to Beasdale. When I queried him about this, he smiled and said, 'It was on the sheet.' He was gone before I could ask him what sheet.

Pondering this and wondering whether I should be comforted or scared by it, I cycled the short distance to Arisaig House. Just before the house there was a path on the left that ran down to Prince Charlie's Cave. This purports to be the place where the bonnie prince hid and rested on the night of 16 July 1746, during his flight from the English Redcoats. However, it seems that he shunned the cave, prepared for him by the loyal Angus MacEachine, opting instead to spend the night in a bed in a house at nearby Meoble – and who among us wouldn't?

Arisaig House wasn't around when Charles made his perilous way through here, but it was built in time to be the reason for the existence of Beasdale station. At least, it used to be the reason, but it burned down sometime around 1935. The current Arisaig House was a second go constructed in the same year that the century had a second go at a world war. This was bad luck for its owners, because the property was snapped up by the Special Operations Executive when the organisation moved from Inverailort. It became the SOE Special Training School STS21, a finishing school for Allied agents before they were dropped behind enemy lines. The crack squad responsible for the 1942 assassination in Prague of one of the leading proponents of the Holocaust and all-round ghastly human being Reinhard Heydrich had their deadly skills honed here, though they themselves met with violent ends not long after carrying out the mission.

The house was ideal for the SOE because it was remote and had only one road in and out, so it was easy to seal off and declare a Special Protected Area. The fact that it was also accessible by train, which meant that the school's staff and pupils could come and go with relative ease, made it a perfect fit.

I was welcomed into the huge kitchen in one of the wings of the house by Sarah, whose family were the current owners. Personable and friendly to this damp stranger who had arrived unannounced so early in the morning, Sarah made me Lady Grey tea (I'd turned down her kind offer of a meat/egg-based breakfast) while feeding me snippets of information about the house. She and her family had run it for three years now as a 'laid-back place where guests wouldn't feel like they were in a hotel but a home'. As homes go, it's quite a place, too. I was allowed to have a nose about – it's all oak panelling and Victorian portraits (an artist called Jemima Blackburn gets a lot of wall space) and high ceilings and tasteful rugs and long ornate coffee tables with carved legs and French doors with vistas of the croquet lawn and the tennis court and the magnificent gardens and Loch nan Uamh. I had no idea this imposing grey stone pile had been built as recently as 1939.

Back in the kitchen, Sarah told me that in the 1980s the house had been a five-star Relais & Châteaux hotel, which makes sense because it does actually resemble a château. The owners back then had sought what they considered a high-class clientele and had not encouraged the low-born locals to darken their doors. Sarah, however, had bravely shattered this unwritten stricture by spending her wedding night there.

'It cost more than a week in Venice.'

At that point Sarah's daughter wandered in, in classic young-woman-with-hangover mode. It transpired that she had also been at the Lochailort Inn the previous night but we didn't recognise each other. Had I been a proper travel writer she would have said, 'Hi, Dixe, great to see you again. That tone poem you recited to the accompaniment of the accordion that made everyone in the pub weep and hug each other and weep again was *amazing*.'

TO DUNCRAIG

The distance as the crow flies between Beasdale and Duncraig is 31 miles. The distance between the two stations as the train chugs is a scarcely believable 409 miles. You scarcely believe me? I can't say I blame you. I wouldn't believe it myself if I hadn't just done the sums. The rail journey requires anyone attempting it to travel all the way back to Glasgow (153¼ miles), then from Glasgow to Perth (62½) and Perth to Inverness (117½) before heading along the Kyle of Lochalsh Line to Duncraig (75¾). If I'd jumped on that 06.25 which so rudely tore me from my dreams – and if all the trains had run on time – I'd have been asking the guard to drop me off at Duncraig at ten past eight that night (after an extra change at Dingwall), a mere 13 hours and 45 minutes later.

Lovely though I'm sure that trip is, there is a sneakier, quicker and far less exhausting way. Taking the train for the short hop up to Mallaig, I caught the ferry over to Armadale on Skye and cycled across the island and back to the mainland via the bridge to the Kyle of Lochalsh, three stops away from Duncraig. It's a lovely little ride across Skye, albeit on major roads the whole way. There are dramatic views of the Cuillin Hills and a chaotic bric-a-brac shop spread across various parts of a house and the front garden. I always pop in and I always end up buying really heavy, bulky books even though my panniers are already full to the brim. I'm not sure why I do this. I did it again on this occasion.

DUNCRAIG

'Sorry, I thought you were a ghost!'

I've only once had this claim directed at me and it came while I was standing in the entrance hall of Duncraig Castle. A few years ago I stayed the night there for a travel feature in the days when it was sort of a B&B. I say 'sort of' advisedly because the owners, who had been the subject of a somewhat scathing fly-on-the-wall documentary series about their life in the castle, had pretty much given up on the place. I think they sold up a few months later and I may well have been their last guest.

'Brideshead after the fall' was how I described the castle at the time. 'Brideshead on the mend' may be the best description for it now. To call its history 'chequered', however, would be like describing Pol Pot's human rights record as 'mixed'.

Unlike Arisaig House, whose Beasdale station was open to the public from the start, Duncraig Castle's station was a private affair. Many are the halts that were opened in the 19th century to appease the landowners over whose estates railway lines were laid, but Duncraig is not one of them. It was built because the man who owned Duncraig Castle also happened to be instrumental in the creation of the railway that ran past it. The man in question was Sir Alexander Matheson, a co-founder of the Jardine Matheson Group and, let's not beat about the bush here, a drug dealer. It's not a profession one readily associates with affluent Victorians. Potted biographies tend to make coy references to Matheson belonging to a 'Hong Kong mercantile family' or some such, but the reality was rather more brutal: he made his staggering fortune selling opium to the Chinese.

Returning to his native Scotland, he set to work on the construction of Duncraig Castle, which was designed by Alexander Ross, 'the Christopher Wren of the Highlands', and completed in 1866. Matheson used his wealth and influence as the Member of Parliament for the area to ensure that the Highland Railway extended all the way from Inverness to the Kyle of Lochalsh. It was not an easy argument to make, given the difficulties of the terrain and the very small populations served along the way. On account of the former, it proved the most expensive line in Britain per mile of track up to that time. It was begun in 1893 and opened four years later. The line proved a bloody venture: no fewer than 70 men were killed, which also made it Britain's costliest ever railway-building project in terms of human life lost.

Having gone to all the trouble of getting the railway line to his castle, Matheson had a halt built nearby for his private use. It's doubtful that he got his money's worth out of it, though: so fabulously wealthy was he that Duncraig Castle, for all its size and ostentation, was merely a summer retreat that he would visit for a few weeks every year.

It would obviously be rude not to take advantage of his spendthrift ways, so once the train had pulled away and burrowed through the gap in the rocks to the east of the sheltered little halt, I sat down on the bench to admire what is a quite wonderful view. The foreground is taken up with a tiny wooded islet called Eilean Lagach. Behind this laps Loch Carron on whose far shore sits the delightful village of Plockton, backed by the wooded hills of Cnoc a Bhlàir and Cnoc na Domhail. Waiting for a train at some stations can feel like watching paint dry; here it's more like watching an oil painting dry. And if it starts to rain you can flee to a tiny wooden hexagonal waiting room built to mirror one of the rooms in the castle. It's no wonder that the station has been given listed-building status.

The affection in which it is held actually kept it alive in the 1960s. In 1964, the station was officially closed on Beeching's recommendation, but the train drivers working the line simply ignored him and continued to stop here. Eleven years later the 'ghost stop' was officially reopened. I'm not sure if this was a victory for good taste, sentimentality or sheer bloody-mindedness, but one of the rebellious drivers is pricelessly quoted as saying, 'We thought that if the English wanted to close a railway station they should pick on Euston or King's Cross.'

There's no road here. A footpath slopes off into the woods to scurry around the loch towards Plockton – it's a fun little stroll and I was looking forward to exploring its pleasures anew. However, first I wanted to take the only other way out from the station: the private drive to the castle. I left my bike and sauntered along the leaf-strewn track, slightly apprehensive about what I might see when I rounded the corner and the castle came into view.

My previous visit, in 2009, was during what we shall call the castle's Dobson Era. It was not a characteristically happy period. Sam and Perlin Dobson bought Duncraig Castle in

2003 and moved in with 17 members of their extended family. Their aim was to restore the almost derelict building – 'There were great holes in the roof and gaps in the walls – water running in all over the place,' Perlin told me – and turn it into a going concern that would give employment to the adults in the group and a memorable childhood to the children. The resultant smorgasbord of backbiting, recrimination and sheer blood-curdling rage was served up for the nation's entertainment on a weekly basis in the BBC's *The Dobsons of Duncraig* in 2004–05. Four years later, there were just Sam, Perlin and their two children left. They had succeeded in making parts of the castle habitable and those rooms retained a good deal of their grandeur, but this was offset by the fact that the rest was a building site full of half-finished solutions to things and 'temporary' fixes that had been in place for years. There was also the mesmerisingly horrible extension in the Brutalist style that jutted out from one end, as if the castle had suddenly been taken violently ill and had projectile-vomited concrete. But to understand how that came about, we need to take a quick squint at the pre-Dobsonian history of Duncraig.

Even after Alexander Matheson's death in 1886, the castle had no year-round tenants. Instead it spent many years being let for the season to affluent individuals such as the Duchess of Somerset and the Duchess of Buckingham and Chandos, who wished to host summer house parties here. In the 1920s, the castle was purchased by Sir Daniel and Lady Hamilton, who were interested in social reform and were the owners of the neighbouring estate of Balmacara. The two facts were apparently not incompatible.

Inevitably, the mansion played its part in World War II, transforming itself into a naval hospital. By the time the war ended, the castle had been bequeathed to the state by Lady Hamilton, who stipulated that it must be used in some educational capacity.

There now began by far the oddest stage in the castle's career, which we shall call the 'Feminism? What Would That Be?' era. From 1945 to 1989, Duncraig was home to an experimental domestic science college for girls. Herein lies the explanation for the Brutalist execration: it provided classrooms for the girls. Why something more in keeping with the architecture of the castle could not have been built remains a bit of a mystery. The experimental college was not, shall we say, steeped in the teachings of radical feminism, but proved hugely popular and was often oversubscribed. Along with art, history and Gaelic, the girls were taught household arithmetic, housewifery, dressmaking and, latterly, hairdressing. Their school song included the timeless lyric:

> Let others laud their French and Greek
> Their Latin and their Trig.
> 'Tis other knowledge that we seek
> We even keep a pig.

When I stayed here, I had a wander around the rooms that once served as the girls' dorms and discovered that their graffiti was still evident on the backs of the window shutters. I kept imagining it must date from the 1880s and had to remind myself that this was a college that began after World War II and was still going in the post-punk world. The classes in housewifery were almost certainly as dull as they sound – Perlin told me that she had come across 30 ancient hoovers when she and her family moved in.

The cause of feminism may have been set back a century or two but at least one of the teachers struck a blow for Scottish nationalism. Back in the 1950s, Kay Matheson (no relation) and various cohorts ventured south to Westminster Abbey and stole the Stone of Scone. This was no pebble, but the ancient rock on which Kings of Scotland had been crowned for hundreds of years before the English absconded with it in the 13th century. In successfully smuggling it out of the abbey and bringing it back over the border, Matheson and her friends became Scottish national heroes.

It was the castle that did for the college in the end – it simply became too expensive to maintain the fabric of the building. Still bound by the terms of the bequest, the local council turned to more tenuous definitions of the word 'educational' to try to make the castle earn its keep (even if it didn't have one). Which is how the production of 'Scottish village bobby' series *Hamish Macbeth* – filmed just across the loch in Plockton – came to be based in the castle for several years. Other bits and bobs of filming also took place there, and if fans of the cult film *The Wicker Man* manage to peep through their fingers for long enough, they'll catch a glimpse or two of Duncraig.

I'd learned by now, however, that no request stop was complete without its commando connection. Duncraig's came in 1942 when the castle posed as a Nazi-occupied French château. The commandos apparently carried out a successful mission that involved negotiating the barbed wire that protected the grounds around the castle (which was serving as a hospital at the time), meeting up with each other by a making a series of owl calls, planting a 'bomb' in a drain timed to go off when Hitler turned up, and leaving again undetected. The fact that Hitler was never blown up while visiting a French château demonstrates that real life can sometimes be harder than the rehearsals for it suggest.

The good news when I emerged from the woods and turned the corner was that something was happening to the castle. Temporary fencing was in place, scaffolding was up and builders were walking around on it. Matt, the man in charge of operations, filled me in. The castle had been bought at last and now belonged to a couple from Surrey who were having the whole place sensitively restored and turned into a B&B. The project would not be finished for several years, even though he himself was living on site and working full time on it with a team of builders. With bated breath I asked about the concrete excrescence.

'It's coming down in the next couple of weeks.'

'Brillstag!' I cried. It was a word I'd started using for some reason.

I'm not even particularly averse to concrete as a building material, but the world became a better place the day that extension was demolished. You probably felt it.

But let's get back to my appearance as a ghost. The young woman I quoted earlier was a friend of the Dobsons. They had gone out for the afternoon and she had worked herself up into a funk, imagining that she had heard a ghost in the house. She was upstairs when she heard me tentatively opening the front door (there was no bell) and, unaware that I was coming, had naturally assumed that I was the spectral presence. I assured her I wasn't, but I don't know that she was ever convinced. To be fair to her, the castle would appear to have something peculiar going on in it. The Dobsons told me that they had often been aware of inexplicable footsteps and 'two girls giggling' in one of the former dorms. Matt, who was living alone in the castle, had also heard the ethereal sounds but wasn't bothered by them. Of course, he might change his mind if 30 ghostly vacuum cleaners start revving up at three in the morning.

DUNROBIN CASTLE

Did you know that the king's brother was killed on active service during World War II? It was news to me. And frankly, it was news I didn't want to hear. That particular conflict had been dogging my steps almost from the beginning of my sally around Britain's request stops. I hadn't planned it in any way. The only stations I knew that were likely to have a connection with the war were Lympstone Commando, Y Fali and Bootle. Yet here I was at Dunrobin Castle, finding out not only that King George VI's brother Prince George* was killed during World War II in a seaplane crash but that his body was brought to the castle, which, inevitably, had become a hospital. All the other dead from the catastrophe (only one man out of 15 survived) were shipped off to Wick. It was clearly too late for the newly ex-Duke of Kent to avail himself of the services of a hospital, so presumably those who had taken charge of his remains felt that a magnificent castle overlooking the North Sea was more in keeping with his erstwhile position in life than whatever was on offer up at Wick. My only consolation in all this is that so far I've not read any claims that the prince was in the commandos.

Like Duncraig, Dunrobin Castle station began life as a private stop for a very rich and powerful man. And that's

---

* He was the proper George – his brother the king was born Albert Frederick Arthur George.

very nearly where the similarities end. Though completely remodelled in 1845, Dunrobin is no Victorian plaything for a member of the nouveau riche but has been the seat of the Earls and Dukes of Sutherland – one of Scotland's seven ancient earldoms – since 1235. Although there have been innumerable additions made to the structure since the 16th century, today's magnificent fairy-tale castle is the confection of Sir Charles Barry, the architect better known for knocking off London's Houses of Parliament. With its turrets topped with conical spires and its lush dressed stone of silver-grey, it doesn't bear any relationship to the first stone fortress on this spot, which was a simple square keep. We know this because, hidden away inside today's monolithic structure, that original keep still exists (albeit in a greatly altered form). It's the reason Dunrobin can make the boast that it is not only a fixture on the Highland tourist trail but also one of Scotland's oldest inhabited houses.

The one glaring blip in the castle's story came in the late 1960s when, out of the blue, it was turned into a boys' boarding school. The experiment lasted only seven years before sanity was restored.

But I'm getting ahead of myself. The station at Dunrobin Castle is very much in the once-seen-never-forgotten category. Its former waiting room is a wonderful black-and-white Arts and Crafts confection oozing workmanship from every finial. It was designed by someone called L Bisset in 1902 and resembles a little timber-framed cottage. It now serves as a museum of railway memorabilia. There's a shed, too, which I was told contained the Duke of Sutherland's own loco. This pulled his private carriage, which bears a passing resemblance to a gipsy caravan. There's a lovely old photo of it in one of the rooms downstairs in the castle.

I freewheeled down the sword-straight drive that leads from the station and took in the magnificence of the place. How come so many other supposedly great homes in Scotland have not looked upon Dunrobin and learned? Below the rock on which the castle stands, the gardens run all the way to the cliff edge. They're such a joy that it is difficult to say whether they are an adornment to the castle or the other way around. They are a bit of a cheat, though, since Barry cheekily stole their basic layout from Versailles. They're also owned by a cat nowadays – a dark smoky-grey long-haired individual who oversees them and their many visitors.

I have a possibly ill-judged fondness for Dingwall (almost certainly based on an admiration for its gloriously unhinged Gaelic name of Inbhir Pheofharain) and I had happily set up my tent in a campsite in the shadow of the stadium of the once lowly but now very nearly mighty Ross County FC. It was all a bit removed from my experience the previous night camping on Beasdale station. After a relaxed dinner of whatever food I had left all thrown into the pan, I found myself in the Mallard, a pub with one foot on the platform of Dingwall/Inbhir Pheofharain station.

At length, a lone man walked purposefully in, swiftly doubling the number of punters. He stood at the bar, this man, his body taut, his youth and hairline receding at roughly equal pace. I could tell in an instant that he was not the sort of happy-go-lucky type to walk into a pub and ask for a Tristram shandy. He bought a pint of lager, then, after two sips, he began muttering to himself. He let himself know that he hadn't been in this pub for years. In case he hadn't heard, he repeated the information. I sensed from his face and tone of mutter that this was not a happy homecoming. Then he turned his muttered ire on me, presumably because the barman had disappeared and I hadn't. He did not look at me as he muttered, but then he did not need to. He muttered about how much he disapproved of my activities. In case I hadn't heard, he repeated the information. A minimalist at heart, he rejoiced in his repeated use of a single well-known intensifier.

'Staring at a [expletive deleted] laptop all [expletive deleted] day then [expletive deleted] staring at it all [expletive deleted] evening.'

This was all before he'd got even halfway through his pint. I wondered if he was one of those men who get angrier as they get drunker. If so, he'd probably started off a bit strong there – if you begin with cold rage you've only got hot rage to go to and the evening was yet young. I wanted to point out that I hadn't actually been staring at a laptop all day. I had been on a ferry. I had been out on my bicycle pedalling across Skye. I had bought books that were comically huge and weighed more than Saturn. I had visited a castle and walked to a village once kept safe by Hamish Macbeth. I had been propelled here over another of Scotland's excessively beautiful railway lines. I had seen the request stops of Attadale, Achnashellach, Achanalt and Lochluichart. In *that* order. I had had a day that would bring joy to the heart of many folk. And anyway, this isn't a laptop but a tablet – if you're going to do shouty mutters, chum, get your basic hardware identification right.

I said none of these things, of course. I didn't even mutter them. Considering my day did make me happier, though, so in a strange way he had done me a favour. It also made me think that I should spend more days like that and fewer when I stare at a laptop all day then stare at it all evening. The mutterer downed his pint and ordered another, so to mutter all the more fulsomely. His humour was not improved when he belatedly asked for some dinner at 9.35 and was told that the kitchen closed at 9.30. He sank half his pint, banged the glass down on the counter and walked purposefully out, his world of Beckettian emptiness following like a cloud behind him. It was a pity there was no latter-day Mrs Cameron-Head in Dingwall or he could have gone round hers for some scran and sympathy.

What do you think would happen if we were all ascribed our own beehive cairn after we died, with an honest inscription to be written by those who outlived us? Would it make us better, kinder people? I idly began composing Mutterer's beehive epitaph.

Remember Matthew 'Mutt' Campbell of Dingwall?
1968–2013
He channelled his regrets into anger at others
And ordered food too late

Then, of course, I started thinking about what my own would say. But that was not a good place to go, so I went somewhere else instead.

TO ALTNABREAC

The very existence of a station at Altnabreac (it's pronounced *alt-na-brek*, by the way, with the emphasis on the *brek*) appears something of a mystery at first and even second glance. We do know that it was opened on 28 July 1874 and built by the Sutherland and Caithness Railway as a stop on their new line from the small village of West Helmsdale far to the south. West Helmsdale had become Scotland's most northerly station just four years previously, when the Duke of Sutherland's Railway took the line up the coast from the railhead at Golspie. The Sutherland and Caithness Line brought the railway network at last to the very top of Scotland and great was the rejoicing in the remote towns of Wick and Thurso, which hitherto had barely been accessible except by sea.

However, look at the Far North Line on a map and you'll instantly notice something very odd: rather than crossing the river at Helmsdale and continuing northeast along the coast to Wick, it veers off drunkenly inland, careering northwest then due north across a veritable no man's land. Only when it reaches the scattering of buildings that is Forsinard, some 20 miles from the coast, does it come to its senses and chart a course northeast towards Halkirk, a small grid-planned village between Wick and Thurso. On its way it racks up an impressive number of stations – take a moment in the sunshine, Kildonan, Kinbrace, Forsinard, Altnabreac and Scotscalder – but not a single village worthy of the name. Indeed, it's an act of generosity to say that these five stations even serve hamlets, for the word suggests a brave little cluster of houses. It's only when the line reaches Georgemas Junction that an actual centre of population – the aforementioned Halkirk – makes a blob on the map that is visible to the naked eye. It's no surprise to learn that, of the five stations, only Forsinard is not a request stop, presumably because it serves a moderately swish hotel that caters for people who want to shoot things.

So why does the railway line plough wilfully across a barely peopled wilderness, missing out the coastal villages between Helmsdale and Wick, which actually have some population to speak of?

According to Brian (we'll meet him in a moment), it was down to Lord Thurso, who he claimed was the driving force behind the scheme to bring the railway to the north coast. The peer was also keen to erect a hunting lodge at Altnabreac and the easiest way to get construction materials to such a remote spot was to take them by train. With this sole purpose in mind he devised a devious and circuitous cross-country route for the railway to follow, putting in stopping points along the way as if on a personal crusade to ensure that every single person in Caithness had their own station. Handily, this version of history also explains how Altnabreac came to have a station when there has never really been anything there to merit one.

Brian's supposition somewhat clashes with the most popular theory you'll hear rolled out by railway enthusiasts, namely that the station was built to serve the nearby hotel, which is plainly marked on current OS maps. This might hold some water if it weren't for the fact that the hotel was built after the station was opened. We know this because the hotel is, in fact, a later incarnation of Lord Thurso's hunting lodge. It should also be noted that the Ordnance Survey has been less than slick in its updating of the map that covers this area, since the hotel closed down in the 1970s. Pity the poor fool caught out in a storm who drags himself across the desolate bog in the hope that the hotel shown on his map might have a room for the night and a chef at large in the kitchen.

Sadly, it appears that Brian's theory regarding the routing of the Far North Line is also a little off beam. My research suggests that the hunting lodge was constructed in 1895, a full 21 years after the line was built. If this date is correct, either Lord Thurso had very slow builders or the idea of opening a hunting lodge struck him somewhat after the railway came into being.

It turns out that the actual reason for the apparently bizarre behaviour of the line is somewhat less fanciful and comes in the shape of the Ord of Caithness. Just to the north of Helmsdale, this great wedge of high ground flush to the coast would have provided quite a challenge to the Victorian engineers charged with building the line. It thus proved far less taxing to dodge around the obstacle by following the Strath of Kildonan inland before heading north over what is relatively flat terrain. Dull, I know, but truth is sometimes less strange than fiction.

Beside me as I write this sits a business card. I'm not, as a rule, a keeper of business cards. Indeed, several times a year I have a thorough clear-out and I'm routinely surprised at how often the names on the cards bring to mind no recollection whatsoever of the human beings they represent.

However, the card next to me right now is one I'm definitely hanging on to, for it will serve as a reminder – not that a reminder will ever be strictly necessary – of one of the most extraordinary experiences of my life. It is not, after all, every day that a fear of your own imminent murder is leavened by the thought that at least it would save you from a rather more unpleasant fate.

What is all the more remarkable is that the following events took place in the vicinity of the most remote station on my itinerary, a place girded round by peat-black lochs and dismal bogs and overshadowed by dark, anonymous plantations of doomed conifers, where nothing of any note has happened these past 70 years save for intense despondent brooding.

So this is the story of Altnabreac and what I discovered there. It is also a salutary tale of how a series of little events, entirely innocent taken in isolation, can assume the form of something monstrous, skewing one's perception of reality so completely that everyday life appears to have morphed into a horror film.

Let us start with that business card. It is a simple affair: it bears a saltire under which sits the title of the man who gave it to me, the title of his wife, their address and, finally, their email address. A friend who is anorak-keen on fonts tells me that the typeface used throughout is English 111 Vivace BT, otherwise known as Shelley Allegro Script, both of which names seem incongruous for a business card emanating from the far north of Scotland. The titles are in black, with the remaining details in blue on a background the colour of cream that has gone missing at the back of the fridge.

The address is succinct – two words and a postcode suffice to distinguish the house from all others and give its approximate location, though the postcode is apparently not one that is often punched into a satnav, for I was the first casual visitor to drop by in four years.

But arguably the card's most interesting feature is its lack of phone number, which is, I suspect, the sort of thing Sherlock Holmes would have referred to as 'singular'. I confess that I also find it rather admirable. I was, after all, the last person of working age in England to purchase a mobile phone.

Perhaps the card's lack of mobile number is merely down to a dearth of coverage in the area around Altnabreac – with a population of less than a tenth of a person per square mile it's easy to see why it might be overlooked. However, I would have thought that there were landlines even in these remote parts, though I can't say for sure that I saw any telegraph poles. Perhaps the gentleman who gave me the card is simply not a telephone-y person – it's not a crime, after all.

Finally, I should add that the card is laminated. The two sheets of clear plastic that encase it overlap the card by some margin, making it difficult to slip into my wallet, whose little pocket was doubtless designed to accommodate cards whose owners have not believed the waterproofing of their contact details to be strictly necessary. I can't help but get the impression that the lamination is also sending the message that this is a card the donor intends the recipient to keep, and perhaps to cherish too. It is not a card to be idly discarded.

So much for the interrogation of the business card. My own one says 'Nothing to see here' in tiny letters on the back, which perhaps says more about me than I'd care to admit.

Anyway, the man who gave me this one also asked me not to mention his name in this book, a request to which I shall scrupulously adhere. I'm not even going to mention the title by which he goes on his card. I shall call him Brian and we'll be seeing a lot of him later.

When I alighted at Altnabreac on that moderately sunny Tuesday afternoon in June, I had, of course, no inkling of what was about to befall me. Perhaps that's as well or I might have opted to forgo the excitement and stay on the train all the way to safe, welcoming Thurso. Would my life have been the poorer for it? I'll let you decide.

ALTNABREAC

When at last I emerged from my train at Altnabreac, I was a little dismayed to note that there were a couple of houses right next to the station. This didn't tally with the mental picture I had drawn of it from looking at maps or indeed the admittedly vague memories I had of the station from previous trips to Thurso. I was expecting – indeed longing for – desolation on a grand scale and a station building that was mouldering sullenly; instead here was a prim bungalow.

Understandably deflated, I turned my attention to the station itself. At least this did not disappoint, for it was impossible to say quite where it ended and the wilds began. The slowly disintegrating paving slabs that marked the edge of the platform and the strip of gravel that formed the platform itself were definitely station matter, as was the little wooden shelter bearing the obligatory 'Keep Scotland Beautiful – Tidy Station – Bronze Award'. (I'd seen these Tidy Station Bronze Awards all over Scotland but never a silver or a gold – though it's possible, of course, that my mere presence on such stations meant they were instantly downgraded.) Everything else was up for debate – trees, pink-flowered ribes bushes and fetching violets had begun to colonise the greensward that swept in from outside the station and which was itself only kept from taking full control of the platform by the band of gravel.

The platform on the far side of what had once been two tracks – for Altnabreac once boasted a passing loop – provided a form of time travel. All that was left to show that it had once felt the scuffle of passengers' footwear was the row of undulating slabs that formed the platform's outer limits. In time, even these would disappear beneath an enveloping shroud of grass and the burial would be complete. Of all the stations I had seen on my tour, many of which had succumbed in part to the irrepressible will of the natural world, Altnabreac was the one that had been most subsumed, and the most likely simply to disappear one day under a mat of green.

Beside the abandoned platform stood a water tank, the railway world's equivalent of the castle keep. A sturdy stone-built oblong with a cistern on top, the structure looked in surprisingly good order, given that – apart from the very occasional heritage trip to Thurso – the last steam train passed through here in 1962. Granted, the cistern was a uniform rust-orange, but it took no great leap of imagination to see a locomotive standing patiently beneath it taking on water before chuffing off into the desert beyond.

On closer inspection, this outwardly proud keep had more the look of a ruined cathedral. A door at one end was greeted at the other by a tall window, now merely a cavity, through which sunshine teemed onto the flag-stoned floor. The altar, pulpit and pews were missing, the light instead falling on the detritus of one person's former home. An armchair, unfolded into a bumpy bed-like state, cut the space in two, while a large orange washing-up bowl full of saucepans and lids sat on the floor beside a mould-ridden wooden chair. In one corner, blue plastic sheeting covered a pile of something I had no desire to see, while another corner had been used as a midden for things plastic, things smashed and things identifiable only by dental records.

Judging by the rust and dust on the saucepans, this home from home had not been used for some considerable time. Nevertheless, I was careful not to move anything, so that if the erstwhile occupier came back one day they wouldn't feel that their space had been violated. Nobody likes that.

Ironically, I'd planned to spend the night at Altnabreac myself, perhaps even camping on the grassy verge of the platform, and taking the first train up to Thurso the next morning. This was due to breeze through at a highly civilised 10.32, leaving me nearly 21 hours to while away. I envisaged another blissful Zen-like sojourn *à la* Sugar Loaf, since I knew that the sole attraction in these parts was the ruins of the hotel about a mile away. However, I was surprised to find, along with the habitual Onward Travel Information Board (highlight: 'Useful Information: The nearest taxi rank is located in Halkirk' – it might perhaps have been more useful to point out that this is an 18-mile walk away), a large framed poster at the station advertising the delights of a circular 16.5-mile trail for walkers, mountain bikers and horse riders that passed right by the station. The poster claimed that the route followed 'well-defined tracks' and, rather conveniently, went straight past the hotel, which meant I could take some suitably morose photographs of whatever was left of it.

The poster, having promised me that I would see hen harriers and bogbeans on my way, issued me with a stern warning: 'Visitors are encouraged to take precautions similar to hill walking. At the very least it is suggested that you carry an up-to-date map, suitable clothing and footwear, packed lunch, a mobile phone and leave word with someone about your route and estimated time of return.' Although I cheerily ticked the boxes concerning clothing and footwear and had plenty of food and water with me, I came up rather short on all the other requirements. My only map was a blurry monochrome small-scale A4 affair I'd printed off at home; I had no mobile, and the only person on the entire planet who knew I was here was the train guard. Still, if you spend your life not risking anything, you barely get to live at all.

Although I had time enough to walk the circuit before nightfall, I reasoned that if I rode my bike I could pedal very gently around and still be back within a couple of hours, thus barely eating into my precious station-based Zen time. Also, it looked as if it might come on to rain later, so cycling gave me a far better chance of being back in time to sit out any deluge in the comfort of the station shelter. I duly set off, quickly passing the only other house in the vicinity besides the prim bungalow. The building had been the primary school up until 1986. A sign affixed to a wall proclaimed, with laudable ambition, 'Altnabreac DC – Twinned with Washington DC'.

Pootling carefully along, enjoying the mini-rollercoaster rides down and up the little dells in the track and glad there had been no rain to fill them, I turned a corner beyond a plantation and the ruined hotel came abruptly into view, standing alone beside a dark lochan. Except that it wasn't a ruined hotel. It was now a completely restored ruined hotel with what looked like a large warehouse tacked on behind it. A hulk of a building, the house made up for its lack of height – a mere two storeys – with a double-gabled frontage, which I discovered later was actually merely a side, and, at one corner, a mock Gothic octagonal tower topped with a turret at whose peak flew the white-on-dark-blue cross of St Andrew.

The building's ochre brickwork stood in unsettling contrast to its woodwork, which appeared to have been freshly coated a bright blood red, as if in readiness for the coming of the Passover angel. Or perhaps these gable ends and dormer windows represented upturned mouths, daubed with lipstick of a shade favoured by 1950s Hollywood starlets. Above them the steeply shelved roofs had been peppered with a dozen or more chimney pots.

The sky, which only a few minutes before had been largely blue and speckled with just the odd gathering cloud, now framed the pile in a dark mass as if it had sucked into itself the colour of the grey slate roofs. For all the house's pristine appearance – if I'd been told that the builders had cleared up and left just a few hours beforehand I wouldn't have been at all surprised – the overall effect was disquieting. The mock Gothic tower on its own might have passed itself off as merely quirky, but twinned with the blood-red paintwork it hinted at something more sinister. Had there been a garden in front of the house it might have softened the scene, made it a little more human, but there was none – the tufted wild grasses of the moor went all but up to the walls, held back only by a stony drive.

So much for first impressions. When I'd got over the shock of discovering that the decaying hotel I had had in my mind's eye for months was nothing of the sort, I noticed that there was a car parked beside the house. Perhaps there was somebody at home? And if there was somebody at home they might be able to fill me in on a few facts about the building's former lives as a hotel and a hunting lodge and I could ask a cheeky question about the counter-cultural choice of exterior colours and then be on my way. I cycled up the drive.

I rang the bell and, as I stood by the front door (which I later discovered was merely a side door), a movement inside the house caught my eye. In a small, barely furnished room, what appeared to be a silver tabby cat was sitting on a table, eyeing me with something akin to disdain. Their innate aloofness is one of the many reasons why cats are superior to dogs and I smiled winningly through the window at this striking representative of his species. In reply, I received only a narrowing of the eyes. I was not to know that this encounter would mark the high point of our friendship.

There being no other response from the household, I was just turning back to my bike to continue on my way when the door opened. I was greeted by a casually dressed but imposing man – I'm just over six foot one and I had to look up – whom I guessed to be in his mid-fifties. I found it hard to place his accent – he could have come from anywhere south of the border and north of Birmingham. A small and thin teenage boy peeped round him. I explained my mission to the man and he invited me in. We walked along a long corridor to a small light-filled octagonal room which was evidently the ground floor of the Gothic tower. We sat in two large armchairs and Brian and I began to talk.

My initial line of questioning concerned the house. I admitted I'd not expected to see it in anything more than a state of total dilapidation.

'It became a hotel in 1960, but closed in 1971,' Brian informed me.* 'It was built by Lord Thurso as a hunting lodge originally.'

It was here that he told me about the railway line apparently being re-routed to bring in the materials necessary for the building of the lodge.

'I bought the house in 1985,' he continued. 'I was living abroad and my sister rang me to say she'd found the perfect place for me to live. So when I was next back in the country we came up to have a look at it. There was a very odd atmosphere to the building, though, and we were so scared by it that we literally ran from room to room and didn't dare go upstairs.'

As Brian began to give out more of the story surrounding the purchase I regretted that I'd never been able to knuckle down and learn shorthand. I also regretted that I'd left my notebook in one of the panniers of my bike. However, I scribbled fast enough around the edges of my small-scale map to be able to tell you that prior to moving into the house – which he only got around to doing in 2004 – he had lived in Africa, America and India. In the first he was doing some sort of noble development work and in the last he was a teacher. I don't think I ever found out what he was doing in America. He did tell me, though, that he paid £30,000 for the house when he bought it, ultimately undeterred by the very odd atmosphere. And in case you're thinking that £30,000 is a pittance – for that is what I

---

* I've since read elsewhere that the hotel closed in 1975, but as that elsewhere was the internet, I'll give this one to Brian.

proclaimed – it was apparently a tidy enough sum in 1985, a fact Brian was quick to impress upon me. I wanted to ask how he could afford a mortgage of that size at the age of – I guessed – about 25 if up until then he had chiefly been engaged in development work. I thought better of it, though. I was, after all, a guest in his house. It's qualms such as these that have kept me from a career as a thrusting investigative reporter.

'It was completely derelict when I bought it and the turret on the tower – the one above us here – had fallen in,' Brian continued, pointing upwards. 'It took four years' work to make the house basically habitable again. I had four friends come up from Newcastle and we rebuilt it using my own designs, including for the swimming pool.'

Ah, so that explained the apparent warehouse I'd identified from the road.

It was then that Brian said the first thing – of rather a lot of things – that made the hairs on the back of my neck prickle.

'I've also built an underground chapel beneath the house because I want to be buried here when I die.'

Building a chapel so you can be buried beneath the house you live in is perfectly normal behaviour. I'm sure many of my friends have done the same, but have never found quite the right time to tell me about it. Indeed, the only thing stopping me from building my own underground mausoleum is that I live in a first-floor flat and the elderly woman downstairs keeps taking my shovel away.

I nodded my head and made a kind of strangulated noise in my throat that, I hoped, expressed mildly surprised admiration. But Brian was on a roll.

'Rudolf Hess was hidden in this house for a while during the war.'

'Gosh!' I exclaimed, already beginning to wonder whether my publishers would frown if my final chapter took up half the book.

When I arrived at Lochdhu – the house being named after the 'black loch' next to which it squats – I knew as much about Rudolf Hess as the next British adult with a passing interest in 20th-century history. If pressed, I'd have told you that he was a high-up Nazi officer who flew to Scotland in the early part of World War II – 1940, perhaps 1941 – to try to negotiate a peace settlement with Britain. His plans came to nothing, however, and he was held captive until the end of the war. He was tried at Nuremberg and incarcerated in Spandau Prison, where, after several decades, he famously became the only inmate. He died in the prison a very old man. I even vaguely remember hearing a news report of his death. Oh, and there was some conspiracy theory in which it was claimed that the man in Spandau was not the real Rudolf Hess at all. And that's it.

What Brian was about to tell me significantly improved my mastery of the life and times of the former German Deputy Führer. Or at least my mastery of one particular theory about his life and times.

'There was a dramatic attempt to rescue Hess made by the Duke of Kent – the second in line to the throne at the time,' Brian began when I pressed him for details. My ears pricked up all the more on hearing this, for I had stumbled upon the news of Prince George's fate only that day.

'He and his co-conspirators took off in a seaplane from Loch More, just over there.' Brian pointed a finger roughly east. 'They were going to take Hess off to a peace conference in Sweden, but they crashed or the plane was shot down. It took a day to find the wreckage and when they did so they found 14 bodies – no survivors. No, actually, there was one survivor who went crawling across the moor and was discovered the next day. The whole thing was covered up, of course, because having the king's brother involved in such a plot would have been a great scandal. There's a little monument somewhere out on the moors, but I expect it's been grown over by now and it would take you forever to find it – it would be like finding a needle in a haystack. Look, shall we continue this in the pool room?'

Brian led the way, apologising over his shoulder that he hadn't offered me anything to drink – I'd been there half an hour or so by then. 'I'm afraid my wife's not in and I don't know how to make tea or coffee,' he explained.

I'll grant you he sounded a little abashed by this admission but, even so, it's a very odd thing in this day and age to come across an adult whose life skills do not run to the making of tea and coffee. I'd only once come across the phenomenon before and then the subject was a Guatemalan man in his early twenties who had only just left home and whose mother and sisters had always made him his coffee (he'd never tasted tea). I took him into the kitchen and opened his eyes to the deep and mysterious ways of the kettle and the teaspoon. I would happily have offered to train Brian up as well, but I was already thinking how nice it would be to leave. Call me a wimp if you will, but I was in a creepy house in the middle of nowhere, miles from the nearest neighbour (Brian told me that no one lived at either of the two houses by the station), with a silent boy and a large man who had told me within five minutes of my meeting him that he'd built himself an underground chapel and tomb, and who now professed an inability to make tea or coffee. Also, as he mentioned this, I noticed that the walls of a corridor heading off to the right of us had been painted with copies of Ancient Egyptian murals.

Now, as we've discussed, memory is a fickle thing. Although the events I'm recalling here occurred very recently and I'm referring to notes I took at the time, my memory has already begun to come unstuck. Half of my brain tells me quite vehemently that this was the first time I had seen copies of Ancient Egyptian murals in the house. The other half tells me that there were Ancient Egyptians processing around the walls of the little octagonal tower room in which we first talked. Let's just say that as Brian's coffee/tea admission was rending the air I became aware for the first time that the house was absolutely teeming with Ancient Egyptian figures. Either way, it did nothing to curb the growing realisation that something here was not at all right.

We happened at that moment to be passing the kitchen. Brian's son, whom I thought he called Kenny, was loitering outside it. Brian had a brainwave.

'Kenny,' he declared, 'you know how to make tea and coffee, don't you?'

Kenny nodded his assent – his mother had taught him. Not wanting to go through the whole 'do you have soya milk?' rigmarole that is the besetting characteristic of vegan life, I opted for a black tea.

'Thank you. We'll be in the pool room,' Brian called back to his son as we pressed on.

As we turned this way and that on our way there I professed wonder at the immense size of the house.

'Yes, and the walls are two feet thick, you know. It used to have 25 bedrooms but we've got that down to nine now – I knocked three bedrooms through just to make my office. And there are ten bathrooms.'

'So you've got one more bathroom than you have bedrooms?'

'Yes.' He smiled, acknowledging the peculiarity of the arrangement.

'And your office must be a good size. Do you mind if I ask you what you do?'

'Oh, this and that,' came the reply. I nodded and said nothing, waiting for Brian to elucidate, but he didn't.

At length we left the corridors behind and came out into a well-equipped gym, complete with punchbag the shape and size of a man. I was so on edge by this time that I was ready to read ill omens even into this, for I could not believe that it was the lean and lightweight Kenny who spent any time punching the man. I told myself it was better not to think about it and, anyway, one door later we were through to the pool room.

To most people, a pool room would be a room with a pool table in it, and if you owned a house with enough space to have its own pool room, you might consider yourself to be one of life's fortunate winners, at least in financial terms. Brian's pool room, naturally, contained a huge swimming pool, its waters hidden by a retractable cover.

My host explained how the high sloping ceiling was created from some super-advanced material fresh out of the lab. It had to be poured in and left to shrink into position or something, and it was guaranteed never to go mouldy, so he never had to have it cleaned. I didn't take it all in because I was too busy staring at the Ancient Egyptian figures that lined the entire length of the wall behind the pool.

In a corner at the far end of the room, a big comfortable-looking settee and armchairs were grouped around the largest television I've ever seen. The sound was low but to compensate for this the screen was blasting out swathes of lurid orange: a tennis court at Roland Garros, as it transpired, for the French Open was on. In the other corner at that end was a shining, shimmering bar stocked with a vast pyramid of bottles on the wall behind it.

'Your friends must love you,' I said, nodding towards the lavish leisure facilities on offer.

'What friends?' Brian replied.

He was half-joking. At least I thought at first that he was half-joking. Then I realised that he wasn't really joking at all.

Earlier he had mentioned his 'four friends from Newcastle' but, now I came to think of it, they made an appearance only in the context of renovating his house and digging the swimming pool. Perhaps they were only friends when he had work to offer them. In fact, I began to consider the possibility that when Brian had said I was the first person to drop by in four years he didn't mean the first stranger to wander in off the path but the first person of any sort.

We made our way to the big armchairs. Like the ones in the octagonal room, they were wide, contemporary and enveloping, inviting the sitter to crash back into them and assume a mien of complete relaxation. I sat well forward in mine, pen poised above the small-scale map perched on my knee. I had all but filled the borders around it with notes, despite having written in a hand so small I wouldn't be able to decipher it myself until I'd rescued my reading glasses from a pannier on my bike.

We returned to the subject of Rudolf Hess. This was good because a plain old conspiracy theory about a leading Nazi was something normal to cling on to among all the abnormalities that surrounded me. I liked having the tok-tok-tok of the French Open in the background too, for it reminded me that there, just out of my line of vision, were normal people doing normal things in a world outside this house. My friend Fiona had gone to Paris to watch the tennis and she might even be in the crowd at the match that was on now. But there was no time to think of that, for Brian had resumed his narration of the Deputy Führer's story and its connection with the house. I scribbled on, minutely.

Before I go on, I should perhaps mention that some elements of the part of the Hess story that I have related thus far aren't strictly correct. Brian mentioned that he had garnered his information from a book called *Double Standards: The Rudolf Hess Cover-up* by Lynn Picknett, Clive Prince and Stephen Prior. Since then I've read the relevant passages and it appears that Brian's memory had played one or two tricks on him.

The first error was a very small one, really. The Duke of Kent was not second but fifth in line to the throne at the time of his death. Had his brother George VI died (or abdicated, as their oldest brother Edward had done) in that summer of 1942, the crown would have gone to his 16-year-old daughter Elizabeth. Next in line was her younger sister Margaret (and what an interesting queen *she* would have made), followed by George's brother Henry, Duke of Gloucester (having skipped past Mary, the Princess Royal, who was pushed down the list by her younger brothers, in keeping with the straightforward sexism inherent in the rules of succession to the British throne). In 1941, the year before the crash, Henry and his wife Alice had a son called William (royal watchers will know that this was the man after whom the current Prince William was named) who would thus have been fourth in line, with the younger of the Georges slotting in only after that. All this proved rather academic, of course, since Elizabeth became queen ten years later and had already mustered up two children of her own, thus kiboshing any title hopes her surviving uncle, aunt and cousins might have harboured. But still, second in line, fifth in line, what does it matter?

Back with Hess, there doesn't appear to be any evidence that the seaplane in which the Duke was flying was shot down – it seems to have rather unambiguously crashed into the side of a hill without the aid of outside agencies. The poor visibility at the time of the crash is a much more likely cause. As for the little monument somewhere out on the moors that would take forever to find, it turned out to be a tall grey stone cross on a plinth and is actually clearly marked as 'monument' on OS maps of the area. It's about two and a half miles southeast of a hamlet called Braemore.

If you can't quite get up the enthusiasm to go and see it for yourself, there's a number of photos of it that hikers have posted on the internet.

Right, now that's all cleared up we can move on.

Brian told me about some of the apparent evidence that the three authors of *Double Standards* used to back up the claim that it was a fake Hess who had been kept in Spandau. This all added weight to the theory that the real Hess had died in the plane crash, which meant that he must have been held prisoner in the vicinity of Loch More, from where the seaplane took off. And what was by far the largest and therefore most appropriate dwelling in the area of Loch More? The house at Lochdhu.

'What's more,' Brian continued, 'Lord Thurso's chauffeur was adamant that during that period of the war he had made deliveries to the house of German goods intended to make Hess's stay here more comfortable. In fact, a strange thing happened when my four friends from Newcastle were helping me dig the swimming pool – we found German beer bottles that dated from the early forties.'

With this exciting revelation hanging in the air I discovered that I had completely filled the margins of my sheet of paper with the small-scale map on it.

'Do you mind if I just go and grab my notebook?' I asked. 'It's in one of my panniers outside.'

He claimed not to mind, so I attempted to make my way back to my bike. Brian had told me the shortest route through the house and I followed his instructions back past the punchbag man and down a dark corridor or two until I reached a door I thought I recognised. When I opened it, my ears were immediately assailed by a scream within. Though I saw nothing, I instantly slammed the door shut, my heart thumping away somewhere north of my chest.

Now, don't get me wrong, I like cats. No, actually, I *love* cats. I have a deep affinity with cats. Cats whose owners say, 'That's funny, little Felix/Suki/Dave doesn't normally like strangers,' greet me like a long-lost friend. But the noise I heard when I opened that door was not that of a cat greeting me. It was the noise of a cat who wanted to rip my throat out and dine on it. For this was no ordinary moggy, and no silver tabby either: this was an Egyptian Mau. Probably descended from African wild cats, the Mau has a top speed of a little over 30mph and was used by the Ancient Egyptians as a hunting cat. Presumably, if I looked closely enough at the murals, I'd find him there.

I suddenly realised just how fortunate I had been that a window had come between us when we first met. I looked at my watch. How could it possibly have been only an hour ago? I had aged two at least. What's more, this fresh encounter had unsettled me again just when the prolonged discussion about Rudolf Hess had eased the needle on the oddness detector back a notch or two.

Still unable to find my way out, it dawned on me that I was in the same corridor in which Brian and I had bumped into Kenny. I strode down to the kitchen. The lad was still there, making our tea and coffee. It had taken him about 20 minutes so far, bless him, and I could see nothing to indicate that either of our orders would be speeding its way towards the pool room any time soon. I hoped he hadn't been looking up instructions on the internet. He stopped what he wasn't doing and told me the way out.

Back in my chair with my notebook now balanced on my knee, I attempted to glean more information about the house or the railway station. I didn't mention the incident with the cat.

Somehow, instead of talking about things local, we got onto the subject of the long periods of time Brian had spent in various continents before settling down in Altnabreac. He painted his story in broad brushstrokes, which I generally find an admirable trait in a conversationalist. However, I couldn't help feeling that he was doing it less to avoid being boring and more because it was the easiest way to remain evasive without seeming to be so. Mind you, I was a total stranger, so I could hardly upbraid him for not revealing every detail of his life to me. I had to remember that, interested though I was in this unarguably idiosyncratic man, I was not his biographer.

It didn't stop me from digging a little deeper than was perhaps polite, though. When the conversation erupted some other item of huge expense that Brian had stumped up for, I took the opportunity of asking him what the 'this and that' that he had told me he did for a living actually consisted of.

'I got lucky with the horses,' he conceded. 'And this,' he added, pointing towards the television. 'Tok tok tok,' went the television in reply. No friendly face of Fiona flashing up on the screen, though.

That was clearly his final word on the matter and the conversation moved on. Then, in the midst of some generalities about his time in Asia, he suddenly declared, 'I married the daughter of a headhunter in Borneo once.'

'Of course you did,' I replied.

I know that's a line that is routinely presented with a side salad of sarcasm, but in this instance I actually meant it. Knowing what I already knew about Brian, I found this latest piece of information quite in keeping with his character. It almost demanded it, in fact. I could tell that he had no doubts about my sincerity, because he looked pleased that I should expect nothing less of him than to have made such an outwardly outlandish match.

'She loved it over here,' he continued. 'She enjoyed going out and killing animals. And she'd throw a net over the loch and catch huge quantities of trout.'

'So, that's interesting,' I thought. It certainly filled in some of the gaps about his wife, whom we'll call Sandie for want of a better name. Previously, all I had known about her was that she was out and about in a car. In the octagonal room, Brian and I had been talking about how far away from everything the house was – it was almost ten miles from the nearest road and 18 from Halkirk, the closest proper village – and he had mentioned as corroborative evidence that his two eldest sons attended some college or other that involved a two-hour school run twice a day. His wife, he added, did both trips every day. The only other thing I knew about her was that she could make tea and coffee and evidently did so at all times for Brian and, presumably, every time Kenny didn't have a spare half-hour to make himself one.

But that last word of Brian's declaration nagged at me a bit: 'I married the daughter of a headhunter in Borneo *once*.' It did rather suggest they weren't together any more. However, asking him whether he was still married to her would have been an insensitive step too far. I also had the horrible feeling that he'd tell me she was dead and then my imagination would run wild as to how she died. Frankly, it felt safer to imagine her in a car heading for home with her two elder sons playing video games in the back. That said, I couldn't help slyly scanning Kenny's face later for signs that he could be half-Bornean.

Since no further information about Sandie was going to be vouchsafed, we pressed on to other topics.

'In Africa I was diagnosed with terminal cancer of the spine.'

I'm afraid I've let the side down here because I cannot recall anything else about this particular episode, aside from the fact that Brian does *not* have cancer of the spine now, terminal or otherwise. By the time I'd recorded this initial pronouncement in my notebook he'd moved on. Thus I cannot tell you whether he was miraculously cured or merely misdiagnosed. I like to think it was the former – anything else would be a disappointment. Had I been engaged in a more conventional conversation, this revelation would doubtless have blazed like a beacon. As it was, there were so many other infernos burning wildly amid our colloquy that this little fire went almost unnoticed.

Brian was now talking about the time he spent in India and, specifically, his three-month stint as a teacher. At which point Kenny came in at last with a tray and two mugs. My black tea was made perfectly. If he'd had half a dozen goes at it before producing this one it had been well worth it. He sat on the settee near us and began to watch the tennis. However, I got the impression that being near us was the reason he was sitting watching the tennis, and I felt rather sorry for him, not for the first time that afternoon.

'Where were you teaching?' I asked Brian.

'Up in the north,' he replied.

At which point I had a premonition – I knew exactly which school he was going to say. I really didn't want my hunch to be correct and, given the vast number of schools that must exist in northern India, the chances of it being so were absurdly slim, but an instinct told me that it would overcome these odds.

'The school was near ...' Brian continued, 'oh, what's the name of that place?'

I wanted to say, 'Shimla,' but stayed quiet.

He turned and asked Kenny, calling him by a name that clearly wasn't Kenny at all, but which was like no name I'd ever heard before either – a mere jumble of syllables. Not-Kenny didn't know. Then a light bulb went on above Brian's head.

'Simla! That's it.'

'Ah yes. Though I believe they call it Shimla nowadays,' I said, just for the sake of saying something. And because I'm a terrible pedant.

'No, it's *Simla*,' Brian insisted. I decided not to challenge him on it.

'And the school was ...?'

'Sanawar,' he declared. '*Send him to Sanawar and make a man of him*, as Kipling said.'

Sanawar or, to give it its full name, the Lawrence School, Sanawar, happened to be where my father was educated (well before Brian was there). It's a boarding school in the Kasauli Hills and I recall being told that you can see Everest from the playground, though you'd be wise not to quote me on that. The forested campus apparently spreads over

139 acres, so for all I know the school may not even have a formal playground as such. My father found himself growing up there because his father was in the Air Force and forever stationed in one or other far-flung corner of India. So, for nine straight months out of every twelve, my father Michael would be at Sanawar and then bravely head off to wherever his parents were to join them for what was left of the year.

If I put myself in my father's shoes and imagine being packed off to boarding school and, worse still, having to endure one endless term every year, I am filled with dread. My father, however, loved it and thrived – spending a great deal of his time climbing trees, according to what he told my mother. He certainly doesn't appear to have made any great scholarly or sporting impact during his time there. I have a few of the Sanawar magazines and have scoured them in vain for a mention of his name among the prize-winners. He didn't even make any of the lists of team members or the results for the school's legendary cross-country runs. But perhaps that's exactly why he enjoyed it there so much.

I barely knew my father – he died when I was four – and I'm a little protective of his memory, even though I have only one very blurred and momentary memory of him myself. Yet somehow I still haven't made it over to India to see where he grew up or where he lived as an adult, and it rankled slightly that Brian had a much better idea of the place where my father spent his formative years than I did. He'd got the Kipling quotation right too – it's up on one of the gymnasium walls at the school and comes from his novel *Kim*.

It was at this juncture in the conversation that I discovered Kenny's real name. I had asked Brian something that involved Kenny tangentially and I found myself having to use his name while simultaneously apologising for not having grasped what it was.

'It's Khenemet,' Brian said.*

But then it would be, wouldn't it? An Ancient Egyptian name for a boy whose father was clearly obsessed with Ancient Egyptians and who wanted to be buried like an Ancient Egyptian beneath his palace. A shiver went up my spine, but Brian was looking over at Khenemet so he missed it.

'Could you spell that for me?' I asked the boy. He seemed pleased to be involved in the conversation.

'It's K–h–e–n–e–m–e–t,' he said softly, remaining patient when I read it back to him with one of the letters wrong.

'You must get bored having to spell it out to everyone,' I joked.

'No, he doesn't,' his father interjected.

At first I thought he meant that his son didn't get bored with spelling out his name, but then it became apparent that he meant that the only reason he didn't get bored spelling out his name was that there was never any need to do so.

I wanted to say, 'What? Don't you ever meet anyone new?' but I couldn't have borne the meek shaking head I'd have been presented with. It was at this point that it came out that Khenemet was home-schooled by his father. I sighed inwardly. 'So, Khenemet,' I thought, 'you have no friends and your two older brothers are at college all day.' It

---

* To protect the innocent, I've not used his real name, which was just as Egyptian, if not more so. The name 'Kenny' is also fictitious.

certainly went some way to explaining his demeanour of quiet obeisance.

Then it was Brian's turn to become chief inquisitor. It seemed only fair. After all, there are few things worse than a conversation with someone who asks no questions about you. He wanted to know about the books I'd written and, specifically, how many copies they'd sold. You'd think that this was the sort of enquiry authors have to deal with all the time but in my experience most people are far too polite to make it. Or perhaps they're exceptionally rude because they're so sure that the numbers are pitifully small that it would be embarrassing for all concerned if I felt obliged to reveal them. After I'd told him how my last book had done he revealed his reason for asking: he was a bit of a publisher on the side.

'I need to get some advice on marketing, really, because the last book I published only sold ...' and then he told me how many copies he had shifted. It was a small number, though not pitifully so.

'What's your genre?' I asked. If he was publishing poetry, for example, then the figure he had quoted was actually not too disastrous.

'The occult,' he replied, and the words fell on the floor between us to lurk there like a dark, unpleasant shadow. In the brief silence that followed, the needle on the oddness detector slid forward several notches.

'Have you heard of Dr Kenealy?' he asked me. I confessed that I hadn't. 'He was the wisest man Britain's seen in the last 600 years.'

Brian's chosen time span struck me as interesting, since he went on to explain that Dr Kenealy had lived out his days in the 19th century. I wondered for a moment what man in the early 1400s had outwised the worthy doctor. Meanwhile, Brian lamented the fact that so few people had heard of Kenealy, given that he had a number of strings to his bow (including, as it happened, proficiency as a violinist). He began to pluck them one by one.

'He was an MP, a poet, the barrister involved in the Tichborne Claimant case – have you heard of that?'

That one did ring a bell, though I had no idea why, and, humiliatingly, I had to ask Brian to spell Tichborne for me so I got it down right.

'And he was Head of the Order of the Druids.' Then I understood why Brian was such a big fan.

Abashed at my ignorance of the wisest man Britain's seen in 600 years, I've since done a little research into Dr Edward Vaughan Hyde Kenealy QC (though he *was* a Queen's Counsel, the 'Dr' was mere affectation). I can't tell a lie – he didn't immediately strike me as a man of wisdom. Indeed, his bizarre, eccentric and sometimes violent behaviour in the Tichborne Claimant case – in which he unsuccessfully defended an impostor who attempted to claim a large inheritance – caused his disbarment the following year. His main claim to fame, it seemed to me, lay in his needlessly dragging out this particular trial for 188 days, with the result that it became the longest one in English legal history at the time. Kenealy also published reams of poetry in journals and several books of mysticism, a brand-new edition of one of which Brian kindly gave me. He told me he'd spent 22 years searching for a copy of the same book and, when he found one, had forked out so vast a sum for it that, when he told me, I hardly believed it possible. He asked me not to mention its title when I came to write this book and, having failed to find enlightenment through its contents, I can assure you I don't think you're missing out by my adherence to his request. I know, I'm a terrible ingrate.

At least I discovered why Brian had mentioned the 600 years thing. Kenealy had calculated that that was the period in between each of the 11 messiahs who had walked among us, starting with Adam and taking in a star-studded list including Zarathustra, Moses, Jesus, Mohammed and Genghis Khan. As far as I can gather, the twelfth messiah appeared to be Kenealy himself, conveniently filling in the vacant 1800s slot. But I digress.

'Where are you staying tonight, by the way?'

The question caught me off guard and I simply offered up the truth. 'I'm just going to wild camp near the station. Maybe even on the platform on that grassy bit.'

The words were no sooner out of my mouth than I wished I could have pulled them back in. My mind swam with visions of being speared to death in my sleeping bag – an Ancient Egyptian spear would be more than a match for rip-stop nylon, of that I could be sure. I imagined becoming a missing person, last seen getting off a train at Altnabreac and presumed dead, possibly sucked into a bog when I had imprudently cycled off the track somewhere.

Brian was surprised that I was camping and then he was surprised that I could get all my camping gear into my panniers.

'It's all very small and lightweight nowadays,' I explained.

'Well,' he replied, 'I would have offered to put you up here for the night but she wouldn't like it.'

I thanked him politely but said I'd be fine – after all, I was not short of isolated places locally where I could pitch my tent.

That isolation, Brian told me, had grown ever more extreme in recent years. 'When we moved here there were 12 houses in the area that were occupied. Now there are only two, and this is one of them.'

The other one was three miles down the track and was lived in by an elderly ghillie and his wife. Come the day they packed up and left or were seen off by a harsh winter – 'Two winters ago we couldn't drive for three months because of the snow' – the inhabitants of the house at Lochdhu would be quite alone with just the bogs and the plantations and the station and the low southern hills for company. Indeed, if we were to have taken the register of all the locals within an eight-mile radius right there and then, it would hardly have used up more than a few seconds: Brian – Yes; Khenemet – Yes; Me – Yes; Ghillie – Dunno; Wife of Ghillie – Dunno. It felt kind of lonely.

But just then Sandie walked in. At least, I imagine she did. I wasn't actually aware of her presence until she was nearly up at our chairs, which were facing away from her. So short was she – a little less than five feet, I would guess – that I confess I thought at first she must be a child, and imagined that this was a daughter Brian had yet to mention. Even when she stopped at the back of our chairs and I could see her up close, I found it all but impossible to tell how old she was. There were two things I could tell about her immediately, though. First, she was clearly *not* the daughter of a headhunter from Borneo. I had no idea what her father might do for a living but this woman was definitely Scottish. Secondly, if the barely concealed rage contained in her eyes was anything to go by, she was a mite unhappy to find me in her house. I didn't take it personally – remembering Brian's 'I would have offered to put you up but she wouldn't like it,' I got the impression that she would have felt the same towards any stranger in her domain.

If I'd hoped that the presence of a woman might dispel the deeply uneasy feeling I had about being here at all, such expectations – scant though they tend to be when you're expecting a headhunter's daughter to join you – were dashed. (Before you get on your high horse, I've no experience of headhunters' daughters and I'm sure the vast majority of them are charming, but I'm just not convinced that we would have struck up an instant rapport – me the vegan and her the compulsive animal killer.) If anything, Sandie's arrival on the stage, even as the daughter of someone who was unlikely to have been a headhunter, only increased my underlying sense of unease. Rather than encountering a potential ally, I was even further outnumbered.

And now I couldn't help but wonder what had happened to the headhunter's daughter.

Brian introduced Sandie to me with more than a hint of forced bonhomie in his voice and a glance towards her that said, 'Not my fault – he just turned up.' However, either Sandie was not blessed with quite as many of the social graces as most of us enjoy or it was as much as she could do to keep her suppressed rage from bursting forth, because she refused to look at me. She stood behind us, focusing on her husband while he tried to explain my apparently inexplicable presence there. But none of the socially expected noises came out of her. There was no 'oh, really' or 'that's interesting' in response to any of the few nuggets of information Brian fed her about me, and soon she was gone again, to stew I knew not where.

I felt it was high time I took my own leave. I knew that my fears were almost certainly groundless and that after I'd left I'd look back and think how foolish I'd been to let my imagination get the better of me, but I had been in the house for over an hour and a half by then and thought I'd probably done my bit for World Literature.

'Well, I really shouldn't take up any more of your time,' I began, tipping myself forward into a standing position.

'Oh,' replied Brian, and then said the words that would plunge me into a whole new adventure, 'don't you want to come and see my tomb?'

And I heard myself say, 'Well, of course I do.'

It was not a complete lie. If this tomb had been beneath a National Trust property with a nice silver-haired volunteer on hand to answer my questions about the artwork and ensure I didn't make off with any treasures, I would have been mustard-keen to have a nose around. It was only when visions of me being held against my will and sacrificed to an Egyptian god at first light the next morning flashed before me that I found myself a little less enthusiastic.

And indeed, had it not been for the fact that I was writing a book, I'm certain I would have politely declined the offer. So I pretended to myself that I was a fearless investigative author and that it was in some way IMPORTANT – my mind had started to capitalise things by this point – that my readership learn of the mysteries of the tomb beneath the house at Lochdhu.

'I'd just assumed that your chapel and tomb would be sacrosanct,' I continued, half in the hope that he would remember that they were indeed sacrosanct and that showing me down there would not have pleased the gods.

'No, no, not at all. Come on.'

And with that, Brian led the way around the far side of the swimming pool. I followed him and Khenemet followed me. I wasn't sure if I felt safer or less safe with Khenemet coming along. Although I didn't feel in any way threatened by him, I was fairly sure that he would do his father's bidding unquestioningly and that made me think the odds were further stacked against me.

Brian swore me to secrecy regarding the location of the entrance to the tomb, so suffice to say you won't find it.

We passed through a large trapdoor and down a surprisingly wide flight of stairs into an arched tunnel. Brian, then me, then Khenemet. The air immediately became much cooler and the sounds of the outside world – the breeze, the occasional cry of a bird – were silenced. There was nothing to be heard now but the dull thud of our feet on the floor.

All I could think of was that I'd seen this tunnel somewhere before. And then I knew where. I'd seen it in every single episode of *Scooby-Doo*. I was now in the interesting position of being very scared while at the same time exclaiming, 'I love this! This is completely brilliant!' and wishing that this *was Scooby-Doo* and that Brian's face was merely a rubber mask I could pull off and cry out, 'Mr Smiiii-iiii-iiiith!' Then Brian would say, 'And I'd have gotten away with it if it hadn't been for your meddling,' and all would be well again.

The tunnel had been beautifully built – its white sides were smooth and shaped as if to admit a tube train. The floor was even – some sort of painted cement, if memory serves – while a few electric bulbs lit our way. We marched on, curving around to the right. After what seemed like 40 or 50 yards the tunnel ended at two white wooden doors. Brian opened one and felt for a light switch in the room beyond. Some strip lights flickered on.

I stepped through the door to join Brian and any trivial thoughts I had about the lighting arrangements were stripped away by the shock of what I saw before me. It wasn't that there were yet more Ancient Egyptians lining the walls – I'd pretty much expected that. Neither was it the simple altar topped with an ankh, the Ancient Egyptian cross with the loop at the top. It was what was guarding the altar. On both sides there were men standing bolt upright. They each held a spear. Their heads were the heads of jackals. They were statues, of course – apologies if you were expecting real men with the heads of jackals – but seeing these life-size, expertly painted figures sent a shiver down my spine the likes of which I hadn't experienced for a very long time. 'If I'm not careful here,' I thought to myself, 'something very bad indeed could happen to me. In an instant this could change from a friendly tour to something rather sinister.'

'Anubis,' Brian commented. He had become noticeably more laconic since coming down here.

Anubis is the god charged with protecting the dead as they journey into the afterlife. If I were one of the dead I'd be glad he was on my side, because he looks like the kind of spear-carrying man-jackal you wouldn't mess with.

Khenemet joined us and Brian closed the door, which I felt was not strictly necessary.

As usual, I had my camera strapped to my belt, so I asked whether I could take some photos. 'Or would that be sacrilege?'

Brian nodded – it would be.

'Pity, because nobody is going to believe me when I tell them about this.'

Denied the opportunity of recording the scene in digital form, I concentrated on fixing it in my mind. The chapel had been laid out in the shape of a Christian cross. We'd entered at the foot, and the altar with its identical twin statues stood towards the far end. The chapel was carpeted and spotless and smelt of newness.

In order to keep talking, I asked after one of the characters on the wall whose appearance stood out from the rest.

'That's Set or Seth,' Brian explained. 'He's the god of ...' To be honest I couldn't really concentrate, so I can't tell you what Brian said he was the god of. I've looked him up since, though, and he turns out to be the god of many things – storms, darkness, chaos, the desert. He's a god with a full workload.

'He was taken up by the Christians,' Brian added, 'and turned into their Satan.'

This information didn't lift my mood any.

We walked further into the chapel. I didn't want to examine the creepy Anubis twins too closely, so I looked left down the arm of the cross. I expected to see some other replica of Ancient Egyptian burial paraphernalia but, to my surprise, there on the wall was a large, competently executed mural portraying an infant Jesus being carried across a river by St Christopher. This was a story I had learned in childhood. The myth goes that, with each step that Christopher took, Jesus became heavier. By the time the disciple had reached the far bank, the future saviour weighed as much as the world. I've never been sure exactly what message this was meant to convey.

I turned around and saw that a mural had also been painted at the right-hand end. This showed an adult Jesus with his arms outstretched and the words 'I am the vine, you are the branches' laid out beneath him. This is the first part of the fifth verse of the fifteenth chapter of John's Gospel: 'I am the vine; you are the branches. If you remain in me and I in you, you will bear much fruit; apart from me you can do nothing.'

What was going on here? It was all very syncretistic. It doesn't take a doctor of theology to point out that Jesus' views on the afterlife may not be entirely in harmony with those of the Ancient Egyptians. Was Brian hoping to get to the Christian heaven, his soul efficiently escorted there by Anubis? Or perhaps he imagined he might meet Jesus in the Kingdom of the Dead and the Fields of Aaru? Or was Jesus acting as backup in case Brian found *post mortem* that the whole Egyptian thing had fallen on its face?

I felt, however, that this was not the time to start querying Brian's core beliefs, and so held my peace.

I was rewarded with a moment or two of light relief.

'I'm not sure if this is sacrilege ...' Brian said, reaching for one of three doors that led off the chapel. He opened it to reveal a room heaving with racks filled with what must have been hundreds of bottles of wine and champagne. His faintly ashamed look led me to believe that these were not intended for consumption in the hereafter.

On the other side of the altar was another door. Brian opened this, too, but it was little more than a glorified cupboard containing a large selection of cleaning materials. To my mind they were arranged with a neatness that bordered on the obsessive, while the number and variety of them seemed excessive for such a small chapel, which, I imagined, saw little use. It was obvious to me that their true purpose was altogether sinister: to ensure that every last blood stain and every drop of gore was obliterated from the scene after each human sacrifice had been made.

'And this is the tomb room,' Brian announced, opening the third door. It led into by far the largest of the three rooms off the chapel. We trooped into it in our usual order – Brian, me, Khenemet. It was some ten yards long and down the middle of its length ran a narrow walkway. On each side a marble-topped platform about waist high provided enough room for six coffins. Khenemet closed the door behind us – this surely was even less necessary – and we stood in the penumbra provided by some feeble light source that shone from somewhere or other.

'Right,' I thought, 'if something's going to happen, it's going to happen in here.'

But what would Brian do? Restrain me somehow and keep me imprisoned here for the rest of my life? Restrain me somehow and kill me in some unpleasant ritual? Or would he not bother with the restraining and just kill me here and now?

'Probably just stab me now,' I concluded – partly to cheer myself up, for the alternatives were not desirable – though there were no knives around that I could see and I had no reason to suspect that Brian was carrying one.

He was standing at the far end now, where, on the right-hand platform, lay a very handsome coffin of a dark rich walnut hue. Even in this half-light its burnished surface shone. Brian laid his hand reverently upon it.

'This is Khenemet's coffin,' he declared.

I didn't know what to say. What do you say when presented with the coffin of a 14-year-old boy who is standing next to you, very much alive?

I turned to Khenemet. 'Is that so? Is that your coffin?'

Khenemet nodded. He didn't seem to think that what I was witnessing here was very strange. Then Brian spoke again.

'Khenemet will be buried here and I will be buried in that space next to him.'

I nodded, as if this was the sort of conversation I had with people ten times a day.

But Brian had obviously decided that he could trust me with a deeper truth: 'You see, Khenemet and I have been together for 30,000 years.'

'Gosh,' I said, rather weakly.

For want of anything better to do, I turned my head round to Khenemet again.

'Is that …? Have you been together for 30,000 years?'

Again he nodded his assent. I turned back to Brian.

'So, is the idea that you'll be reincarnated together or something?'

'No,' he replied, 'it's just symbolic.'

I asked about who would occupy the other spaces, then wished I hadn't. We seemed to be building up to some sort of climax and I was momentarily convinced that he was going to scream 'You!' and set about me.

'My wife doesn't want to be buried here. She doesn't like it down here.'

At last I felt some kindred feeling for Sandie.

'But I hope my descendants will want to be buried here.'

What else we spoke about in that small dark room under the ground with its coffin and its youthful intended occupant I cannot remember. I can only recall the sense of overwhelming relief when Khenemet opened the door again and we filed out into the strip-lit chapel. If I was going to die, at least I was going to do so in the light. We headed for the white double doors.

'You know,' Brian said, 'you're only the sixth person ever to see this chapel.' And then he plunged us into total darkness.

I immediately realised the significance of his words. There were five people in his family, so I was the very first outsider who had been in this chapel. And now he was going to kill me.

In the darkness, I swayed away from him. He had been standing immediately to my left when he had flicked the light switch. I tensed myself to resist the thrust of a knife towards my ribs. 'This is it,' I thought. 'It's coming now.'

After a few seconds I heard a noise. It was a door handle. The door was thrust open and the dim light from the corridor spilled into the chapel.

'Sorry,' said Brian. 'I should have opened the door before I turned the light off.'

And breathe.

So anyway, it's just like Boris Becker said: 'Nobody died.'

And, of course, nobody was ever likely to die either. I'm sure Brian never entertained the thought of harming me in any way for a single moment. Indeed, unless you were trying to lull your victim into a false sense of security, it would be perverse indeed to make him a gift of a book, then kill him half an hour later. If nothing else, you might get blood all over the cover.

I left shortly afterwards. As we said our goodbyes on the driveway outside the house, Brian gave me his card. Khenemet had trailed outside after us but Sandie failed to make an appearance, even to assure herself that I was leaving. I thanked Brian for his time – I'd been there for two hours. I thanked Khenemet for the tea – he was embarrassingly pleased that I'd done so. Brian looked me firmly in the eye as we shook hands and said, 'It's nice to talk to someone who understands.' I've replayed in my mind many times the tone of voice and the body language he used as he said that, but I still don't know whether he intended the final word to mean that I empathised with his views or merely comprehended them. Whichever it was, I fear he may have ascribed to me more understanding than I actually possessed.

I cycled off down the track along Loch Dhu. A few minutes later, when I felt I was at a safe distance, I recorded a short video of myself in order to capture a sense of my emotional state. Watching it now, I think it's fair to say I was a little perplexed by what had happened, even though nothing had actually happened ('I've just had one of the weirdest experiences of my life,' were my first words). More than anything I was relieved to have escaped, for that's what it felt like, despite the fact that I was never held against my will at any point. It's instructive that I was sufficiently spooked to feel the need to continue cycling away from the house while recording my impressions, even though it was difficult enough to cycle along the track with two hands on the handlebars, let alone one.

Now that I was free again, my thoughts turned back to Khenemet. Some might say that having apparently very little contact with anyone from the outside world and living above your own coffin equated to a rather unorthodox upbringing. All the same, his home-schooling days should now be behind him. At the time of my visit he had already passed a smattering of GCSEs, but his father confessed that those were in the subjects he himself could teach well and that there were educational holes that needed filling. I asked whether Khenemet would be joining his older brothers at the college and was told that he would be starting in September. I hope he makes some good friends there.

As I cycled east, continuing the circular route I'd seen on the noticeboard at the station (what a long time ago *that* felt), my thoughts turned to where I might sleep that night. Understandably, I was no longer enthusiastic about camping out at the station. I resolved to find somewhere out of the way around the back of some plantation and sleep with one eye open. I reached Dalnawillan Lodge, which Brian had mentioned a couple of times. It looked like several small houses all cobbled together. It was grey and though there was still glass in the windows it was obviously abandoned and a more unwelcoming place you couldn't hope to imagine. Nearby, I crossed a bridge by another, much smaller house, which also appeared to have been left to its fate, but I heard a dog bark at me from somewhere so I assumed this was where the ghillie and his wife lived. I wasn't tempted to stop. It was when I took out my small-scale map to make sure I was still going the right way that I saw it showed some sort of track I hadn't noticed before. It led off from Loch More – where the Duke of Kent and (some would add) Rudolf Hess had apparently taken their last few steps on this Earth – and seemed to link up with a road.

An hour and a half later I was in a packed hotel bar in the village of Halkirk ordering a nice long pint of normality with a packet of ready salted humdrum on the side. There have been few times in my life when I've felt quite so glad to hear the babble of other people, so stupidly happy to catch the odd sentence of ordinary everyday inane chatter. They made the world of Altnabreac and Loch Dhu seem fantastical.

I've been to Thurso often enough now to consider it, in common with Talsarnau, one of my set of little homes dotted around the country. There's a campsite on the cliff-tops there that has cracking views across to the island of Hoy in Orkney. It suddenly occurred to me that the campsite was only another seven miles north of me. I finished my pint, saddled up and was pitching my tent just before darkness fell.

TO LONDON

I spent the next morning pottering around Thurso –
buying more bulky books in the second-hand bookshop;
checking out the brand-new health-food store;
and downing a huge soya decaf latte (yes, I know –
sometimes I'm hard to parody) in my favourite coffee shop
while checking my emails. I took the lunchtime train
down from Thurso to Inverness and had a wander about
on the dinky little islands on the River Ness until it was
time to make my way to the station for the sleeper train
back home to London.

I felt the jolt of excitement that I always feel on a sleeper
when that first judder of the cabin tells me we're off and
running. I lay on my bed, staring out of the window as the
Highlands swept past me in crepuscular light that
imperceptibly turned to night.

I was sad that my adventure among the railway request
stops of Britain was over. It would certainly be one I
wouldn't forget for a month or two. I had met an upside-
down woman (and given her some half-eaten hummus);
hung out with commandos; got roaringly sober on a pub
crawl; Zenned my way to blissfulness near a Welsh mountain
top; made my peace with a member of the police force
(just 130,000-odd to go); been inside a real live signal box
and witnessed levers being pulled and everything; had a go

on the Denton Flyer; attempted a joke in the bar of the Berney Arms; misinterpreted lapwing behaviour; seen a little bit of Siena come to Lincolnshire; had a go on the Denton Flyer (again); held an elderly man's head together (not particularly well, as it turned out, but well enough); slept the night in an outsized Wendy house; faced certain death in a fake Egyptian underground tomb; and carried my ukulele around several thousand miles of track only to find by the end that I hadn't got around to taking it out of its case even once (though those who have heard my guitar playing might look upon this as a victory for the Forces of Good).

Had I learned anything about life? My attempt to read *The Consolation of Philosophy* had been even more desultory than my first go at it as a teenager. That told me something about myself that was perhaps slightly uncomfortable.

I had learned something else, though, just thinking about poor old Boethius awaiting execution and imagining Philosophy coming to him and sharing his final hours on Earth. It was the same idea that had sometimes crept up on me when I was sitting on my own on a platform, dwelling upon what my life would look like if I made it to old age. It was something that had come home to me with greatest clarity when I was in the gloomy inner sanctum of the tomb looking upon Khenemet's coffin and wondering if I would ever see daylight again. It's not deep or original or even particularly life-affirming, although it does at least have the virtue of valuing human relationships. I shall render it first into cod Latin, so that it may take on the form, if not the substance, of an eternal verity:

*Veraciter mortem solum confrontare
non multus cachinni est.*

(Facing death alone really isn't much of a laugh.)

At fairly regular intervals stations appeared through my window, at first without lights then exotically lit up as if Important Things might happen there. From my position, lying on my back on my bed, I missed out on the legs and the head of each station but could take in each of their torsos — the upper parts of their windows, their electronic screens and their name boards — so I always knew where I was.

    Aviemore

        Kingussie

            Newtonmore

                Dalwhinnie

                    Blair Atholl

                        Pitlochry

                            Dunkeld & Birnam

                              Perth

                                  Gleneagles

                                    Dunblane

And somewhere before Stirling, I fell asleep.

    Meanwhile, in my rucksack, nestling safely in the silicon semiconductors of my tablet, was a reply from Verena.

TRAVEL INFORMATION

Here are some handy contact details for the major train companies I used while visiting the nation's most interesting railway request stops.

Arriva Trains Wales

ATW covers the whole of Wales and includes the Heart of Wales Line and the Cambrian Coast Line, both of which provide rich pickings for request-stop hunters. The Explore Wales Pass allows passengers to travel over the entire ATW network with a 50 per cent discount on the Ffestiniog Railway (which I used to get me up to the Conwy Valley Line).
Web: arrivatrainswales.co.uk
Tel: 0870 9000 773 (Welsh Language service: 0845 6040500)

East Coast

Although East Coast doesn't have any request stops of its own, it does provide a useful means of getting to those on other networks. Its services shoot up and down the spine of Britain from London to the East Midlands, Yorkshire and Humberside, Northeast England and all the way north to Aberdeen and Inverness in the Highlands of Scotland.
Web: eastcoast.co.uk
Tel: 08457 225 225

First Great Western

The Night Riviera service from London to Penzance is a memorable way of getting to FGW's many request stops in Devon and Cornwall. Its network also covers South Wales, the Cotswolds and large parts of Southern England, including London.
Web: firstgreatwestern.co.uk
Tel: 08457 000 125

Greater Anglia

The fabulous Berney Arms and other notable East Anglian request stops come under the aegis of Greater Anglia, whose routes cover Cambridgeshire,

Norfolk, Suffolk, much of Essex and some of Hertfordshire, with trains leaving London from Liverpool Street station.
Web: greateranglia.co.uk
Tel: 08456 007 245

Northern Rail

Home to Burnley Barracks, Entwistle and the many request stops along the Cumbrian Coast Line, Northern's network spreads over the whole of northern England from Crewe, Stoke, Buxton and Nottingham in the south to Carlisle and Newcastle in the north.
Web: northernrail.org
Tel: 0845 0000 125

ScotRail

The Caledonian Sleeper service is one of the great rail journeys in Britain, especially if you travel all the way up to Fort William or Inverness and thus don't have to rouse yourself too early. ScotRail's trains cover the whole Scottish network, which includes the plethora of request stops on the Far North Line.
Web: scotrail.co.uk
Tel: 08457 550 033

Virgin Trains

Like East Coast, Virgin does not have any request stops but is a handy mode of getting to them – especially those on the North Welsh mainland and Anglesey. The West Coast Line from London takes in the West Midlands, North Wales, Manchester, Liverpool, the Lake District, Glasgow and Edinburgh.
Web: virgintrains.co.uk
Tel: 08719 774 222

FURTHER USEFUL CONTACTS

National Rail Enquiries

Web: nationalrail.co.uk
Tel: 08457 48 49 50 (24 hours)

A to B Magazine

The Bike/Rail page is full of excellent information on when and where you can travel on trains, coaches, trams and ferries with a bicycle.
Web: atob.org.uk/bike-rail

SELECT BIBLIOGRAPHY

A History of the Parishes of Saint Ives, Lelant, Towednack and Zennor,
John Hobson Matthews, Short Run Press (2003 reprint –
original published in 1892)

Anglesey at War, Geraint Jones, The History Press (2012)

Anglesey Railways, Geraint Jones, Gwasg Carreg Gwalch (2005)

Berney Arms Remembered, Sheila Hutchinson, Sheila & Paul
Hutchinson (2003)

Branch Lines to Exmouth, Vic Mitchell & Keith Smith,
Middleton Press (1992)

British Railway Stations, J Horsley Denton, Ian Allan (1965)

Country Railway Routes: Craven Arms to Llandeilo, John Organ,
Middleton Press (2008)

*Dates of Opening and Closure of Railway Stations in the South West
of England*, G L Crowther, G L Crowther (2001)

Double Standards: The Rudolf Hess Cover-up, Lynn Picknett,
Clive Prince & Stephen Prior, Little, Brown & Co. (2001)

East Anglia by Rail, ed. Trevor Garrod, Railway Development
Society (1984)

Furness Railway: Its Rise and Development 1846–1923, W McGowan
Gradon, privately printed (1946)

Great Wales Rail, Cambrian Coast Line Action Group (1989)

*Great Western Railway Stations 1947: A Photographic and Track
Diagram Survey*, R J Smith, Robin Smith (2010)

Heart of Wales Line, ed. Neil Sprinks & Geoffrey Body, British Rail
(Western) and Avon-Anglia Publications & Services (1981)

Heart of Wales Line Guide, John Russell et al, Heart of Wales Line
Travellers' Association (1999)

Llanrwst & District Official Guide, no author or publisher credited
(1937)

Mapping the Railways, David Spaven & Julian Holland, Times
Books (2011)

Old Newton St. Cyres: Memories of Boyhood in a Devonshire Village,
    A G Abraham, Arthur H Stockwell Ltd (1972)
Pearson's Railway Rides: The Cumbrian Coast, Michael Pearson,
    J M Pearson & Son (1992)
Rails Round the Cumbrian Coast, Richard Kirkman & Peter van
    Zeller, Dalesman Books (1988)
The Consolation of Philosophy, Anicius Manlius Severinus Boethius
    (trans. H R James), Elliot Stock (1897)
The Conwy Valley Line, W G Rear, Foxline (1991)
The Cornish Riviera, S P B Mais, Great Western Railway Co. (1934)
The Illustrated Heart of Wales Line, Rob Gittins & Dorian Spencer
    Davies, Gomer (1985)
The Newquay Branch and its Branches, John Vaughan, OPC Railprint
    (1991)
The Switzerland of Wales: Penmaenmawr and Dwygyfylchi, M H Parry,
    Penmaenmawr Town Improvement Association (1905)
The Tarka Line, Terry Gough, The Nostalgia Collection (2011)

I'm also indebted to the creators of and contributors to the
following websites:

1745 Association: 1745association.org.uk (particularly
'Bonnie Prince Charlie's Long March' by Peter D Brown)
Bugle Inn, Bugle: bugleinn.co.uk
Cumberland and Westmorland Archives: cumberlandarchives.co.uk
Friends of the Far North Line: fofnl.org.uk
Friends of the West Highland Lines: westhighlandline.org.uk
Lelant Village: lelant.info
Luxulyan Village: luxulyanvalley.co.uk (particularly 'Luxulyan Valley
– An Historical View' a 2008 essay by Stephen Austin)
Moidart Local History Group: moidart.org.uk (particularly the
wartime memoirs of Ernest Dale, which can also be read here:
waryears.wordpress.com)
Ormerod Family: ormerod.uk.net
Rail Accident Investigation Branch: raib.gov.uk
Secret Scotland: secretscotland.org.uk
Undiscovered Scotland: undiscoveredscotland.co.uk

INDEX

AUTHOR'S ACKNOWLEDGEMENTS

I'd like to thank the following people, all of whom have helped this book to come about:

Ben Brooksbank
Brian and Khenemet at Lochdhu
Carl Palmer for his typeface
  identification skills
Celt Roberts for information
  on the Talsarnau tsunami
Claire Kennelly for Burnley
  Barack Obama tips
Claire 'Klur' Robertson for
  nom de guerre co-ordination
Clive Wills
Ellen Rossiter at Greater Anglia
Everyone at the Camping and
  Caravanning Club site at Dingwall
Fiona McGlade for
  pseudonymal advice
Gareth Edwards (not *that*
  Gareth Edwards)
Hazel and Geoff Wills
Helpful unnamed woman
  at Machynlleth station –
  you know who you are
James Davis at First Great Western
Jannine Russell at First ScotRail
John and Scott at Dunrobin Castle
John Allison at the Highland
  Railway Society
John Gelson at East Coast
Joselyn Rankin at Northern Rail
Lewis Brencher at Arriva Trains Wales
Luke Gosset
Matt Wakeford at Duncraig
Matthew Gorton at First Great Western
Maxwell Adams for refreshments
  and lots of excellent information
  about Lelant
Melissa Z Harrison for various acts of
  helpfulness and Darwin's barberry-
  based knowledge
Mo Campbell, her sword and her pond
Naomi Woodstock from
  Haven Holidays

Niamh O'Mahony
Rosie from Falmouth
Sarah at Arisaig House
Simon Jones
The Cambrian Line cleaner at Arriva
  Trains Wales
The diligent staff at the British Library's
  Rare Books Reading Room
The excellent couple who gave
  me a lift into Tywyn
Tracy Clifton at Virgin Trains
Verena van den Berg, whether upside
  down or in a bin

With particular thanks to:
Rowland Farrer for permission to use
his recollections of Burnley Barracks;
Jenifer Shimon for permission to use
her late mother Dorothy Meade's
recollections of Lelant; and Sheila
Hutchinson for permission to quote
from her book *Berney Arms Remembered*.

'The Slow Train' is reproduced
by permission of the Estates of
Michael Flanders and Donald Swann
2013. Any use of Flanders and Swann
material, large or small, should be
referred to the Estates at leonberger@
donaldswann.co.uk

I would like to extend grateful thanks
to my literary agent Ben Mason. My
gratitude also goes out to Donna
Wood and Caroline Taggart for their
fine editing skills, to the design team
at AA Media and to Harriet Yeomans
for drawing the map. Finally, I'd like
to thank my ever-patient editor Helen
Brocklehurst for her support and advice,
much of which was extremely sage.